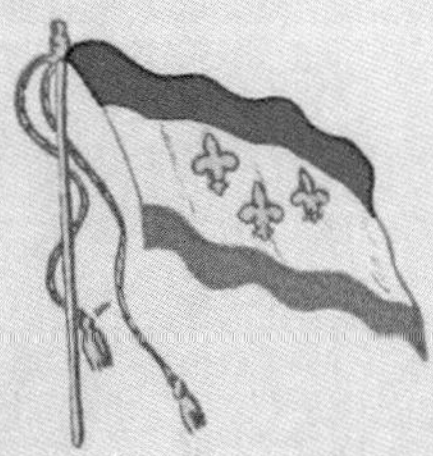

OFFICIAL FLAG OF THE CITY OF NEW ORLEANS.

THIS flag was accepted by Mayor Behrman and raised over the City Hall, February ninth, nineteen hundred and eighteen. It was designed by Bernard Barry and Gustave Couret, assisted by Miss Ida Barrow, who first conceived the idea of the adoption of a flag for the City of New Orleans.

"This flag commemorates the birth and the infancy of New Orleans, while it symbolizes the ideals of good government and the triumph of DEMOCRACY."

Courtesy of W. J. WAGUESPACK.

Marula

An imprint of Arcadia Publishing

The New Orleans Book
Orleans Parish School Board

A Marula Historical Reprint
Originally published in 1919

Published by Arcadia Publishing
Charleston SC

ISBN 978-0-7385-9471-2

Printed in the United States of America

For all general information contact Arcadia Publishing at:
Telephone 843-853-2070
Fax 843-853-0044
E-mail sales@arcadiapublishing.com
For customer service and orders:
Toll-Free 1-888-313-2665

Visit us on the Internet at www.arcadiapublishing.com

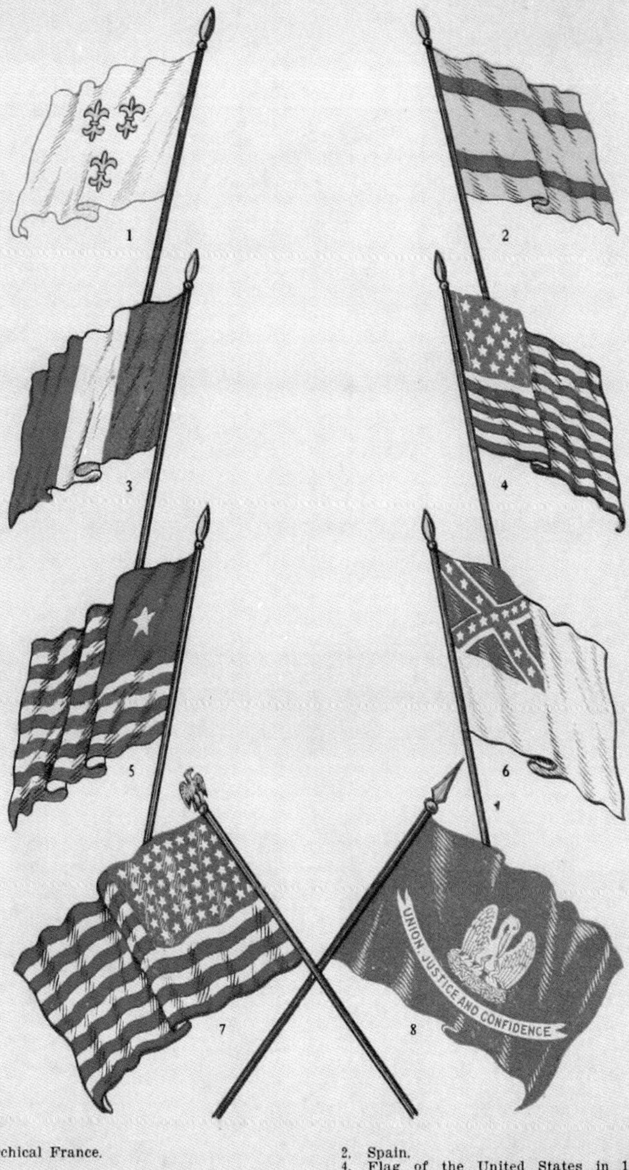

1. Monarchical France.

2. Spain.

3. First French Republic.

4. Flag of the United States in 1803, when Louisiana was ceded to the United States by France, Napoleon Bonaparte, First Consul.
   In 1812, when Louisiana was admitted into the Union.
   In 1815, when the Battle of New Orleans was fought.

5. State Flag, adopted by the Louisiana Convention which passed the Ordinance of Secession.

6. Confederate Flag, Act of Confederate Congress, 1863.

7. The present Flag of the United States.

8. The present State Flag, adopted by the General Assembly of Louisiana, Act 39 of 1912.

THE NEW ORLEANS BOOK

PUBLISHED BY

ORLEANS PARISH SCHOOL BOARD

New Orleans.
SEARCY & PFAFF, Ltd.
720-728 Perdido Street.
1919.

INTRODUCTION.

IF the opportunities within her reach are intelligently realized, New Orleans will become one of the great centers of the world. Love of country is a feeling inherent in every normal boy and girl. Community patriotism—an outgrowth of the modern conditions of life—takes the form of great pride in one's native city, or in the city one has adopted as one's home, and inevitably leads to good results.

We want to inculcate in the children of our city a keen, vivid interest in its past history, in its present, and in its future. Economy in government, good order, cleanliness, and honesty must be the outcome of the education of the children, if our city is to take and maintain its place in civilization. That the growth of a city is measured by the civic interest of its people is a recognized fact. New conditions demand that all children should be taught they are the coming responsible heads of the community.

There was a time when the national government was controlled principally by men from small towns or farms. Today, our Presidents are city men who are calling into their cabinets advisors from our great municipalities, thus proving, "He who makes the city makes the world."

PREFACE.

IT is only meet that the public should know how this study of New Orleans was made possible. The accomplishment of the task was at first doubtful; but the passing weeks revealed the lively disposition of the gentlemen of New Orleans to assist in making New Orleans known to the children of the Southern metropolis. To the courtesy, civic interest, and co-operation of those gentlemen whom it was our pleasure to interview and otherwise communicate with, is due the existence of this book.

Our kind readers will no doubt sometimes be surprised at the relative size of some of the illustrations. We crave their indulgence. Such discrepancies are the result of the very limited cost of the book, which prevented all the illustrations being made to order, and caused dependence upon the generosity of friends of the work, for the majority of the illustrations.

To the following gentlemen and organizations, we desire to extend special thanks for information, advice, criticism, or illustrations: Robert Glenk, T. P. Thompson, Gaspar Cusach, Norman Walker, W. O. Hart, J. Zach. Spearing, Judge I. D. Moore, Prof. Ellsworth Woodward, S. Locke Breaux, L. E. Bentley, E. E. Lafaye, Dr. Jos. Holt, Dr. G. F. Patton, Dr. I. M. Cline, Dr. W. H. Robin, Stanley C. Arthur, Leonard Nicholson, George G. Earle, Sidney Lewis, Chris Reuter, Tiley McChesney, the Louisiana State Museum, Southern Pacific Railroad, Association of Commerce, Board of Trade, and the officials of the city.

We wish to express our appreciation of the unfailing courtesy and co-operation of the gentlemen of the New Orleans Board of Public School Directors and the Superintendents of the New Orleans Public Schools. It is our sincere wish that "The New Orleans Book" will attain the end they desire, namely, the dissemination of knowledge of New Orleans, fostering of love of our unique city, and development of a true civic spirit, active in times of peace, in reform, and improvement along lines conservative of the city's individuality and, yet, abreast with real progress,—and steadfast, true, and self-sacrificing in times of trouble and trial which, in the progression of the world, must necessarily come upon New Orleans in the future as in the past; but, as in the past, to be heroically borne and overcome, thus giving rise to a still nobler period.

THE AUTHORS.

NEW ORLEANS, LA.,
September, 1915.

PREFACE TO SECOND EDITION.

In order to profit by the experience gained in teaching The New Orleans Book during the past four years, the Orleans Parish School Board having acquired the copyright to this book appointed a Committee on Revision and a Committee of Editors to revise and edit the manuscript preparatory to printing a second edition. These Committees were composed as follows:

Committee on Revision: Mrs. Ellen W. Gardner, Miss Stella Herron, Miss Caroline Pfaff, Miss Sadie Vickers, Miss Ray Abrams, Miss Augustine Aurianne, and Miss Josephine Thomas.

Committee of Editors: Mr. Henry M. Gill, City Librarian, Pres. A. B. Dinwiddie, President Tulane University, and Mr. Norman Walker, Editor, Times-Picayune.

The Board extends to the members of these Committees its heartiest appreciation of their invaluable work and feels confident that the book will serve its purpose of disseminating facts concerning New Orleans, the City of Opportunity.

ORLEANS PARISH SCHOOL BOARD.

NEW ORLEANS, LA.,
August, 1919.

CONTENTS.

ILLUSTRATIONS.

ILLUSTRATIONS—Continued.

CHAPTER I.

Geographical Conditions.

SECTION 1. LOCATION OF NEW ORLEANS.

Location. Bienville selected the present site of New Orleans for his capital, because he realized that one day his little settlement would grow into a great and prosperous city through the advantages offered by the Mississippi and the agricultural possibilities of the country. Almost a hundred years later, Jefferson secured Louisiana for the United States. His principal object was the possession of New Orleans, which he predicted would become the commercial metropolis of the South.

New Orleans, Louisiana, is in the south central part of the United States, 29 degrees, 56 minutes, 59 seconds North Latitude, 90 degrees, 4 minutes, 9 seconds West Longitude. Although one hundred ten miles from the Gulf of Mexico, New Orleans is a seaport, for it is situated on the Mississippi River, which can float at this point the largest sea-going vessels.

Advantages of Location. The Mississippi River, with its tributaries, offers seventeen thousand six hundred fifty miles of navigable waterway, extending through twenty-two states. Because of its location, New Orleans should be the center of trade between the Mississippi Valley and Central and South American countries. The Panama Canal brings a large portion of the oriental commerce through this port. The prosperity of a city depends not only upon its commercial facilities, but also upon the resources of the adjacent region. In this respect, New Orleans, the gateway of the fertile Mississippi Valley, is equalled by few cities.

SECTION 2. EXTENT OF NEW ORLEANS.

Extent. The corporate limits of New Orleans embrace the whole of Orleans Parish, an area of one hundred ninety-six square miles. There are only a few cities in the United States that cover more territory. The boundary line of Orleans Parish is very irregular, but it may be given approximately as Lake Pontchartrain on the north, the Rigolets separating Orleans from St. Tammany Parish on the north, Lake Borgne on the east and south, St. Bernard Parish on the east and south, the Mississippi River on the south, with the exception of Algiers, which is across the river, and Jefferson Parish on the west. Part of Orleans Parish extends over the river, embracing Algiers and the surrounding districts.

SECTION 3. TOPOGRAPHY.

Topography. The topography of this region has undergone great changes. This has been proven by a study of the soil and by historic records. Even in the memory of the present generation, there were swamps where now stand beautiful residences. These changes have been largely effected by the Mississippi, to which mighty agency New Orleans owes its very existence. Ages ago, an arm of the Gulf of Mexico reached to the Ohio River. In this bay the river deposited its sediment until not only the bay, but much of the Gulf, was filled.

As the Mississippi River carries hundreds of millions of tons of silt into the Gulf every year, this process of land building continues. Even after the land was raised above the sea-level, the river did not cease its great work. Swollen by the floods and melting snows along its upper course, it would annually overflow this region, leaving a deposit of alluvium

Thus, year by year, until the levees shut out the floods, New Orleans was built up. According to the records of George G. Earl, Superintendent of the Sewerage and Water Board, the highest portions now have an elevation of fifteen feet; but, in some places, the city is slightly below Gulf level. There is a gradual slope back from the river front, where the land is highest, and a lesser slope back from the lake shore. A slight elevation extends across the city along Metairie Ridge, City Park, and Gentilly Terrace. The section extending between Lakes Borgne and Pontchartrain as far as the Rigolets is almost entirely swamp land. Small tracts of this have been reclaimed for market gardens.

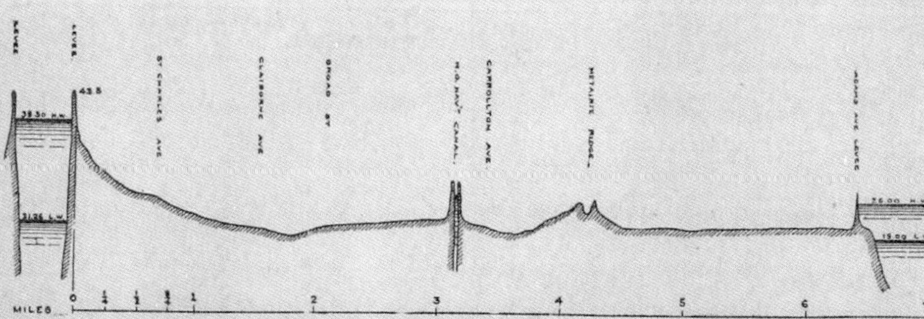

Cross Section Showing Land-slope from the River to the Lake.

SECTION 4. SOIL FORMATION.

Soil Formation. The causes of these slopes and ridges will be understood by studying the work of rivers in building up their flood plains. A swiftly flowing river can carry a large amount of detritus, but when the current is checked it is forced to drop its burden. The greatest check to the current of a river overflowing its flood plains occurs as it leaves its channels; consequently, the heaviest and coarsest sediment is deposited there. The river banks are thus built higher by each flood and a system of natural levees is produced. The finer silt is carried farther before being released. This causes a marked difference in the formation and composition of front and back lands along a river. The formation of the land along the bayous is similar to that along the river; it is high near the streams and slopes back into lowlands or swamps. This accounts for the ridges along Bayou St. John and Bayou Sauvage. The course of a former outlet of the Mississippi River is marked by the ridge along Metairie and Gentilly Terrace.

Present Work of the River. Levees restrain the flood waters; but the river has not ceased its work. The current grows sluggish along the inner curve of the river, and here a bank or "batture" is built up outside the levee. The current is correspondingly swift along an outer curve, where it wears away the bank. This is occurring at Carrollton Bend and at Greenville Bend (between Westwego and Carrollton). The batture from Felicity Street to below Canal Street has increased so much that the levee has been moved to take in the newly formed land. Within the history of New Orleans, the site of the present Customhouse was on the river front and Tchoupitoulas Street was the highroad along the bank.

SECTION 5. INUNDATIONS.

Causes of Inundations. New Orleans has suffered from overflows of the Mississippi and Lake Pontchartrain. Floods from Lake Pontchartrain have resulted from two causes: (1) Backwater from crevasses along the river filled Lake Pontchartrain; this water, when prevented by prevailing southeast winds from reaching the Gulf, flooded the region about the lake. (2) The same result was produced when violent storms piled up the waters of the lake.

SECTION 6. LEVEES.

Along the River. Levees of great size and strength have been built along the Mississippi's course through the State of Louisiana. Nowhere in the world, not even in Holland, where the people hold back the waters of the sea, are the levees as large as those built by the Parish of Orleans to check the encroachments of the "Father of Waters."

Size and Length. The base of these great levees is as thick through as a city block, and in places the crown or top is fifty feet wide and five feet above the highest water ever recorded at New Orleans. The largest levees are along Carrollton Bend, called Carrollton Reach Levee, and in front of the Third District. The great size of these levees is easily realized because of the unobstructed view. There are levees of almost the same height before the business section, but the slope is so gradual it is scarcely perceptible. The levee at Canal Street commences at the Louisville and Nashville depot and slopes up until it is two to three feet above high-water mark at the river front. The Orleans Levee Board maintains twelve miles of levee on the left or east bank of the river and over thirteen miles on the right or west bank, besides the fifty-two miles of rear protection levees.

Bank Protection. The levees are protected from erosion, or wearing, by wooden revetments or by a coating of concrete. Willow mattresses, sunk below the surface of the water, prevent the caving of levees along banks where the current washes with greater force. The work of bank protection is relegated to the United States Government. From 1907 up to date, the Government has expended over a million dollars in this character of work.

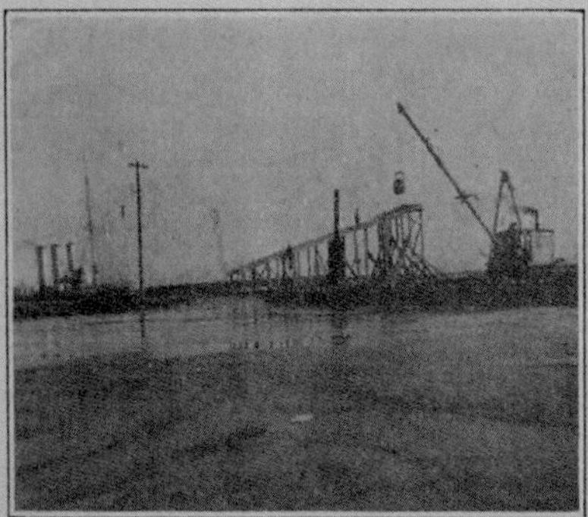

Scene in Third District showing levee construction, mud pumped through elevated sluices.

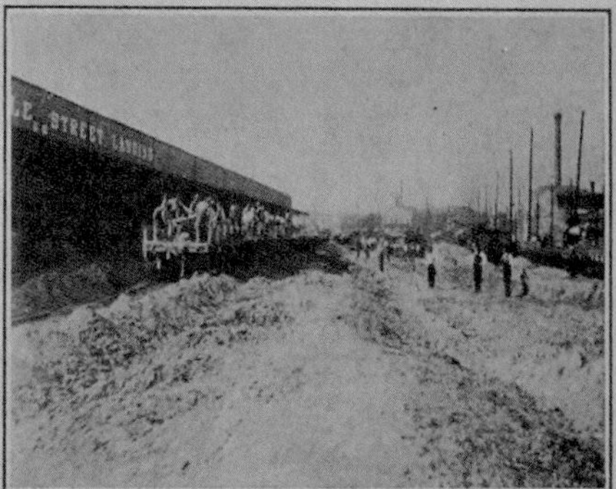

Scene in Third District showing levee construction, material being brought on cars.

Construction of Levees. The Orleans Levee Board is charged with the construction, repair, supervision, and maintenance of all levees in the Parish of Orleans. The method of construction depends largely upon the facilities at hand for obtaining the necessary earth to build the levee.

Frequently the dirt is brought on barges, or in cars, if there are railroad tracks near. Great cranes unload the barges or cars and place the dirt in the required position. The force of running water is sometimes applied to levee construction. The material used to build the levee is shot through long elevated sluices by a continuous stream, and the mud thus produced is deposited through troughs at regular distances along the line of construction. Low dams hold this slush within a certain area, where, after the water has drained off, the dirt is shaped into a levee. Where the use of machinery is not practicable, the dirt has to be hauled by mules or wheeled in barrows; and the levees have to be built with wheel and drag scrapers.

Protection Levees. Levees are maintained along the lake shore, the parish lines, the canal banks, and Bayou St. John, as well as along the river front. The purpose of protection levees is to prevent backwater from crevasses or lake floods from entering the city. These levees are not nearly so high as those along the river, but they aggregate about fifty-two miles in length.

Swamp Reclamation. Since the construction of levees that afford effectual protection to the city, attention has been directed towards reclamation of swamp lands. Cypress trees and tangled undergrowth once covered an extensive area of marsh where streets are now laid out and houses are being built. Most of the reclamation has been effected at the city's expense by means of the drainage canals. The entire area from People's Avenue to the New Basin Canal and from the river to the lake is now drained. Land companies have reclaimed many sections in, and near, New Orleans.

Other reclamation projects are now being considered and, when completed, all of the swamp lands in the rear of the city will be reclaimed by drainage canals and levees.

SECTION 7. CLIMATE.

Conditions that Affect Climate in New Orleans. The climate of New Orleans is affected by (1) latitude, (2) nearness to large bodies of water, (3) direction of prevailing winds, (4) levelness of the surrounding country.

Latitude. New Orleans is about seven degrees north of the torrid zone. The thirtieth parallel of latitude crosses Africa and Arabia through burning deserts, but New Orleans, at the same distance from the equator, has mild and pleasant summers.

Nearness to Large Bodies of Water. Regions adjacent to large expanses of water are less subject to extremes of temperature than inland sections, because water neither heats nor cools as rapidly as land. The extensive water surface formed by the network of bayous and lakes which indent the coast of Louisiana materially affects the climate. Especially is this true in New Orleans, which is made almost an island by Lake Pontchartrain, Lake Borgne, and the Mississippi River. The warm Gulf Stream lessens the severity of winter.

Direction of Prevailing Winds. For almost six months of the year the city is swept by southeasterly winds from the Gulf. These are saturated with moisture, which lessens the intensity of the sun's rays by day and prevents rapid radiation by night. During the winter months, the prevailing winds are from the north and northeast, but, having to cross Lake Pontchartrain, they are tempered before reaching New Orleans. The atmosphere, though laden with moisture, is not heavy nor oppressive. Breezes from the Gulf impart a fresh and vigorous tone during the summer and moderate the cold in winter.

Levelness of the Surrounding Country. There are no heights of land in the vicinity of New Orleans to obstruct the winds or prevent the distribution of moisture.

Temperature. The summers are long, but the maximum temperature never exceeds and seldom equals that of inland cities much farther north. The mean temperature for July and August, the hottest months of the year, obtained from records extending over a period of forty-two years, is 82 degrees. Excessive heat is rare and heat prostrations are few. On the other hand, the winters are exceedingly mild.

There is ice on an average of less than four times a year, and the ground seldom freezes. All but the most delicate plants can remain out of doors during the winter with only a covering of burlap or paper to protect them from frost. The lowest temperature ever recorded at New Orleans did not descend to zero, being seven degrees above zero on February 13, 1899. The season of greatest cold occurs during December and January.

Rainfall and Moisture. There is no distinctive rainy season in New Orleans, as many outsiders suppose. The average rainfall is about equal for all the months of the year, increasing slightly during the summer. The inhabitants appreciate this provision of nature, for rainy days are few, and frequent showers serve to cool the atmosphere. Spring and autumn, having very moderate rainfall, are always pleasant seasons. The annual monthly rainfall averages four and five-tenths inches.

Healthfulness. Few places have a more uniformly delightful climate than New Orleans. Residents of New Orleans have no need to seek mountain and seashore resorts in summer, for breezes from the gulf and lake keep their own city pleasant during the summer months, while strangers flock to the Southern metropolis to enjoy the winters, where trees are green and flowers bloom, where outdoor life is uninterrupted and fires may be dispensed with many days in the season.

SECTION 8. WEATHER BUREAU.

Weather Bureau. Climate exerts so much influence over the lives, habits, and occupations of people that the United States Government has established the Weather Bureau under the Department of Agriculture. The work of this Bureau is to study the rise and fall of temperature, the direction and velocity of the wind, the amount of rainfall, and the barometric pressure, in order to anticipate unusual weather conditions, and to give information and warning with regards to floods.

New Orleans Station. There is a station in New Orleans fully equipped for making observations and forecasts. The offices are located in the Post Office building.

Observations of local weather conditions are taken twice daily at about two hundred observing stations in the United States. Trained observers, using delicate instruments, determine weather changes with utmost accuracy. Complete telegraphic reports are immediately sent to Washington, District of Columbia, where expert forecasters determine the weather conditions that may be expected to prevail during the next thirty-six to forty-eight hours. Reports are also sent to some of the larger stations, where similar calculations are made for their respective vicinities.

Distribution of Forecasts. Within two hours after the morning observations have been taken, the forecasts are telegraphed from the forecast stations to nearly two thousand distributing points. Countless individuals receive the daily weather news from these points by means of telegraph, telephone, or mail. The principal features of current weather conditions throughout the country are represented on a map.

Value of Forecasts. The extent to which the Weather Bureau, in the collection and publication of data and the issue of weather forecasts and warnings, affects the daily life of the people is increasing yearly. Warnings of storms and hurricanes, issued for the benefit of marine interests, are the most important and valuable. These are displayed at more than three hundred points along the coasts and along the shores of the Great Lakes. So nearly perfect has service become that scarcely a storm of marked danger to maritime interests has occurred for years for which ample warnings have not been issued from twelve to twenty-four hours in advance. West Indian reports are especially valuable, as the approach of those destructive hurricanes which sweep the Gulf and Atlantic coasts from July to October can thereby be accurately determined.

Change of Temperature Warnings. The warnings of those sudden temperature changes known as cold waves are probably next in importance. These warnings, issued from twenty-four to thirty-six hours in advance, are scattered throughout the threatened region by flags at Weather Bureau stations, by telegraph, telephone, and mail service; planters, florists, shippers and many others profit by this knowledge. Fruit, sugar, tobacco, strawberry, and market gardening interests are protected by forecasts of frost or freezing weather. Savings to growers in a limited district through the instrumentality of such warnings have been estimated at thousands of dollars for one cold spell.

Flood Warnings. The commerce of our rivers is greatly aided and lives and property in regions subject to overflow are protected by the publication of river stages and the issue of river and flood forecasts. These are based on reports received from about five hundred special river and rainfall stations. The value of this service was strongly emphasized during a great flood, in March, April, and May, 1912, in the Mississippi Basin, which was one of the greatest in its history, the stages in some places being the highest ever known. Yet, notwithstanding the enormous volumes of water, the forecasts and warnings were accurately verified as to location, stage, and date.

TOPICS. **Section 1.** Location of New Orleans; **Section 2.** Extent of New Orleans; **Section 3.** Topography; **Section 4.** Soil Formation; **Section 5.** Inundations; **Section 6.** Levees; **Section 7.** Climate; **Section 8.** Weather Bureau.

REFERENCES: Geological Survey of Louisiana; Waring and Cable, History and Present Conditions of New Orleans, 1880; Report of the Orleans Levee Board; Reports of the Weather Bureau, Bulletin Y.

CHAPTER II.

History of New Orleans.

SECTION 1. FRENCH DOMINATION.

1. LOUISIANA BEFORE 1718.

Early Explorers of Louisiana. In 1528, Pamphilo de Narvaez led an expedition from Cuba into Florida. Defeated by the Indians, he retreated to the coast, only to find his ships gone. Some rude craft were built with which he set sail. After several days' sailing, they passed the mouth of a great river and drank of its water; but the mighty current dispersed the boats, and Narvaez was never heard of again. Three boats reached Texas, and, after six years' detention by the Indians, several of the survivors, led by Cabeza de Vaca, the treasurer of the expedition, managed to reach a Spanish settlement in Mexico.

Eleven years later, Hernando de Soto sailed from Cuba with a large force and landed on the coast of Tampa Bay, determined to conquer the territory explored by Narvaez. After wandering through what is now Georgia, Alabama, and Mississippi, having his army diminished by Indian attacks and malaria, he at last, in the third year of the expedition, reached the Mississippi River at a point slightly south of Memphis. Here he crossed the river and wandered as far west as the Red River, but becoming ill he returned to the banks of the Mississippi, where he died. His followers, fearing attacks of the Indians should they hear of their leader's death, placed his body in the trunk of a tree and buried him in the great river. Unable to reach Mexico by land, they built seven brigantines and, led by Moscoso, de Soto's successor, one-half of his followers finally reached Tampico River in Mexico.

Expeditions of Père Marquette and La Salle. In 1673, having heard from the Indians, of a great river that flowed to the west, Père Marquette, a Jesuit missionary, set out from Quebec accompanied by Joliet, a fur-trader, to explore and claim it for France. In their birch bark canoes they descended the Mississippi River as far as the Arkansas; and, convinced that it flowed south into the Gulf of Mexico instead of west, proceeded to return to Canada. Worn out by the hardships, Père Marquette died before the party reached Canada and Joliet proceeded alone to bear the news to Quebec.

Inflamed with the desire of establishing France's power through the heart of the continent from the mouth of the St. Lawrence to that of the Mississippi, Robert Cavelier, Sieur de La Salle started from Canada in August, 1681, and

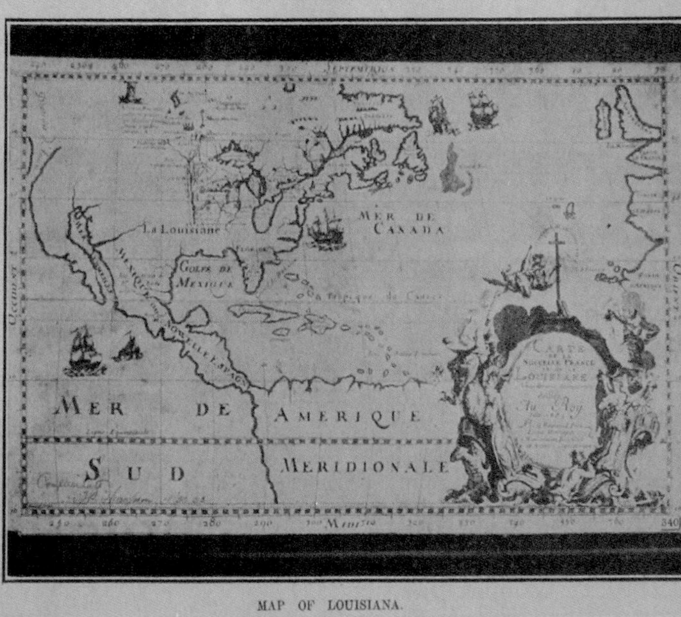

MAP OF LOUISIANA.

entered the Mississippi on February 6th, 1682. When he at length reached the mouth of the river, he claimed for France all the land watered by the Mississippi and its tributaries, and named it Louisiana in honor of Louis XIV, King of France. It was the desire of La Salle to establish a chain of forts from the St. Lawrence to the Mississippi. On his return to Canada, he went to France, where the government fitted out an expedition for him. In 1684, he landed on the coast of Matagorda Bay in Texas, having failed to find the mouth of the Mississippi. Soon he lost his vessels. In attempting to find the Mississippi River and reach Canada by way of that river, he was murdered by one of his followers.

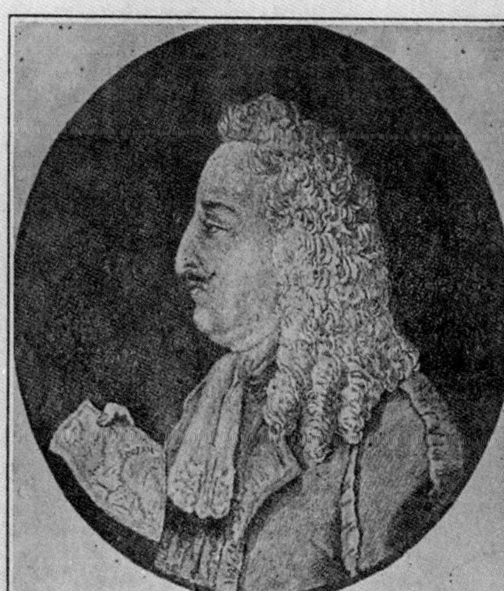

LA SALLE.

France at the Close of the Seventeenth Century. France had risen, through the skill of Louis XIV. and the genius of his ministers, to the dominance of the affairs of Europe. Though an able ruler, Louis, "le Grand," was not far-sighted. After the death of Colbert, the great financier, he gave no attention to the development of the colonies of France, which had been one of the cherished plans of the able Comptroller. In 1689, Count Pontchartrain was entrusted with the difficult task of relieving France of her financial troubles. The treasury was depleted by the constant strain upon it caused by the continuous European wars, the development of the interior of France, material encouragement given to commerce and manufactures, erection of such costly structures as Versailles, the Louvre and the Hotel des Invalides. The nation was groaning under the burden of taxation which had been thus necessarily increased. In the endeavor to solve this mighty financial problem, Pontchartrain, following Colbert's policy, turned his attention to the development of the colonies. He began with Louisiana, as yet a wild, trackless wilderness, extending from the Province of Canada on the north and the English colonies on the Atlantic, to the Rocky Mountain, the Spanish province of Mexico, and the Gulf of Mexico on the south. As the seventeenth century saw the struggle among the European nations for control of Europe, so the eighteenth century was to see the conflict for supremacy in North America carried on between France and England. As a preparation for this struggle, France proceeded to establish settlements in her territory along the Gulf.

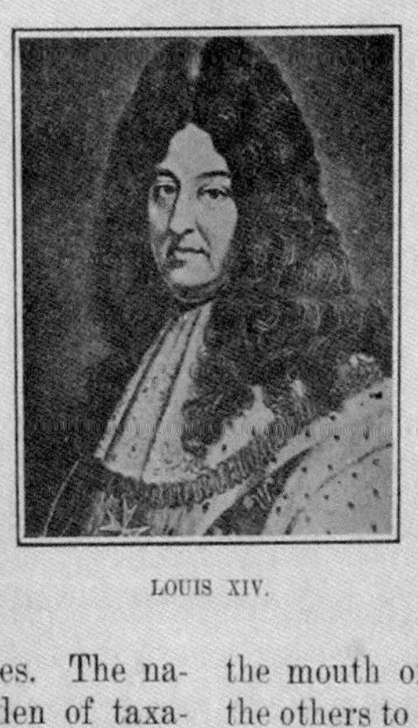

LOUIS XIV.

Early Colonization of Louisiana. Pierre Le Moyne d'Iberville was chosen in 1698 to settle Louisiana. An able seaman, brave, energetic, inured to hardships by his life on the frontier of Canada, Iberville was in every way suited to the accomplishment of the difficult task. With four ships and two hundred emigrants, he crossed the Atlantic, and after touching at San Domingo and Pensacola, at which latter place he found the Spaniards already established, anchored in Mobile Bay. After cruising among the islands along the coast, they reached the mouth of the Mississippi on March 2, 1699, and for the first time since La Salle's memorable visit, the solemn notes of the Te Deum resounded through the dismal swamps. Iberville ascended the Mississippi as far as Red River and returned by the same route to the mouth of Bayou Manchac, where, leaving the others to continue their way by the river, he, accompanied by three companions and an Indian guide, entered Bayou Manchac; thence he proceeded through Lakes Maurepas, Pontchartrain and Borgne, to Mississippi Sound and Mobile Bay, which he thus reached before the river party. As he had found no spot on the river free from the annual overflow, he erected a fort on the east side of Biloxi Bay (named after an Indian tribe), where is now Ocean Springs, and called it Biloxi. Iberville left Louisiana in order to take part in the war of the Spanish Succession (Queen Anne's War), and entrusted the governorship to his younger brother, Bienville. A settlement was made on Mobile Bay, to which the capital was removed from Biloxi. In 1704, a ship bringing twenty girls for the colonists arrived. Internal dissensions, lack of funds and food, low class of immigrants, unfavorable natural conditions, and fever visitations, retarded the development of the colony.

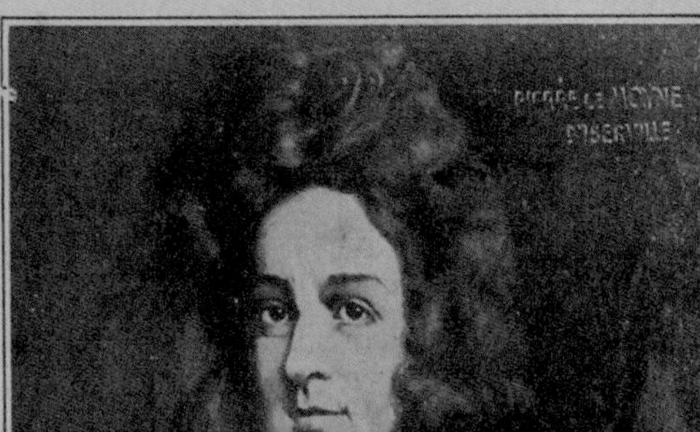

PIERRE LE MOYNE D'IBERVILLE.

Louisiana a Proprietary Colony 1712-1717. Louis XIV. became tired of the burden of Louisiana, and granted the province, with exclusive control of the trade as far north as Illinois, to Anthony Crozat, a wealthy Paris banker, who was to give the king a share in the precious metals and stones. Cadillac was appointed governor by the proprietor, with Bienville as lieutenant-governor. A trading post was established at Natchitoches and at a few other places, and trade with Mexico was vainly sought. Cadillac declared war against the powerful Natchez Indians for having murdered some Frenchmen, and sent Bienville with a small force against them. He succeeded by strategy in decoying the leaders into his hands and forced them to accept his terms. De l'Epinay now became governor, but met with no better success than Cadillac. As Crozat had parted with a large part of his fortune in the endeavor to make money out of Louisiana, he decided to restore the king's gift by resigning the charter.

2. PROPRIETORSHIP OF THE COMPANY OF THE WEST.

Company of the West. In 1717, the French Government chartered a company to take over Louisiana. At the head of this company was John Law, a Scotchman, who, by his bold financial schemes, had dazzled the regent, the Duc d'Orléans, and obtained great influence in the management of the government's finances. The company received a twenty-five-year charter, and promised during that period to send over six thousand white persons and three thousand African slaves. There were at that time seven hundred whites in Louisiana. Law's great insight into the condition of the country was displayed in his advertising among the people of the Lowlands of Europe for emigrants to Louisiana; he established a band of these Germans on his own land grant on the Arkansas River. Bienville was reinstated governor, and immediately made plans for a settlement on the Mississippi River.

Founding of New Orleans, 1718. Iberville had proven the land along the left bank of the river, south of Bayou Manchac, to be a real island, surrounded by the waters of the Mississippi, Bayou Manchac, the three lakes, and the

Gulf of Mexico. Bienville chose for the site of his settlement an elevation on this island one hundred ten miles from the river's mouth, between the head of Bayou St. John and the river. This location presented many advantages over the surrounding country; the land was higher; it was accessible by two waterways, by the Mississippi and by the lakes and Bayou St. John; it was well known to the Indians of that district as the home of the Houma Indians, hence could be a good Indian trading post. Even though this land was elevated above the rest of the country, it was subject to frequent overflows, and was then scarcely more than a swamp presenting elevations, and had all the disadvantages of an uncleared lowland in a semi-tropical climate. To this spot, in 1718, Bienville sent the Sieur le Blond de la Tour and fifty men to clear the undergrowth and lay out the city. De la Tour, assisted by Pauger, arranged the settlement in the shape of a rectangle facing the river, and in the middle marked off a square to be used as a Place d'Armes, to the rear of this to be the church, school and government house. Barracks and a few huts were erected, and to this crude settlement Bienville gave the name of La Nouvelle Orléans in honor of the Regent, the Duc d'Orléans. Storms and fever visitations, prevented the immediate growth of the little settlement.

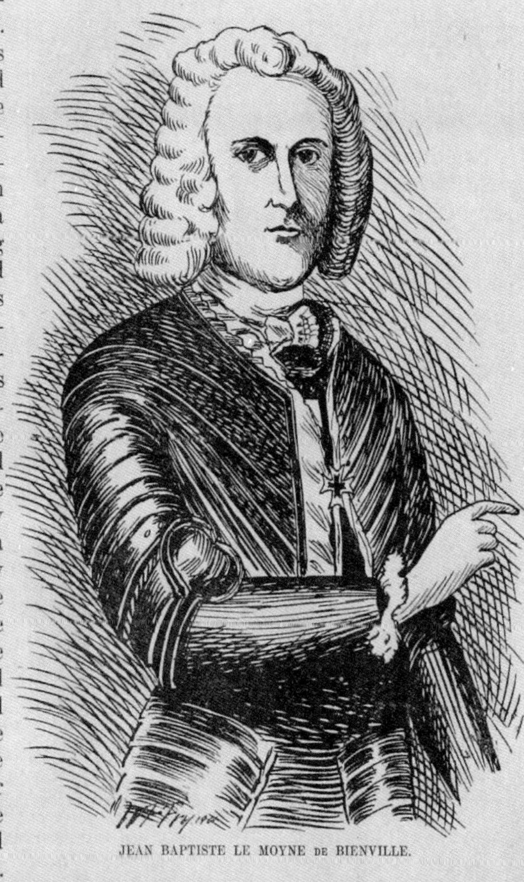

JEAN BAPTISTE LE MOYNE DE BIENVILLE.

New Orleans, the Capital, 1722. When Bienville had requested that New Orleans be made the capital of the colony, the directors refused, saying it could not be safely reached by large vessels. In 1722, Bienville had his chief engineer, Pauger, examine the mouths of the Mississippi; he reported eighteen feet of water in southeast pass, and suggested that if dikes were built along this pass and the others closed, the current would, by its own power, keep sand out of this pass. It was in accordance with this plan that, a century and a half later, Eads constructed the jetties. Bienville had one of his vessels taken through the pass of the Balize. The directors, on receiving the reports of these investigations, yielded to Bienville and New Orleans was made the capital. According to Père Charlevoix, who visited New Orleans in this year, the town consisted of a hundred disorderly, barrack-like buildings, a wooden storehouse, and two or three homes that would not ornament a French village; nevertheless, he foresaw a great future for this city, found its location superior to that of Rome and Paris, and declared it would be "one day—and perhaps that day is not far distant—an opulent city and the metropolis of a great and rich colony." Three years previous, the first negro slaves had been introduced, five hundred in number. The position of New Orleans near the mouth of the river controlled the southern entrance to the whole country between the Alleghenies and the Rockies, for the province of Louisiana was then only accessible by the rivers draining its vast extent, all of which contributed their waters to the Mississippi long before it reached the point opposite La Nouvelle Orléans.

Failure of Law's Bank. Law's great bank in Paris failed at this time, ruining the majority of those connected with him. The poor Germans whom he had located on the banks of the Arkansas managed to reach New Orleans, and there prayed Bienville to send them back to their homes. He persuaded them to settle along the river above the city. Thus was formed the nucleus of the German settlement on the banks of the Mississippi which is to this day called German Coast.

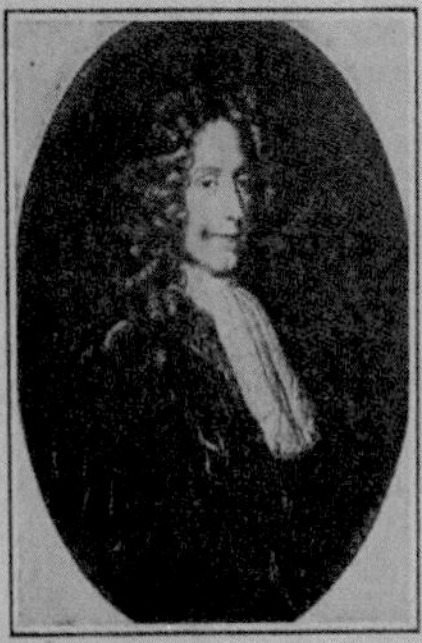

JOHN LAW.

As slaves continued to be received, laws had to be made for their governance; Bienville drew up the Black Code, a set of laws which has been equally well praised and blamed. About the most important provision was that forbidding the intermarriage of the black and white races, which is still enforced in Louisiana. Bienville was now recalled and Perrier appointed to succeed him.

Governorship of Perrier. Perrier accomplished many improvements. He had a levee eighteen feet wide and nine hundred feet long constructed in front of New Orleans and continued for eighteen miles above and below the city. The inhabitants furnished their slaves to do the work and the government fed them while they were so engaged. To protect the city against Indian inroads, a stockade with eight little forts was erected. The first sanitary measure was now undertaken, namely, as Perrier termed it, ventilating the city by clearing the forest between the city and Lake Pontchartrain; lack of funds and means prevented its completion. Taxation was unknown; hence the only revenues available for public improvements were those furnished by the home government.

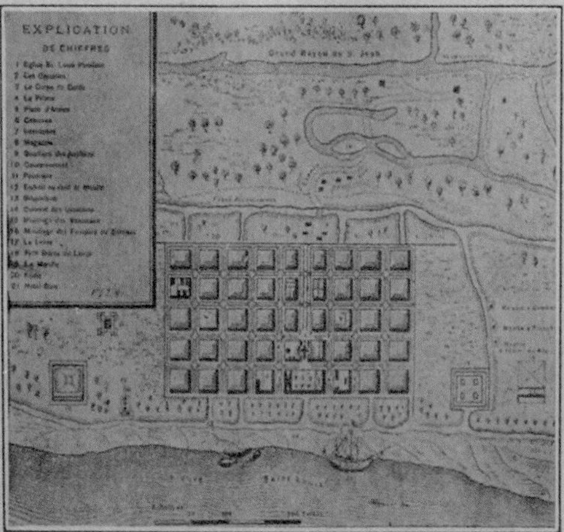

MAP OF 1728.

Need of Women. There were few women of good character in the colony; consequently many of the better settlers, missing their home-life in France, desired to return. It thus became evident that, if the settlement were to be permanent, the men must have good wives to make homes for them. An experiment in Indian wives was tried; but as one dusky bride, on returning from France, where her marriage to a French officer had been performed at court with great pomp, grew tired of civilization and, having sought again the haunts of her tribe, was influenced by them to betray her husband's post, it was deemed an unwise innovation. When Bienville left the colony, in 1724, he promised to send a band of good women over as soon as possible. In 1727, the "Casket Girls" (Filles à la cassette), so called because of each having received a box containing her trousseau, arrived and were placed under the care of the Ursulines until they should be married.

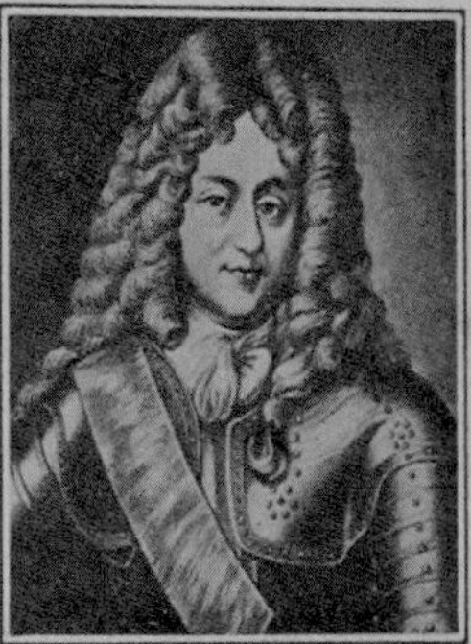

DUC D'ORLEANS.

Education. In 1726, Bienville sold to a company of Jesuits a plantation which, by later extensions, up to 1745, occupied about the area of the present First District. Here, in 1727, the Jesuits established a church and mission center. Their plantation became the first agricultural school of Louisiana, for here they introduced the cultivation of the orange, fig, sugar cane (1751), indigo plant, and myrtle, from which was obtained myrtle wax; these became staple crops and the industry and enterprise of the Fathers a good example to the other colonists. The order was suppressed through political reasons in 1763 and their great plantation confiscated by the king of Spain and sold for about one hundred eighty thousand dollars.

A convent of Capuchins was established adjoining the church, of which they took charge, besides conducting the regular parish school. The boys, however, had to be sent to France for a good education.

The girls of New Orleans were more fortunate, for, in 1727, Bienville had induced the Ursuline Nuns to establish a convent there. They were first located in Bienville's former home, until their convent on Chartres and Ursuline Streets was completed in 1730; this building is the oldest in the United States, west of the Alleghenies, and the school conducted by the sisters was the first in the United States to be opened for girls.

Life in New Orleans in 1730. The city extended from Bienville to Ursuline Streets, and from the river to Dauphine Street. The Place d'Armes was located in the central square facing the river, and to the rear of it was the church and convent of the Capuchins; farther down, on what are now Hospital and Ursuline Streets, were the convent of the Ursulines, the hospital, and barracks; the homes of the colonists clustered about the Place d'Armes and these principal buildings; the homes were built of wood and soft brick, and, like all pioneer homes, presented little comfort. Greased paper or linen was used in the windows instead of glass, and torches or the ill-smelling myrtle wax candle furnished artificial light. Nevertheless, according to the letters of Sister Madeleine Hachard, an Ursuline nun, to her family in France, the people dressed, had the same manners, and partook of the same foods as the people in France. Sister Madeleine wrote that the ladies knew how to paint and rouge as did those in France, and that their manners were as charming; she was much surprised to enjoy café au lait and chocolate for breakfast. There were now five thousand whites and two thousand blacks in the colony; the white population consisted of French, Germans, and Canadians; the blacks were negroes from Africa.

Natchez War. The greed of the French commander at Fort Rosalie in Mississippi, for the best lands, had urged him to seize the White Apple village from the Natchez. As a result, the Indians fell upon the fort and settlement and massacred two hundred men, taking the women and children into captivity. Perrier fitted out an expedition and marched against them; but they managed to escape by strategy. They took their last stand at Sicily Island in the northern section of the state; here, after being forced to give up their white captives, the greater number of the braves escaped to the Chickasaws. In consequence of this drain upon its funds, the Company of the West gave up its charter. Louisiana again became a royal colony. Perrier was recalled and Bienville reappointed as governor.

3. NEW ORLEANS, 1731-'63.

Negro Insurrection, 1732. In the attempt to put down the Natchez, the Louisianians had even armed and trained their negro slaves. The negroes then rose in revolt. The insurrection was not suppressed until the leaders had been put to death—the women on the gallows, and the men on the wheel. The heads of the men were put on posts at each end of the town to arouse fear in probable future insurrectionists.

Chickasaw War. Bienville saw the necessity of defeating the Chickasaws, the harborers of the Natchez warriors, if peace were to be restored in Louisiana. In 1736, he marched against them in northern Mississippi. Through English help, they were able to defeat Bienville's army, taking many captives; these poor unfortunates were burned by the Indians as Bienville withdrew the remnant of his army. He fitted out another expedition, which was even more overwhelmingly defeated. Repulsed by the Indians and worn out by the trials and hardships of the colony, the Father of Louisiana asked to be recalled. His request was granted and the Marquis de Vaudreuil, "le grand Marquis," was appointed to succeed him.

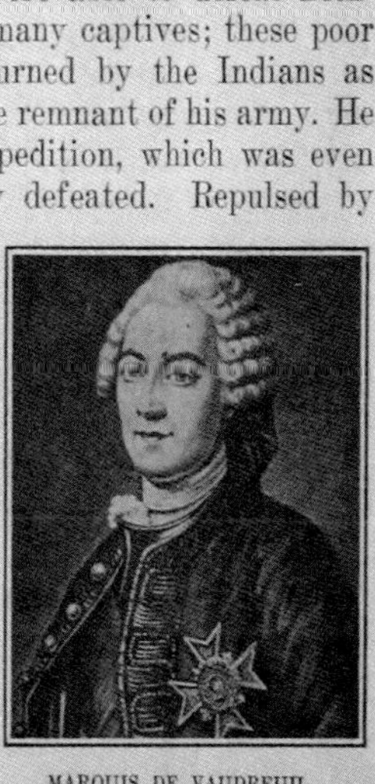

MARQUIS DE VAUDREUIL.

Improvements. De Vaudreuil's rule was a period of development. The levees, so necessary to the good of the country, were extended and made better. In 1737, Jean Louis, a poor sailor, laid the foundation of one of the city's greatest institutions—the Charity Hospital. Its first quarters were in a building on Rampart Street, between St. Louis and Toulouse. English occupation of the Ohio Valley drove out many of the French settlers, who then flocked to New Orleans. This sudden influx of people forced the government to erect more commodious barracks in the lower part of the city by the river front, where is now Barracks Street. Sixty more girls of good character were sent over in the care of the Ursulines. New Orleans became the trade center of the colony. Hides, tobacco, indigo, rice, and a little cotton and sugar were sent to her by the other sections of Louisiana for export. Cotton was introduced in 1740. As a slave could pick not more than six pounds a day, it was not extensively raised until after Whitney's invention of the gin, when, with the gin, a negro might clean a thousand pounds a day. The Jesuits brought in sugarcane in 1751 from San Domingo and cultivated it on their plantation. A few years later, Dubreuil devoted a large plantation to the cultivation of sugar-cane, building thereon the first sugar mill in Louisiana; his plantation was located where Esplanade Avenue is to-day. The method of granulating was unknown; the sugar produced was hard, sticky, gluey; tafia, a drink resembling rum, was made from it. The export of this sugar to France was attempted in 1765, but was given up owing to a large portion of it having leaked out of the barrels.

Obstacles to Progress. One of the great hindrances to progress was the unstable condition of the currency, which was changed three times during this period; finally the king and Council of State of France interfered and put a stop to changes in the currency. Lack of money also militated against the colony's advance. The monopoly system, by which the government gave or sold to an individual or company the sole right to operate an industry, is of its very nature detrimental to the good of a community. The Louisiana government not only supported monopolies, but even arbitrarily regulated the price at which produce, such as tobacco, rice, etc., should be sold. Again, the people had no voice in their government; frequently laws and regulations were formulated in France by people ignorant of the conditions in Louisiana.

Fourth French and Indian War. France and England, during these years, were approaching their final struggle for commercial, naval and colonial supremacy. Rivals in Europe, India and America, the two nations, for over half a century, had kept the world of that day in a constant state of war. In North America, France had established her power in Canada and Louisiana, and, by a system of forts extending from the mouth of the St. Lawrence to that of the Mississippi, had sought to make her position invulnerable; her last step in that direction had been the erection of Fort Duquesne at the juncture of the Alleghany and Monongahela Rivers, where they unite to form the Ohio River. This position at the head of the Ohio Valley might be said to be the key to the whole system of French Forts. The English had established their control on the Atlantic coast from Maine to Florida. The Virginians realized the importance of Fort Duquesne and sent Major George Washington to dislodge the French. He failed, and a British army led by Braddock against it in 1755 met with crushing defeat. The war that then began is known in Europe as the Seven Years' War. At first, victory favored the French; but in 1757, William Pitt, becoming Prime Minister of England, changed the tide of victory to the English side.

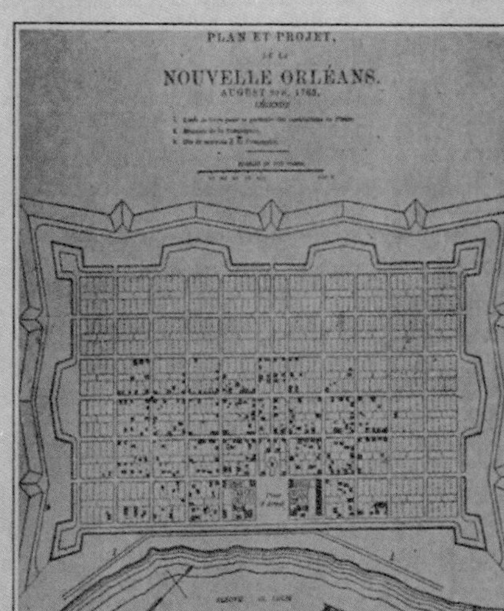

MAP OF NEW ORLEANS, 1763.

The war was practically ended by the surrender of Quebec and Montreal to the English; the former in 1759, and the latter in 1760. Peace was not concluded until 1763, when a treaty was signed in Paris. By this treaty, France ceded to England Canada, Cape Breton Island, and Louisiana as far west as the Mississippi River, excepting the Isle of Orleans. England had captured Manila and Havana from the Spaniards, but returned them on Spain ceding Florida to her.

Government Under French Rule. The Louisiana province was governed by a Superior Council, composed originally of two members, namely, the governor and commissary. Gradually the membership was extended to twelve persons. This council was the supreme legislative and judicial body in the colony. That does not mean that all laws for Louisiana were made in the colony; many were made in France, and all others had, of course, to accord with French law. "The Custom of Paris" became the basis of colonial law. Louisiana was divided into nine districts, each having a commandant and judge, but these were subject to the Superior Council. The people, unlike the English colonists, took no part in their own government; however, on the whole, considering the times, the colony was governed well and liberally. There was broader religious toleration in Louisiana than in most of the English colonies along the Atlantic coast.

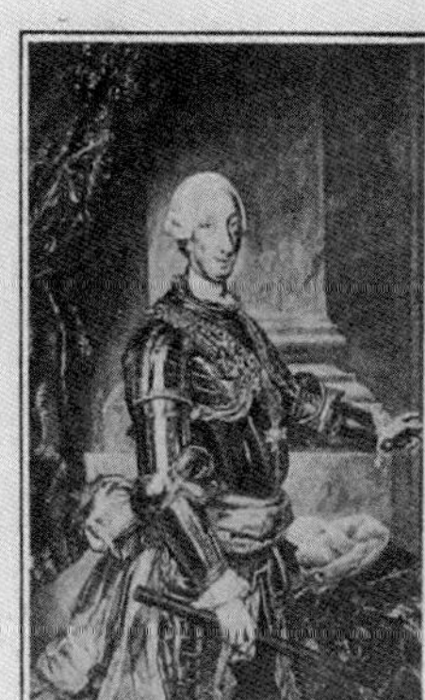

CHARLES III OF SPAIN.

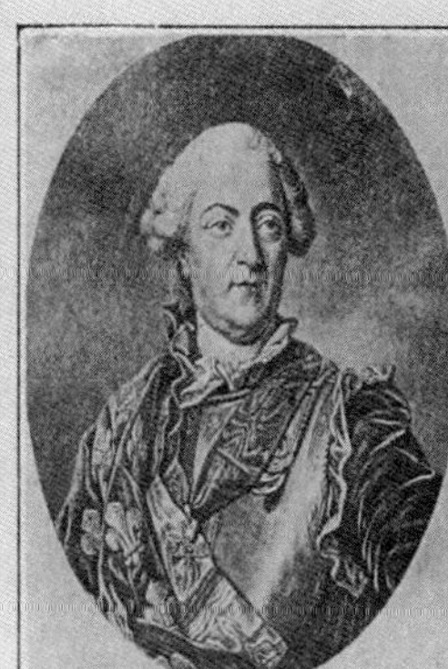

LOUIS XV.

Changing Ownership. In 1763, the Treaty of Paris was concluded between France and England; by this treaty, England gained all the territory east of the Mississippi, except the Isle of Orleans. On November 3, 1762, Louis XV. had, by the secret treaty of St. Ildefonso, given all Louisiana, west of the Mississippi, and the Isle of Orleans to his cousin, Charles III. of Spain. Governor Kerlerec, the successor of Vaudreuil, had been recalled to France, and, on charge of having misappropriated the colony's funds, had been thrown into the Bastile. d'Abbadie then became governor. It was not until October, 1764, that the French king notified the governor of the transfer of Louisiana, nearly two years previous, to Spain, and ordered him to surrender Louisiana to accredited Spanish commissioners when they should present themselves. The people heard the tidings with dismay, and could not be convinced that it was final. A convention assembled in New Orleans and sent Jean Milhet, one of the wealthiest merchants, with a petition to the king entreating him to take them back under French control.

SECTION 2. SPANISH DOMINATION.

1. MANIFESTATION OF THE SPIRIT OF LIBERTY, 1766-1768.

Don Antonio de Ulloa. Four years after the cession of Louisiana to Spain, the Spanish government sent over Don Antonio de Ulloa as governor of the province. Ulloa was a distinguished scientist, but, by his lack of judgment and tact, unfitted to occupy his new position. He wrote from Havana to Aubry, successor of d'Abadie, of his appointment as governor, and of his early arrival in Louisiana; yet, when he reached New Orleans, he refused to present his credentials, and removed neither the French officials nor the French flag. Louisiana had a joint Spanish and French government. For seven months Ulloa absented himself from the city to await at the Balize for the coming of his Peruvian bride. Among the few beneficial acts of

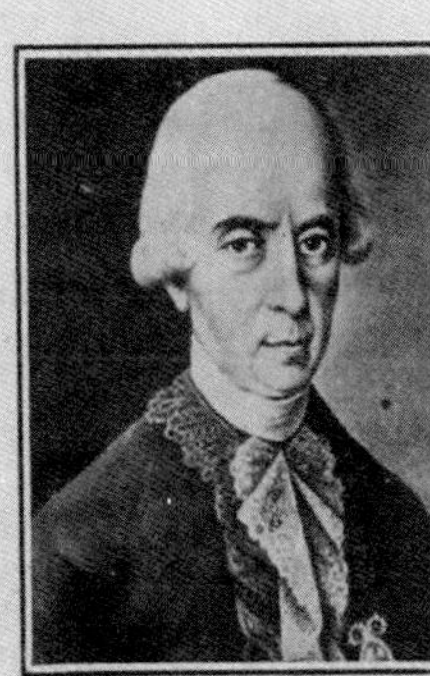

DON ANTONIO DE ULLOA.

this governor were his trade regulations. He ordered the merchants not to sell their goods until "just and intelligent persons" had inspected them and listed the prices.

Conspiracy of October, 1768. The merchants called upon the Superior Council to prevent the enforcement of these regulations. Led by Lafrénière, Doucet, the Milhets and others, a conspiracy was formed for the expulsion of Ulloa and the seizure of the city. Noyan and Villeré, with their followers, secured control of the city, forcing Ulloa to flee for safety to a Spanish vessel in the harbor. The patriots drew up a memorial of Ulloa's outrages and sent a copy to him in Havana. They then formed the project of organizing a republic and union of all American colonies. The plan failed. The times were not yet ready for such a change.

2. ESTABLISHMENT OF SPANISH CONTROL, 1769-'70.

Suppression of the Revolution. Spain decided to keep Louisiana. It would serve as a good bulwark between the English possessions and valued Mexico. Don Alexandro O'Reilly became the new governor, and with three thousand six hundred Spanish troops and twenty-four vessels, arrived at New Orleans in August, 1769. The leaders of the conspiracy of '68 thought of leaving the colony. Aubry, who was in constant communication with O'Reilly, advised against this, saying they would be treated with clemency. However, events proved the contrary. They were entrapped, and five of the principals, including Lafrénière and Noyan, were shot October 25, 1769; six others were confined in various prisons.

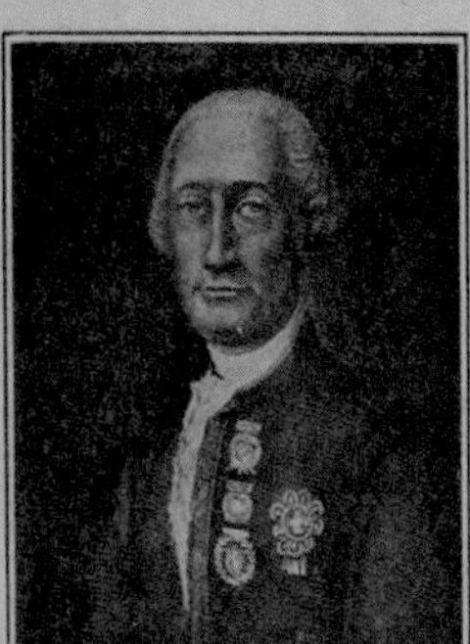

DON ALEXANDRO O'REILLY.

Change in Government. O'Reilly abolished the Superior Council and replaced it by the Cabildo, in which some of the memberships were held for life. The governor presided over the Cabildo in person. Spanish laws were substituted for the French, but as both were based on the Roman code, this did not cause much change. The Spanish language became the official tongue, though French was permitted in notarial and judicial acts in the parishes. A system of taxation was organized which provided a regular revenue for the city; a shipping tax was devoted to the construction and improvement of the levees. Commerce was greatly benefited by the opening of free trade with Cuba. A census taken gives the population of New Orleans at three thousand one hundred ninety, of which one thousand nine hundred one were free persons, one thousand two hundred thirty slaves, and sixty Indians; there were four hundred sixty-eight houses.

3. SPANISH DEVELOPMENT OF NEW ORLEANS, 1770-1800.

Improvement of Trade Laws. When O'Reilly came to New Orleans, the English controlled the trade. This was soon stopped by English ships being prohibited entrance into the port. Under certain restrictions, trade was allowed with Campeachy and the French and Spanish West Indies. Trade in slaves from these islands was forbidden because of the revolutionary spirit existing there, but encouragement was given to the Guinea slave trade. Governor Galvez permitted free trade with France and the Thirteen American Colonies in 1778. Merchants from Boston, New York and Philadelphia soon opened business houses in New Orleans.

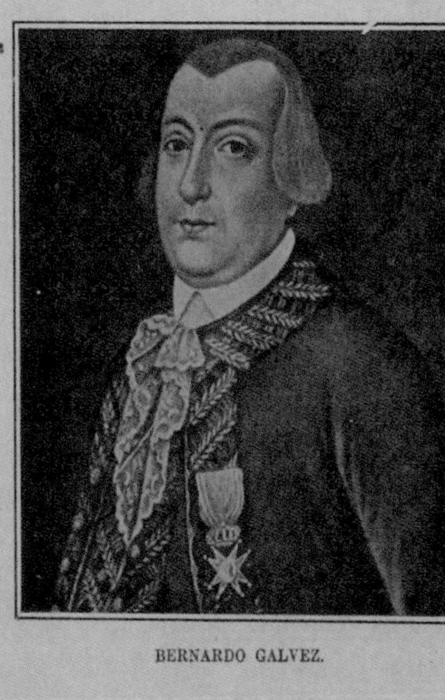

BERNARDO GALVEZ.

Assistance Given to American Revolution. Galvez allowed Oliver Pollock, an American merchant, to collect arms and ammunition and send them by a fleet of canoes to Fort Pitt for delivery to the Americans. In 1779, Spain allied herself to the Thirteen Colonies and France against England. Galvez immediately marched against Fort Manchac, Baton Rouge, Mobile and Pensacola, and drove the English from these forts. The Treaty of Paris, 1783, confirmed Spain in the possession of this territory, granted free and open navigation of the Mississippi River to the subjects of Great Britain and the United States, and gave thirty-one degrees North Latitude as the southern boundary of the United States.

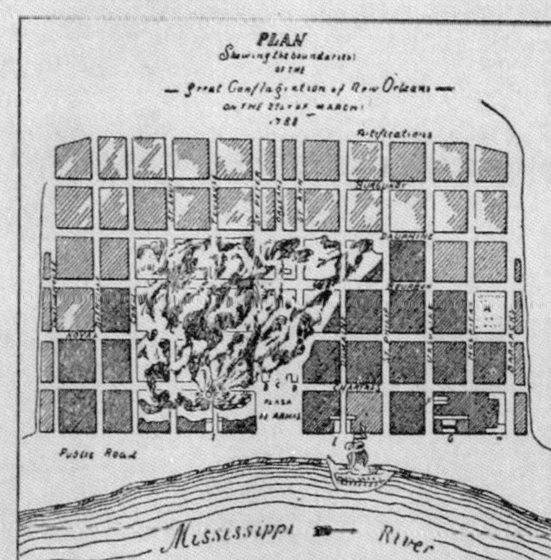

PLAN OF THE GREAT CONFLAGRATION, 1788.

Great Fires of 1788 and 1794. The conflagration of 1788 originated in a Spanish official's private chapel on Chartres Street, near St. Louis. It destroyed the central portion of the town, where were the commercial quarter, the principal residences, government house, arsenal, prison, church, and Capuchin convent. Nineteen squares were devastated, with a loss of eight hundred fifty-six houses. In 1794, some children accidentally set fire to a hay store on Royal Street. Two hundred twelve homes were destroyed. The cathedral, recently rebuilt, escaped. The financial loss occasioned by this fire exceeded that of the first, and has been estimated at two million six hundred thousand dollars. Camps were opened in the Place d'Armes and on the levee to shelter the homeless population.

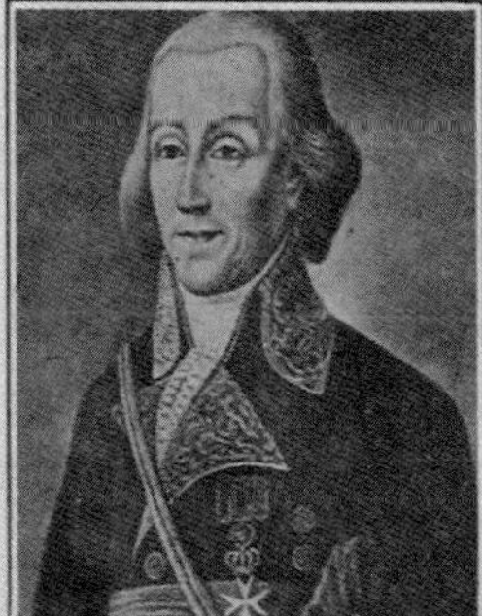

BARON DE CARONDELET.

Spanish Rebuilding of the City. The conflagration had a most beneficial effect on the city. It was seen that the material generally used for buildings was highly inflammable and assisted the fire in its ravages. Carondelet urged the use of tile roofs instead of shingles, and even offered a premium on them. The old city gradually rose up as we see it to-day, with its Spanish-American architecture—walls of adobe or brick, white or yellow lime-washed stucco, heavy doors and windows, balconies, portes-cochères, arcades, and inner courts; two-story homes replaced the former low one-story.

Work of Don Almonaster y Roxas. Don Almonaster y Roxas was the greatest benefactor of New Orleans in that period. He opened his purse freely to his city in her hour of need, for all purposes. He rented in perpetuity from the city the squares flanking the Place d'Armes, and where now stand the red Pontalba buildings, erected a fine row of brick buildings, which were immediately occupied by "boutiques," the retail stores. In 1784, he had the Charity Hospital, which had been destroyed by a hurricane five years previous, rebuilt in brick at a cost of one hundred fourteen thousand dollars. Three years later, he gave the Ursuline Nuns a chapel of stucco brick. The rebuilding of the church was begun in 1792 at his expense and, when completed two years later, became the

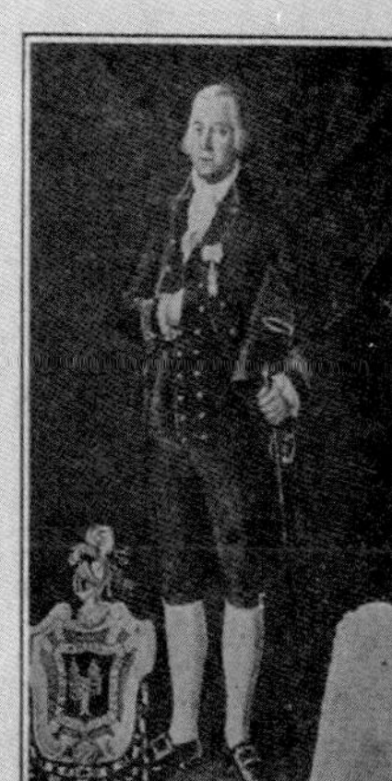

DON ANDRES ALMONASTER Y ROXAS.

cathedral, as Florida and Louisiana had been united into one diocese, with the bishopric in New Orleans. The cathedral was constructed of brick, and appeared much as it does to-day. Owing to cracking, the belfrys, which were added in 1815, were changed in the fifties. Don Almonaster gave not only to charity and religion, but to the government as well. In 1795, he gave the city its town hall, or hall of the Cabildo, now commonly known as simply the Cabildo; there has been one great change made in its appearance since the time of its founder — the addition of a French roof. Here, the Spanish Cabildo held its sessions and the formal transfer of Louisiana from France to the United States took place.

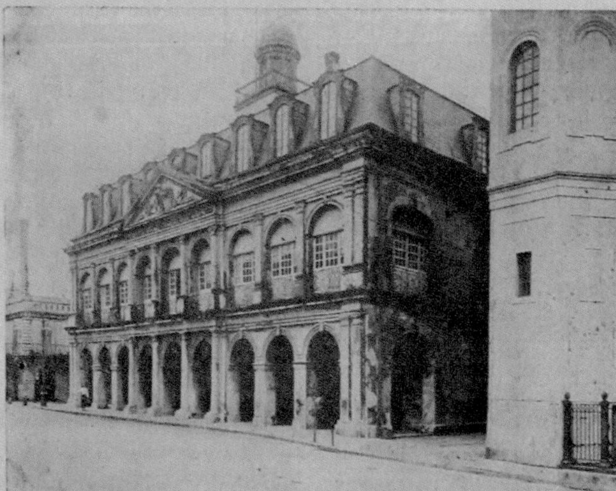

CABILDO AS IT APPEARS TODAY.

Government's Improvements. The barracks, begun by Kerlerec as places of refuge for the French settlers driven out of other places captured by the English, were well completed and nearby a military hospital and chapel were built.

Where now stands the Customhouse, a little wooden one was erected; the "Old French Market," the "Halle de Boucheries," was also built then. By 1796, the excavation of Carondelet Canal and the "old basin" was completed; thus New Orleans was connected with Bayou St. John and Lake Pontchartrain, and the city's drainage begun.

San Domingo Refugees. The revolutions in San Domingo caused many of the planters to come with their families and slaves to New Orleans. They brought with them the French revolutionary ideas of the period, which they easily introduced by means of such songs as the "Marsellaise" and the "Ca Ira."

Carondelet's Fortifications. Though the Kentucky farmers needed open waters to the Gulf for the transportation of their crops, they turned a deaf ear to the invitation of the messenger from Carondelet that they oppose the United States. Fearing lest these farmers should plan an attack and to protect the city against possible inroads of the Kentuckians and put down the developing revolutionary spirit within the city, Carondelet had the city fortified. Though these fortifications could not have accomplished the first purpose, they did secure the sec-

VIEW IN THE INTERIOR OF THE CABILDO.
Showing the Grand Staircase and Wrought Iron Door.

VIEW OF THE CORRIDOR OF THE CABILDO.
Showing Massive Arches.

ond; there were five forts connected by a wall, in front of which was a moat. Fort St. Charles was on the lower river front and Fort St. Louis on the upper; each of these consisted of a fort and a parapet eighteen feet thick, faced with brick; they could each accommodate one hundred fifty men, and were armed with twelve twelve and eighteen-pounders. Fort Burgundy was at the corner of Canal and Rampart; Fort St. Joseph on the present Beauregard Square (formerly known as Congo Square); and Fort St. Ferdinand at the corner of Rampart and Esplanade Avenue. The wall connecting these forts was fifteen feet high, and the fosse, or moat, seven feet in depth by a width of forty feet; Carondelet Canal kept the water in it about three feet high.

Granulation of Sugar, 1795. The indigo crop had not been a success because of the unfavorable climate and the devastation of an insect that fed on its leaves. Etienne de Boré decided to cultivate his entire plantation in sugar. This plantation was where Carrollton now is. He hired a skillful sugar-maker, a San Domingo refugee, to granulate the sugar. Mr. de Boré's family and friends had pleaded with him not to be so rash, but to no purpose. A number of planters went to de Boré's for the experiment. They gathered around the little mill to watch the process. Suddenly a cry arose, "It granulates!" De Boré's fortune was made and the famed Louisiana industry brought to light, opening wide a great door to prosperity.

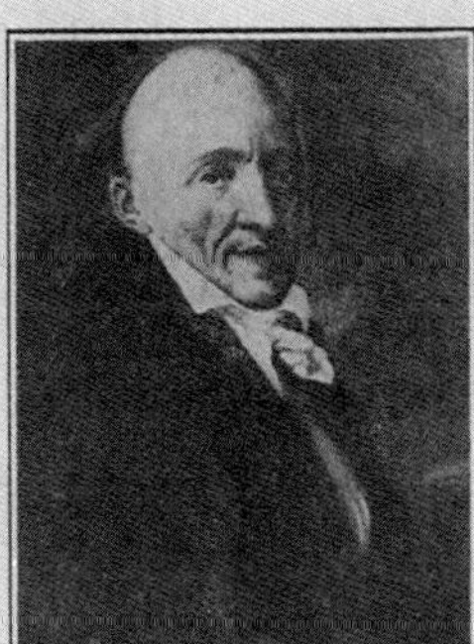

ETIENNE DE BORE.

Commerce. By the Treaty of Paris, 1783, the Mississippi River was free to Great Britain and the United States for navigation; but Spain did not intend to hold to this clause. Those Americans who had crossed over the Alleghany Mountains to seek homes in the rich valley of the Ohio took advantage of this privilege to build up a flatboat trade with New Orleans, exchanging their produce of hides, meat, flour, corn, etc., for manufactured goods. As early as 1786, some of these flatboats were seized and confiscated. The enraged Westerners threatened to capture New Orleans, but waited for Congress to treat with Spain. Spain had two plans, namely, to induce the Kentuckians to come in as immigrants, or to generate among them the spirit of insurrection against the "negligence" of Congress, and thus separate the West from the East. Some Westerners did come, and located about the town of New Madrid. General James Wilkinson, a shrewd Kentuckian, sent a number of flatboats laden with Western produce to New Orleans in 1787, and, by working on Governor Miro's political fears, opened up the river trade. France controlled the city's Atlantic trade. The port of New Orleans was neither closed nor open; commerce could be carried on, but there was danger; all depended on the caprices of Spanish officials. In 1793, Spain granted to all her colonies free trade with Europe and America.

Carondelet succeeded Miro as governor. He endeavored through an agent, one Thomas Powers, to bribe the Kentucky leaders into separating from the United States, but in vain.

New Orleans was opened to the Americans as a point of deposit for three years, free of duty or charge on produce, except a reasonable price for store rent. The commerce of New Orleans improved by leaps and bounds. The levee was the scene of noisy, excited bustling and business. Before the people could realize it, the three years had passed. The United States demanded that Spain evacuate her territory, as agreed in the two treaties. Morales, the intendant of the colony, closed the port of New Orleans and assigned no other place to the Westerners. American indignation rose high. President Adams prepared an expedition to capture New Orleans. Its advance was prevented by the approaching retirement of Adams and Spain's disapproval of the intendant's act.

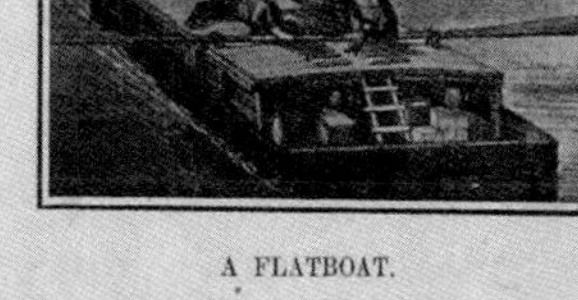

A FLATBOAT.

4. NEW ORLEANS, 1800-'15.

Buildings. The Spanish governors lived in a plain, one-story brick house at the corner of

Toulouse and the Rue de la Levée; it faced the river, had a parterre to one side and on the other a latticed screened gallery; the kitchen and stables were in the well-fenced rear yard. The Orleans legislature occupied the building from 1803 until it was burnt in 1827. The Charity Hospital and Military Hospital have also passed away. The Cathedral and Cabildo are still intact, and are splendid types of the Spanish architecture then prevalent. Brick or

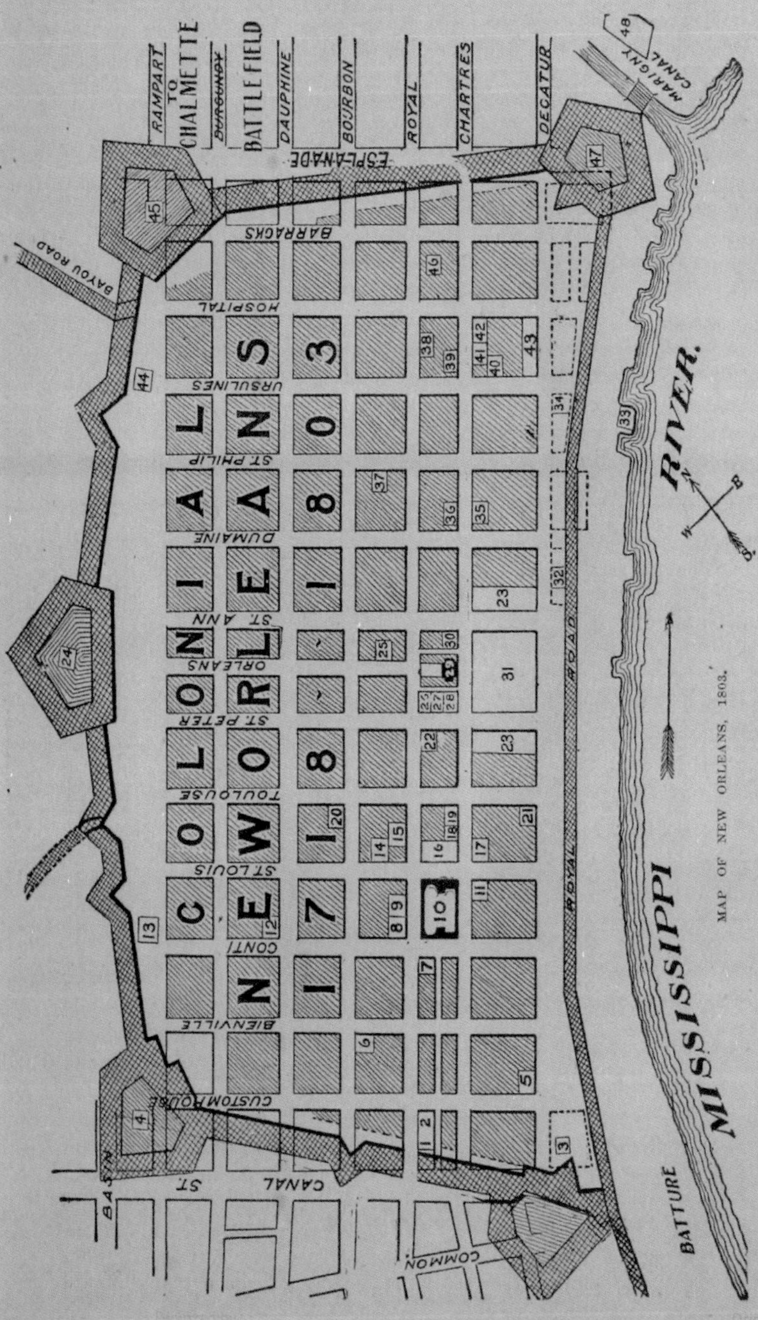

MAP OF NEW ORLEANS, 1803.

1. Merchants Exchange.
2. La. State Bank.
3. Fort St. Louis (site).
4. Fort Burgundy (site).
5. Bienville's House (site).
6. Old Absinthe House, 1798.
7. Mortgage Office.
8. Branch U. S. Bank.
9. La. Bank, 1804.
10. Court House, 1910.
11. Where defenses of N. O. were planned, 1814-15.
12. Audubon's Studio (site).
13. Italian Church.
14. Antoine's Restaurant.
15. Spanish Commanderia, 1769.
16. St. Louis Hotel (site).
17. Residence Mayor Girod.
18. Home of Judah Touro.
19. Hotel d'Orleans.
20. French Opera House.
21. Government House, 1761 (site).
22. First Skyscraper, 1774.
23. Pontalba Buildings.
24. Fort St. Ferdinand, 1766 (site).
25. Old Theatre d'Orleans.
26. Spanish Calabozo, 1769 (site).
27. Spanish Arsenal, 1770 (site).
28. "Cabildo."
29. St. Louis Cathedral.
30. "Presbytere," 1813.
31. Jackson Square.
32. French Market, 1813.
33. French Navy Yard, 1728 (site).
34. Waterworks Pump, 1813 (site).
35. Lafitte's Rendezvous (site).
36. Where Jackson was Tried (site).
37. Theatre St. Philip, 1798 (site).
38. Spanish Barracks (site).
39. Gen. Beauregard's Home.
40. Old Ursuline School, 1730.
41. Archbishop's Palace, 1727.
42. St. Mary's Archbishop's Church, 1780.
43. Typical Antebellum Slave Quarters.
44. Orleans College, 1811 (site).
45. Fort St. John (site).
46. Spanish Barracks (site).
47. Fort St. Charles (site).
48. Birthplace Jno. J. Audubon (site).

stucco with a covering of cement were used in building; the structures were massive, with arches and arched doorways, balconies and courtyards; they were to stand the wear of time and weather. The old French Market is also the product of these times, as is shown by the materials of which it is made and the large, cool arches. Many private buildings in the Vieux Carré date from this period.

People. The city was cosmopolitan in its population. There were the native Creoles, French, Spanish, English, Americans from the States, Germans, Italians, refugees from San Domingo and Martinique, emigrants from the Canaries, gipsies, negroes and Indians. The French were the shop-keepers and farmers; the Spaniards, in the government's employ; the Catalonians, the shop and saloon-keepers. The American, English and Irish element formed the chief commercial class. The dairymen and truck-farmers were mostly Canary Islanders or Islinques; the fishermen, Italians; gipsies, who had given up their wandering life, turned musicians and dancers. The "Kaintocks," Kentucky flatboatmen, formed a large, though floating population; they brought down the river on their flatboats the raw produce of the west and, after the sale of their cargoes, would give themselves up to riotous times. The Creoles cordially disliked them, as is shown by the custom among Creole mothers of telling a naughty child, "Tu n'es qu'un mauvais Kaintock."

Jackson Square. The Place d'Armes, now called Jackson Square, was the promenade of 1800. Here, the troops were reviewed and the children played of an evening, on the barren ground, beneath the shadow of the wooden gallows, which stood about where General Jackson's statue is to-day. The Cathedral, Capuchin convent, Cabildo, and government warehouses faced the square; the leading "boutiques" and restaurants were around, and to one side was French Market, where handkerchiefs, shoes and hats were sold along with meat, fruit and vegetables. The public landing was along the levee in front of the square. Here, on a holiday, the populace congregated; excitable Louisianians, ever ready to defend their honor with their rapiers; Canadian trappers and hunters; Attakapas 'Cadians in home-made cottonades; indolent gentlemen banished for interference with the king or politics; fascinating Quadroon beauties from San Domingo; quiet, energetic Germans from German coast; brilliantly uniformed Spanish soldiers; ex-galley slaves and convicts. Peddlers wheeled their goods about in coffin-shaped vehicles; turbaned women balanced large cans of milk and coffee on their heads. In the morning, the colored marchandes kept the air resounding with cries of "callas tous chauds," and at dusk, "belles chandelles."

Streets. The streets were regularly laid out, and drained by wooden gutters; but there was no pavement. Pedestrians were accommodated by a wooden banquette four or five feet wide; between the sidewalks, the streets were, according to the state of the weather, either a marsh or a mass of dust. Wagons sank to the hub as they worked their way through them. Chartres Street and the Rue de la Levée were the principal thoroughfares.

Lights. The streets were lighted by oil lamps swung at the street intersections from ropes caught to the corners of the houses; their dimness forced the people to carry lanterns if they wished to see their way. The homes were lighted by myrtle wax candles, placed, for protection against drafts, within huge glass vases, open at the bottom to facilitate their being put over the candles.

Water Supply. There were neither cisterns nor water system. The people drank filtered river water, and, for household purposes, used dug wells on the premises.

Servants. The servants were negro and Indian slaves. But it was the negro mammy who was the ideal servant as cook, nurse, and second mother to the children, despite the fact that she taught them the wretched patois, "gombo," of the Louisiana negro. This dialect consisted of a few hundred words, and lacked grammatical structure; it was originated by the primitive negroes of Africa, who found the French language too difficult. The manual work of the colony was done by slaves; people made a business of owning slaves, training them, and renting them out to those who did not possess any. The servants always dressed plainly; the women wore on their heads the brilliant bandannas, "tignons." Indian slaves were troublesome, and at length became so dangerous the United States government freed them; a little later there was a negro uprising, which was only overcome after considerable loss of life.

City Guardians. The military had the duty of preserving order. For this purpose a small band of soldiers was kept on duty at the calaboose, and at stated intervals paraded through the streets, or appeared on the scene of disorder after the trouble had subsided. At night, it was their duty to call out the hour and the state of the weather. Their costume was very imposing; it consisted of a deep blue frock, crossing over which were black leather straps to uphold a cartridge box, bayonet and scabbard; knee-breeches completed the outfit. They were armed with an old flint-lock musket and short sword.

Promenades and Drives. The favorite walk was along the levee; there, at the ends of the streets, were a few backless benches where the promenaders met to rest and chat. Bayou Road, leading to Gentilly and Metairie, was the evening driveway of the citizens.

Entertainment. The city boasted of one theatre, on St. Peter Street, between Royal and Bourbon; it was a long, low cypress structure. A company of San Domingo actors and actresses rendered comedy, vaudeville, and comic opera in 1799. After a few years, the troupe declined, and were replaced by local talent.

Dancing. Of all amusements, dancing was the most popular. In a long room, about eighty feet by thirty feet, in a wooden building on Chartres, between St. Ann and Dumaine, the light-hearted people met twice a week to enjoy the Terpsichorean art; one evening was for adults and the other for the children. The dancers paid fifty cents a head. Elevated boxes along the wall accommodated the mammas and young wall flowers; seats to the front of these were for the fair dancers; the men were allowed to stand. The music was furnished by gypsy violinists.

Duelling. There existed among the men of that day the "code d'honneur," by which a gentleman fought another for anything, from an accidental mashing of a sensitive corn to an attack on his life or character. French custom considered a man's honor satisfied by the first drop of blood. The Creole fought with colichemards, Creole rapiers, sword canes, or pistols. There were three noted duelling grounds, viz.: St. Anthony Square, in rear of the Cathedral, which was then thickly hedged in; "The Oaks," in City Park, where the more talked-of duels took place; and "Les Trois Capalins," three sister trees, on Metairie Road.

The First Newspaper. 1794 saw the first newspaper, "Le Moniteur de la Louisiane," published in New Orleans. It was not very newsy, being more of a journal of government proceedings. Ten years later, the first English paper, the Gazette, was edited.

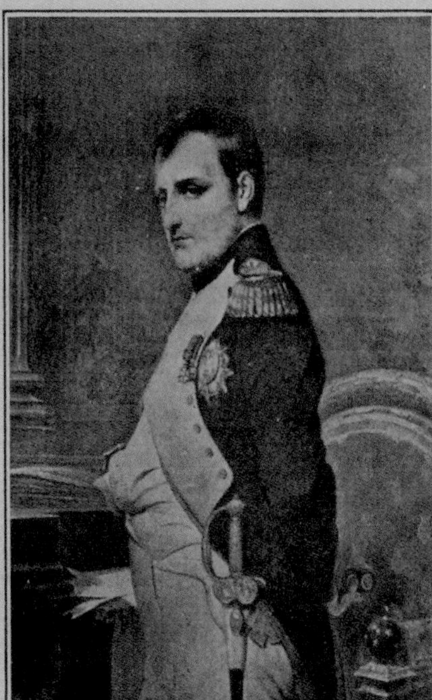

NAPOLEON BONAPARTE.

SECTION 3. TRANSITION PERIOD.

Louisiana Coveted by the United States and France. The United States realized the necessity of possessing Louisiana for the development of the western section, and proceeded to look to its acquisition. Napoleon, the First Consul of France, desired to re-establish the colonial power of France in North America, and looked with a pleased eye upon Louisiana.

Secret Treaty of Ildefonso, 1800. Napoleon persuaded the king of Spain to secretly cede Louisiana to France in exchange for a province in Italy. This transaction first became known in America in November, 1802.

Unsettled Conditions in Louisiana. Not until March, 1803, did the French Colonial prefect, Laussat, land in New Orleans. With Governor Salcedo and Marquis de Casa Calvo, a former governor, he began preparations for the reception of General Victor, who was to receive the formal transfer of Louisiana from Spain. Once more the people were astir. They knew not what to expect of the lately established Republican Government in France.

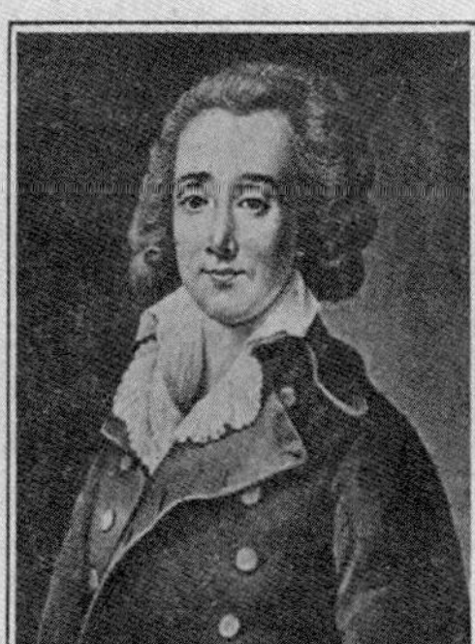

LAUSSAT.

Purchase of Louisiana by the United States, April 30, 1803. President Jefferson realized the great danger to the United States in having a foreign power in possession of the mouth of the Mississippi. He appointed Monroe and Livingston to treat with Napoleon for the purchase of the "Isle of Orleans." Napoleon refused this offer, but, instead, proposed to sell the whole of Louisiana for fifteen million dollars. The two commissioners realized the good quality of the bargain, and made the purchase April 30, 1803, trusting to Jefferson to secure its ratification by Congress. This Jefferson accomplished the following October, and obtained the authorization to take possession of the ceded territory.

The Transfers. Instead of General Victor's arrival in July, there came to New Orleans the news of the purchase of Louisiana by the United States in the preceding April. On November 30, the troops were drawn up in the Place d'Armes and, in the hall of the Cabildo, Governor Salcedo delivered the keys of the city to Laussat. Casa Calvo addressed the people in the name of the Spanish King, and released them from their allegiance to Spain; the Spanish flag was lowered and that of France hoisted. Twenty days later the same ceremony took place, with a

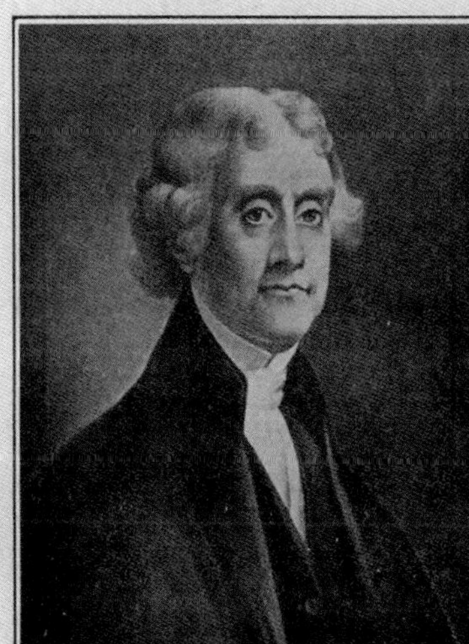

THOMAS JEFFERSON.

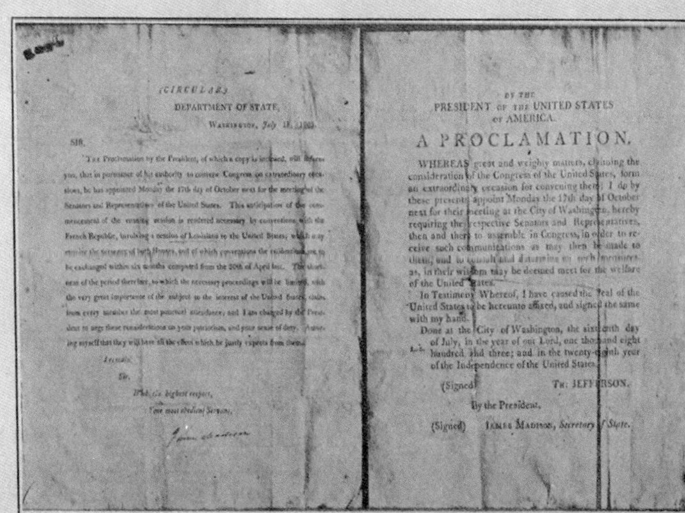

(CIRCULAR.)

DEPARTMENT OF STATE,

WASHINGTON, *July 18, 1803.*

SIR,

THE Proclamation by the President, of which a copy is inclosed, will inform you, that in pursuance of his authority to convene Congress on extraordinary occasions, he has appointed Monday the 17th day of October next for the meeting of the Senators and Representatives of the United States. This anticipation of the commencement of the ensuing session is rendered necessary by conventions with the French Republic, involving a cession of Louisiana to the United States, which may require the measures of both Houses, and of which conventions the ratifications are to be exchanged within six months computed from the 30th of April last. The shortness of the period therefore, to which the necessary proceedings will be limited, with the very great importance of the subject to the interest of the United States, claim from every member the most punctual attendance; and I am charged by the President to urge these considerations on your patriotism, and your sense of duty. Assuring myself that they will have all the effect which he justly expects from them.

I remain,

Sir,

With the highest respect,

Your most obedient Servant,

[illegible]

BY THE PRESIDENT OF THE UNITED STATES OF AMERICA.

A PROCLAMATION.

WHEREAS great and weighty matters, claiming the consideration of the Congress of the United States, form an extraordinary occasion for convening them; I do by these presents appoint Monday the 17th day of October next for their meeting at the City of Washington, hereby requiring the respective Senators and Representatives, then and there to assemble in Congress, in order to receive such communications as may then be made to them, and to consult and determine on such measures as, in their wisdom may be deemed meet for the welfare of the United States.

In Testimony Whereof, I have caused the Seal of the United States to be hereunto affixed, and signed the same with my hand.

Done at the City of Washington, the sixteenth day of July, in the year of our Lord, one thousand eight hundred and three; and in the twenty-eighth year of the Independence of the United States.

(Signed) TH: JEFFERSON.

By the President.

(Signed) JAMES MADISON, *Secretary of State.*

COPY OF JEFFERSON'S PROCLAMATION OF A SPECIAL SESSION OF CONGRESS TO RATIFY THE PURCHASE OF LOUISIANA FROM FRANCE.

change in the dramatis personnæ; Laussat transferred the province to the two American commissioners, Claiborne and Wilkinson; the former took charge of civil affairs and the latter of the military. With such sudden changes of nationality, in which the Louisianians were handed about from one nation to another, without ever being consulted, is it any wonder that they appeared apathetic and uninterested?

SECTION 4. AMERICAN DOMINATION.

1. New Orleans, 1803-'15.

Commerce. The purchase of Louisiana by the United States had an immediate effect on New Orleans trade. The first half of 1803 showed an increase in tonnage of thirty-seven per cent over that of 1802; the exports exceeded two million dollars and the imports two million five hundred thousand dollars. The flatboat trade became enormous; their mooring was above the city, along what is now Tchoupitoulas Street.

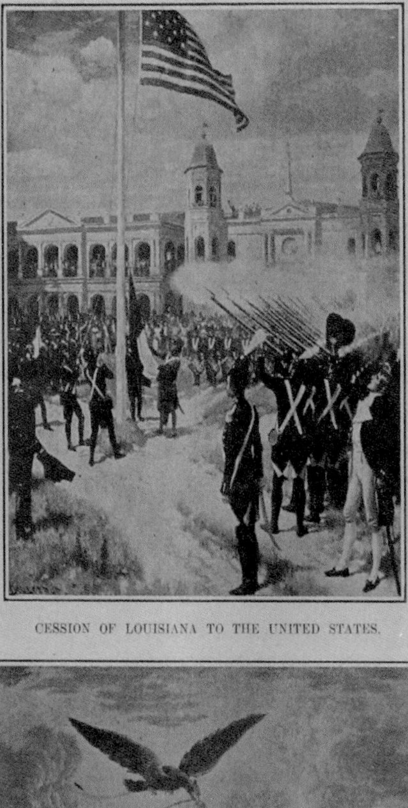

CESSION OF LOUISIANA TO THE UNITED STATES.

Suburbs or Faubourgs. Above the Terre Commune, Common Street, was Mme. Gravier's plantation, part of the former Jesuit grant. In 1788, some streets were opened and lots marked off; it grew very little at first, until the coming of the Americans; it then became the commercial center of the city. The street names commemorated the first owners, or the use the place was put to; as, for example: Gravier Street, from Gravier, the original owner; Poydras Street, from the great philanthropist, whose home was located there; Magazine Street, from the Spanish name for the great tobacco warehouse that stood on Magazine

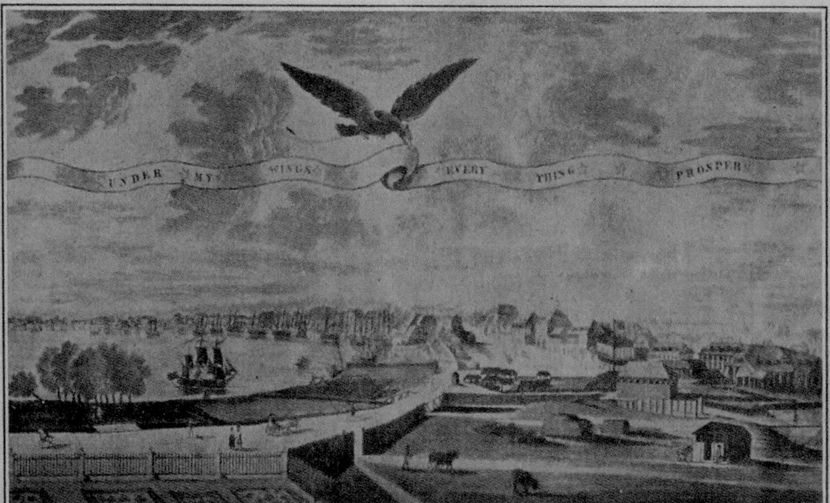

A VIEW OF NEW ORLEANS FROM THE PLANTATION OF MARIGNY, 1803.

and Common; Camp Street, from a slave camp located there, between Poydras and Girod. The aristocratic suburb was along the Bayou St. John road. Below the Vieux Carré was the Marigny plantation, which, when inherited by Bernard Marigny, was opened up as a faubourg and settled by the French. To-day it is one of the most densely populated portions of New Orleans.

Orleans Territory, March 26, 1804. Congress divided Louisiana into two parts; the extent of the present state was known as Orleans Territory. The President appointed a legislative council and named Claiborne governor; certain Spanish land-grants were nullified and an official inspection made of all titles; the slave trade was interdicted. The Louisianians became indignant at the last regulation; insurrectionary sentiments were placarded on the streets, copied by crowds, and when the police attempted to remove them they were driven away. However, the trouble went no further. But slaves continued to be smuggled in by way of the lakes and different bayous and inlets.

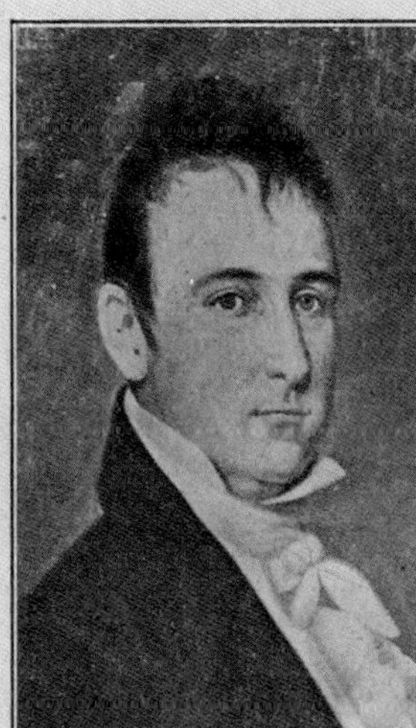

GOV. W. C. C. CLAIBORNE.

City of New Orleans, March, 1805. New Orleans was incorporated as a city by the charter of March, 1805. The people, in electing aldermen, exercised the right of suffrage for the first time.

Concessions to Orleans Territory. In March, 1805, Congress allowed the people of Orleans Territory to elect the House of Representatives, and promised them statehood when the population should equal sixty thousand souls.

Restless Spirit in City. The spirit of the populace was restless, owing to the unsettled conditions, viz., the war between Spain and Great Britain; presence of Casa Calvo and Morales; and possibility of war between the United States and Spain. Casa Calvo and Morales were put out of the colony and the trouble with Spain passed over. Claiborne, writing to the President in November, 1806, said: "Were it not for the calumnies of some Frenchmen, who are among us, and the intrigues of a few ambitious, unprincipled men, whose native language is English, I do believe that the Louisianians would be very soon the most zealous and faithful members of our Republic."

Aaron Burr's Conspiracy. In June, 1803, disappointed, but undaunted, by his political defeats in the east, Burr came to Louisiana bringing letters of introduction to the best people of New Orleans. He bought a large tract of land on the Red River and was believed to be intent on establishing a separate government in Mexican territory and of probably including in this a portion of the Louisiana territory. He was arrested by order of President Jefferson; was tried at Richmond, Va., on a charge of treason; but was acquitted, 1807.

West Indian Immigration. The population more than doubled itself between 1803 and 1810. The war between France and Spain caused many whites and mulattos of San Domingo to become exiles; between May 19 and July 18, 1809, thirty-four vessels from Cuba brought to New Orleans over one thousand eight hundred whites, almost as many free persons of color, and about two thousand slaves; in all, about five thousand seven hundred ninety-seven souls. Others followed from Cuba, Guadeloupe, and other islands, until the total reached ten thousand. Very few ever left the city. The Creoles of the West Indies were united with the Creoles of Louisiana by strong ties; they had the same religion, language, and political ideas, and had met with similar misfortune. This was the period of Creole domination; the city had few German and Irish citizens; the two thousand free persons of color were an indolent class; the floating population of sailors from all parts, bargemen, flatboatmen, and raftsmen from the wild region of the Tennessee, Ohio, and Cumberland Rivers, were unruly and riotous, engaging in riots and brawls, and giving themselves up to shameful excesses on completing their journey. Strife pervaded the town. A riot was nearly caused by a newspaper article that reflected on Napoleon. Plays were put upon the theatre boards which caused the Ursulines to appeal to the governor for protection against public derision.

Admission of Louisiana as a State, April 30, 1812. The population of Orleans Territory had now reached the 60,000-mark required by Congress as necessary for her admission as a state. A convention met in New Orleans in November, 1811, to draw up a constitution; it was adopted as the State Constitution, January 28, 1812, and, on the following April 30, Louisiana was admitted into the Union as a state.

The "New Orleans." January 10, 1812, was a red-letter day in the city's commercial history. On that day, the "New Orleans," a steam-propelled vessel, planned by Fulton but owned by Nicholas J. Roosevelt (a relative of Ex-President Roosevelt) arrived on her maiden trip from Pittsburg. It was only five years previous that Fulton had invented the steamboat.

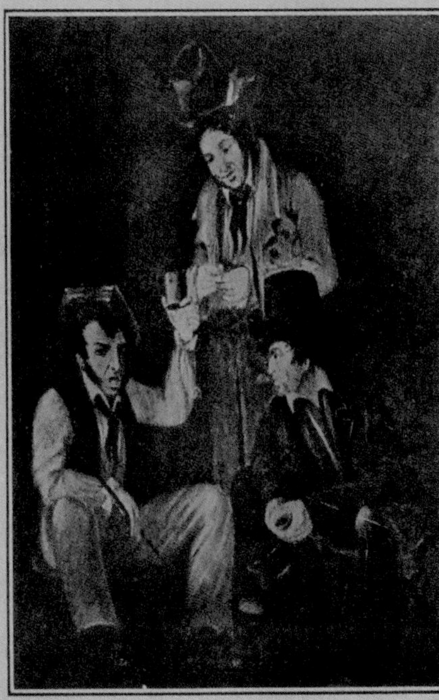

JEAN AND PIERRE LAFITTE AND DOMINIQUE YOU.
From a Portrait by Jarvis, 1812.

Outlook on City's Future, 1812. The future of New Orleans appeared, assured to be prosperous, once international politics should be cleared. Cotton, by Whitney's invention of the gin had become one of the world's greatest industries. Steam navigation closely united New Orleans with the distant parts of the Mississippi Valley. Statehood confirmed the people in the possession of their government and liberty.

War of 1812. England's violation of the United States' rights as a neutral and her assumption of the right to search American vessels and impress seamen on board, whom she considered English citizens, precipitated war between the two nations. The War of 1812 was the aftermath of the Revolutionary War and settled the remaining disputed points.

Defenseless Condition of New Orleans. New Orleans was left undefended by the attempt to make Canada the seat of the war. Wilkinson was ordered to occupy that part of Florida west of the Perdido River. The Creeks massacred 350 whites at Fort Mimms, Mississippi. Drunken Choctaws roamed the streets of New Orleans. Lafitte and his smugglers held Barataria Bay and appeared daily in the city. Crevasses occurred, as well as fires. Though Claiborne labored assiduously, it was many months before he could muster the 1,000 men called for by the President. In the meantime, Napoleon's abdication enabled England to throw more energy into her campaigns. In August, Congress ordered Jackson to proceed to New Orleans for its defense. The British had established themselves in Florida and were offering large rewards to all who would join them, especially the Baratarians.

The Baratarians. The Baratarians were a band of French and South Americans, who claimed to be engaged in smuggling, not in piracy. The Lafitte brothers had obtained control over these daring characters and organized them into a band. The English failed in their attempt to secure their assistance; instead, Lafitte offered their services to Claiborne, who refused them, since he looked upon them as smugglers and outlaws, and Commodore Patterson and Colonel Ross were on their way to destroy their rendezvous on Barataria Bay. This was accomplished a few days later; the Lafitte's escaped to the German coast, while their followers made use of any available refuge.

Andrew Jackson's Arrival. The arrival of Andrew Jackson on December 1st, created confidence and enthusiasm among the New Orleanians. He immediately set to work; fortified Fort St. Philip, demolished its wooden barracks, mounted additional cannon; inspected the country in and about the city, and instructed Governor Claiborne to have obstructed all bayous on the "Isle of Orleans" leading to the Gulf. Through some unexplained oversight, Bayou Bienvenue was not closed. By December 14th, the British fleet of eighty sail, led by Cochrane, the dreaded ravager of the Atlantic Coast, was in possession of Lake Borgne. Claiborne informed the Legislature of the arrival of the British fleet and advised its adjournment; the Legislature did not comply with this advice, so Jackson, declaring the safety of the city required it, proclaimed martial law. Jackson later was fined $1,000 for this, but was subsequently reimbursed by the United States Government. Jean Lafitte now offered the services of the Baratarians to Jackson, who accepted them. Jackson's army was a motley crew; every man capable of bearing arms was mustered into service; it was about 6,000 strong, composed of Tennessee riflemen under Generals Carroll and Coffee, Creoles and French, freemen of color, Choctaw Indians, even prison inmates.

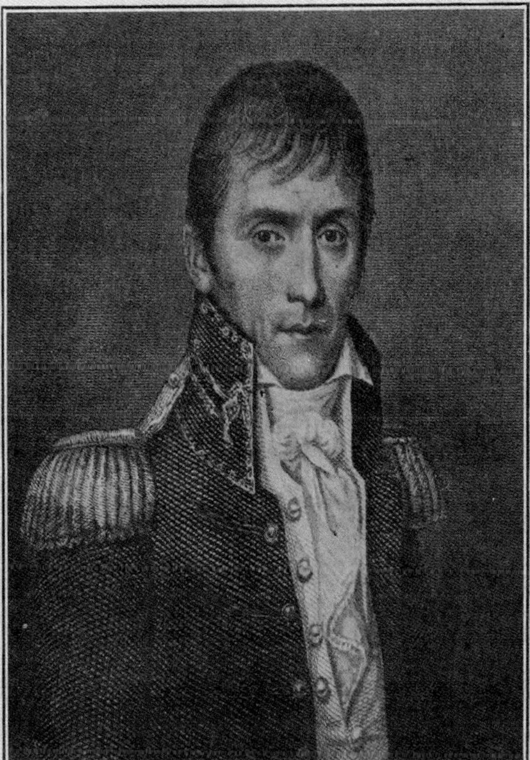

ANDREW JACKSON.

From a miniature presented by Andrew Jackson to Edward Livingston, March 1, 1815, painted by Jean Francois Valle in New Orleans, by Jackson's orders.

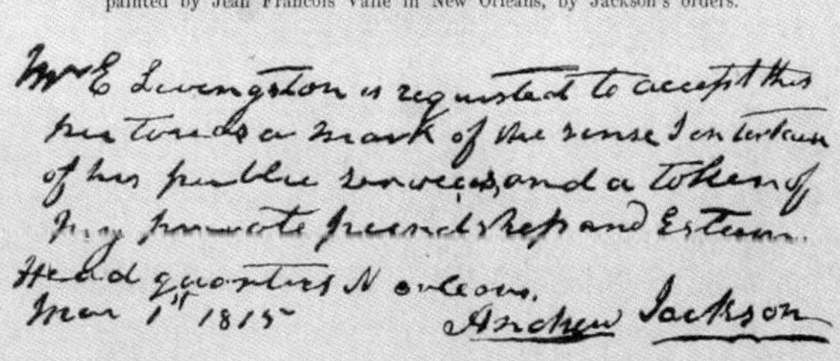

Mr E Livingston is requested to accept this picture as a mark of the sense I entertain of his public services, and a token of my private friendship and esteem.
Head quarters N orleans
Mar 1st 1815
Andrew Jackson

FAC-SIMILE OF NOTE FROM ANDREW JACKSON TO EDWARD LIVINGSTON.

Advance of the British. Cochrane commanded the fleet and Sir Edward Pakenham the land forces. The English forces numbered 14,450, among whom were veterans of Wellington's famed Peninsular campaign. Of the total number 3,600 were on the main line, 6,000 were in reserve, and the rest were stationed at different points. The fighting began on December 23. Reconnoissance of Lake Borgne revealed the unclosed entrance to Bayou Bienvenue; the American picket stationed there was easily overpowered, and the English boats passed up the bayou into Villeré's canal. At half-past eleven in the morning, General Keane's division came out upon the open plain at the rear of General Villeré's plantation, seized the home, and formed their camp. There was not a foot of fortification between the English camp and New Orleans. Major Villeré had been locked up in his home. He realized the necessity of informing Jackson of the location of the British in order to save New Orleans and save his honor from being tarnished with the suspicion of his being in league with the British. He made a bold dash for liberty, sped past his guards, and, unscathed by the shower of bullets sent after him, reached the swamp forest in the rear. Here he hid in the thick moss up in the trees until the English gave up the search; his faithful dog having followed him, Villeré was forced to kill the animal in order to keep his own hiding place in the tree concealed. He reached the city in time to inform Jackson of the enemy's advance. Major Villeré's foot race, though little known, was far more hazardous than Paul Revere's midnight ride. The English, by halting for reinforcements, gave Jackson time to prepare for them. That evening, he sent the schooner, Carolina, to open her broadsides on the British camp, while he attacked by land. The fighting lasted until stopped by the heavy fog. The next morning, Jackson removed two miles nearer to New Orleans, to Rodriguez's canal; here, he established his fortifications, threw up breastworks, dug trenches, and put his ten guns to oppose the twenty-eight of the British. Skirmishing occurred nearly every day; but still the enemy made no great attack. Their delay strengthened Jackson's army. On December 30th, 300 Acadians arrived; two days later, 500 men from Baton Rouge; on January 2nd, 2,250 Kentuckians, poorly clad and armed; the citizens of New Orleans immediately collected $16,000, which was spent for clothing for them, the garments being made by the women of the city.

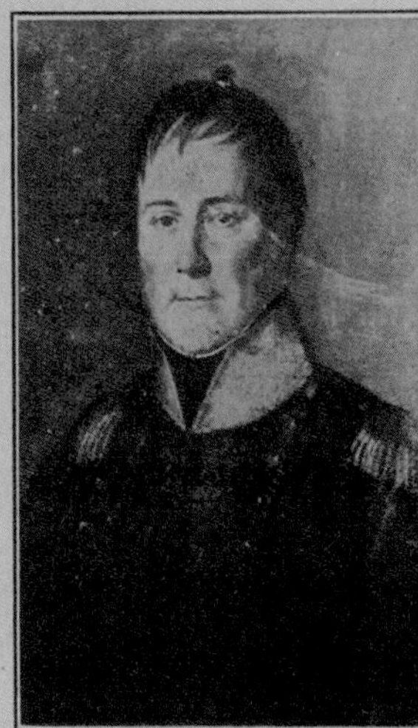

GEN. JACQUES VILLERE.

Battle of New Orleans, January 8, 1815. General Lambert's division at last arrived. The British planned to make four simultaneous attacks: one on the opposite side of the river and three on the New Orleans side. The first attack was delayed, the time allowed the troops being too short; hence, though it was successful, it occurred too late to be of any help. The English formed about 400 yards from the American line, in a close column of sixty men front; burdened with heavy fascines of ripe sugar cane, ladders, and weighty knap-sacks, they could move but slowly; with cheers still on their lips they fell before the guns of their enemy. The accuracy of the American fire tore

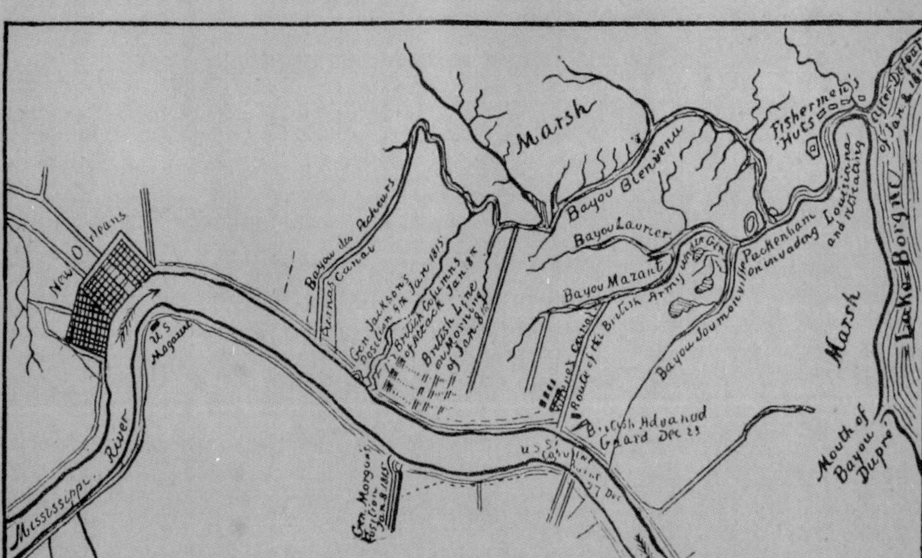

BATTLE OF NEW ORLEANS.

out whole files of men. The British retreated and formed again, to meet with worse defeat. The soldiers could not be rallied for a third attack. Sir Edward Pakenham and General Gibbs had fallen mortally wounded, and General Keane was severely injured; this left General Lambert in command. The English continued the fire from their batteries until two o'clock in the afternoon; but the Battle of New Orleans was over at nine-thirty in the morning, when the attempt to storm the American line was abandoned, one hour after the signal had been given to begin fighting. January 9-18, an ineffectual attack was made on Fort St. Philip. The only explanation for the defeat of so splendid an army by one so small and so poorly equipped is the deadly marksmanship of the Kentucky sharpshooters and the slowness of the British advance.

Effects of the Great Victory. Rejoicing in New Orleans knew no bounds. A public reception in the Place d'Armes was tendered General Jackson, during which he was, as the victors of old, crowned with laurel; he then attended the solemn services of thanksgiving held in the Cathedral. There was little to mar the general joy, as only six of the defenders had been killed and seven wounded. The kindly assistance that would have been given to their own was generously extended to the thousands of English wounded. On February 13, 1815, Admiral Cochrane wrote General Jackson that a treaty of peace had been signed between the United States and Great Britain on December 24, 1814. Jackson received the official news on the following March 17th. On March 16th, Claiborne wrote to Mr. Monroe, Secretary of War, as follows: "Our harbor is again whitening with canvas; the levee is crowded with cotton, tobacco, and other articles for exportation. The merchant seems delighted with the prospect before him; the agriculturist finds in the high price for his products new excitements to industry." The discordant elements from that time gradually became welded into one harmonious whole. The patriotism of the Creoles was no longer doubted. Fighting side by side on the battlefield developed a feeling of brotherhood between the Creoles and Americans, and union of the two people by intermarriage cemented the bond thus established.

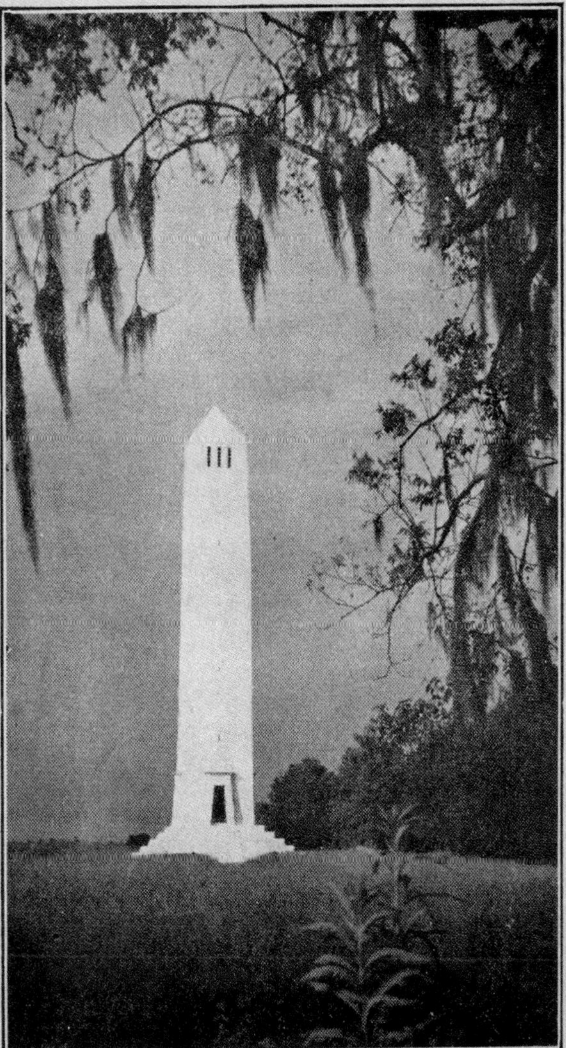

THE BATTLE MONUMENT.

Marking the spot where General Andrew Jackson's Standard flew on his lines along Rodriguez Canal. Officially unveiled January 8th, 1915, at the 100th anniversary of the Battle of New Orleans.

2. FROM 1815-'60.

Commerce, 1815-1840. Steam navigation first appeared on the Mississippi in 1812. A movement was started after the War of 1812 to have the steamboats ply on the river. In 1817, 1,500 flatboats and 500 barges brought the produce of the great valley to New Orleans; four years later, 287 steamboats, 441 flatboats, and 174 barges moored along the city's river front. The Faubourg Ste. Marie, the American section of the city, became the trade center; because of the slack water in front of its batture, the flatboats moored there; thence arose great storehouses for the products brought down from the valley. The Vieux Carré retained

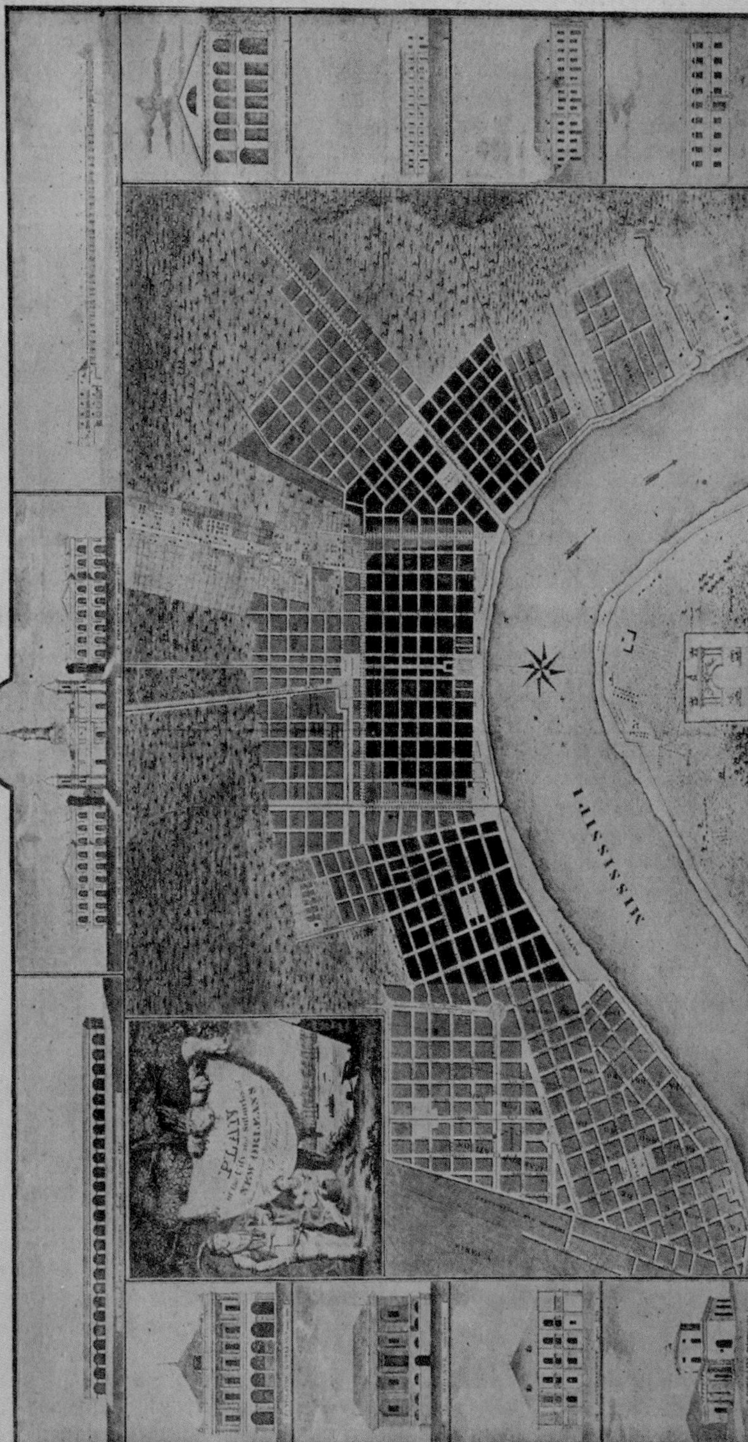

MAP OF NEW ORLEANS, 1815.

control of the trade in coffee, indigo, sugar, rice, foreign fruits and wines; but cotton, tobacco, pork, beef, corn, flour, and northern and British materials were received into the American section. In 1825, New Orleans imports and exports were valued at $17,000,000. The value of trade increased 75 per cent. between 1820 and 1830, and by 1835 was valued at $53,000,750; this increase was partly due to the extraordinary rise in prices throughout the country.

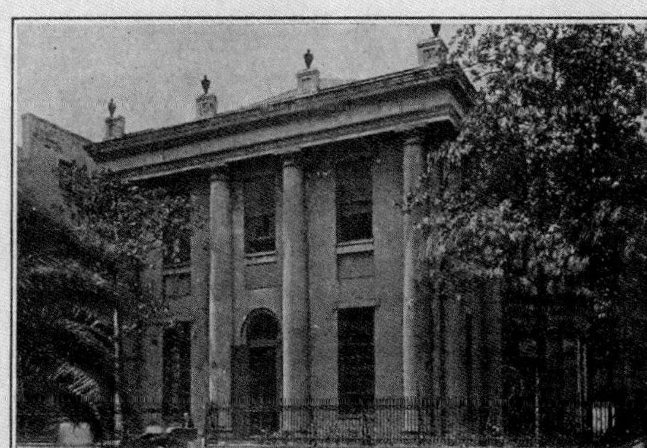

VIEW, AS IT APPEARS TODAY, OF THE BANK OF LOUISIANA BUILDING, CORNER OF ROYAL AND CONTI STREETS, ERECTED IN 1826.

Credit System in Business. There was an ever-increasing demand for cotton, and the rich agricultural resources of Arkansas, Mississippi, and Louisiana offered great returns even for the investment of borrowed money. Thus the credit system became the rule among the cotton, sugar, and tobacco planters of these sections. New Orleans advanced them millions in money at a high rate of interest, and huge quantities of supplies which were kept on hand in the city. In this way, New Orleans merchants and bankers enslaved the agricultural community, who were able to buy and sell only through them. Reckless borrowing and lending kept the planter in constant debt and the city without capital. Planters' notes were based on the value of their slaves and tilled lands and, regarded by results, were almost imaginary; but the system caused a great amount of business, which in turn called in numberless immigrants.

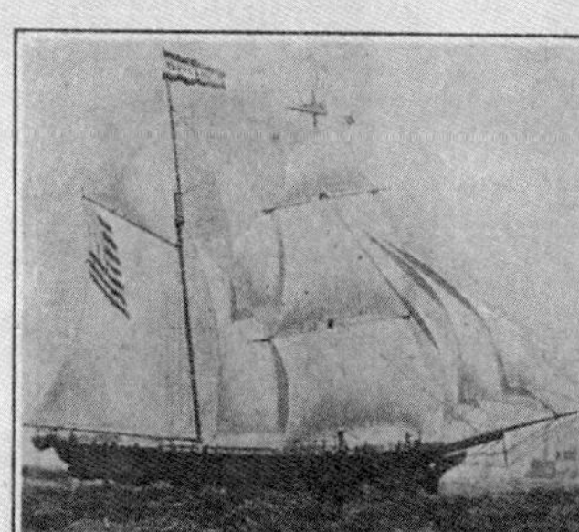

THE TALLULAH.
Clipper engaged in slave trade to New Orleans.

Position of New Orleans Among Cities of the United States. In 1840, New Orleans was fourth in population, New York, Philadelphia and Baltimore taking the lead. In 1847-'48, she actually exceeded New York in exports of domestic products, and in total exports was surpassed only by New York; but her imports were far less; New York imported ten times as much and Boston over three times; her principal imports were coffee, iron, hardware, and French fancy fabrics. By 1850, Boston had taken fourth place among the cities of the United States, and New Orleans dropped to fifth.

Cause of Loss of Valley's Trade. The opening of the Erie Canal, 1825, connecting Lake Erie, by way of Buffalo, with New York City, and of the Ohio Canal, 1832, linking the Ohio River to Lake Erie, established a short, easy, and safe communication between the Ohio Valley and the Atlantic coast, and thereby with Europe. It was only a natural consequence that the Ohio Valley trade should take this quicker and less hazardous course to the New York markets and thence to Europe, instead of the long one to New Orleans and then through the Gulf of Mexico, around Florida, and across the Atlantic to Europe. The establishment of these canals opened up a direct course to the world's centers. In 1835, Ohio State sent 86,000 barrels of flour, 98,000 bushels of wheat, and 2,500,000 staves through Buffalo to the Atlantic ports. A second factor in alienating the valley trade from New Orleans was the danger to navigation on the Mississippi and Ohio Rivers; 1824-'27, property loss on the two rivers aggregated one and one-third millions; these losses were later considerably reduced by the Federal Government's efforts. Again, the cost of running steamboats on these rivers was six times as heavy as on the Great Lakes. Neither were the mouths of the Mississippi clear; sand bars continually formed and, in this period, Northeast Pass, considered the deepest, had a depth of twelve feet. The opening of railroad communication after 1840 severed the last tie that bound the northern valley commerce to New Orleans.

Slavery—Effects. The institution of slavery, of its very nature, is an obstacle to industrial development. The African slave labor in and about New Orleans was also of a most inferior grade. Wild men, as were these negroes, do not become civilized and masters of crafts in one generation. Slavery kept out the class of immigrants that were adepts in mechanical and productive arts, the people who rapidly develop a nation's resources. One-third of the increase in population between 1830 and 1840 was composed of slaves and free persons of color; this last class, under the conditions of the times, were a heavy burden; the remaining two-thirds of the increase were Irish and Germans of the very poorest class.

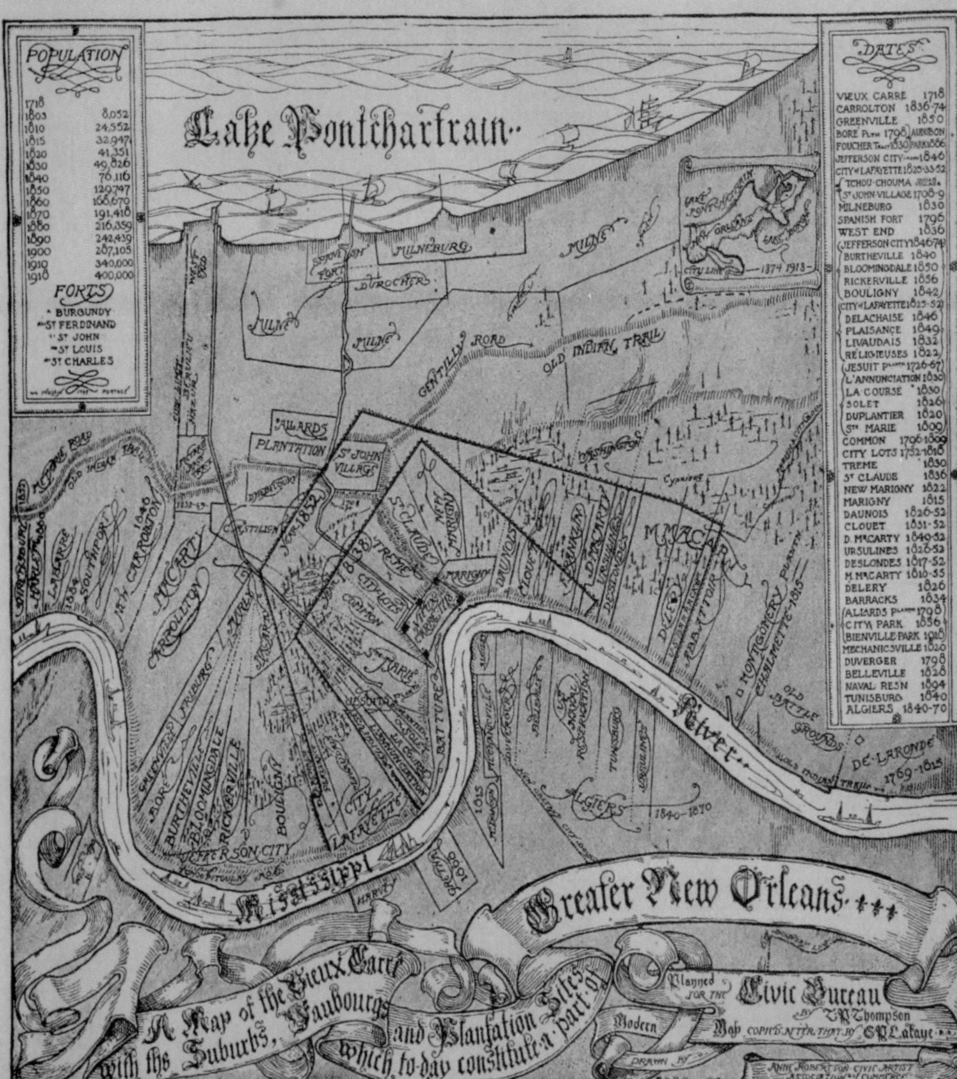

PROGRESS OF THE GROWTH OF NEW ORLEANS.

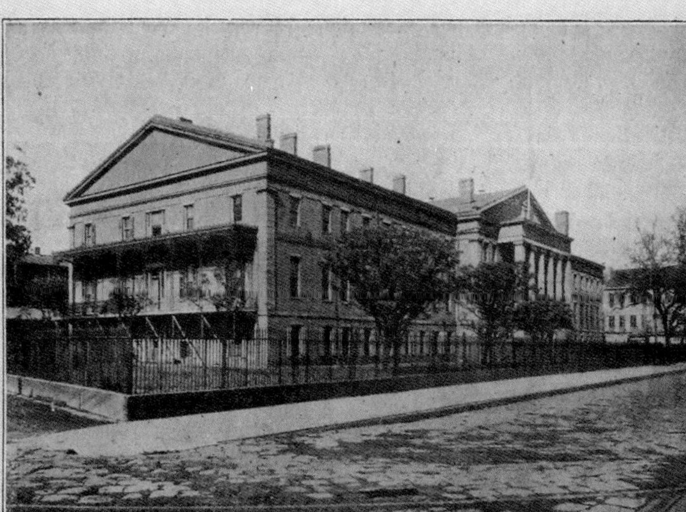

UNITED STATES MINT.

corporation should be established in Louisiana; thus the banking monopoly was given to a few houses that bore up under the financial stress and resumed payment of specie in 1843 with $4,500,000 in their vaults and $1,250,000 in circulation.

Railroads. The first railroad was completed in New Orleans in 1830; it ran out Elysian Fields and connected the city with Milneburg. Captain Grant, the builder of the road, was the originator of the raised platform; it was not until 1858 that it was adopted throughout England and Europe. In 1837, two railroads were planned to join New Orleans to the great central railroad system of the United States in the Mississippi Valley, and with Texas; the first was to stretch north to Jackson, Mississippi; the second, westerly to Opelousas, Louisiana. The state assisted

Mulatto Exodus. The free mulattoes were nearly one-third as numerous as the whites in 1840. They were held in contempt by all, especially by the Americans. The abolition movement created an antagonistic sentiment towards them. The result was that during the decade more than 9,000 left the city. No evidence has been found of their ever returning. Their departure raised the proportion of whites in the community from 58 per cent. to 78 per cent.

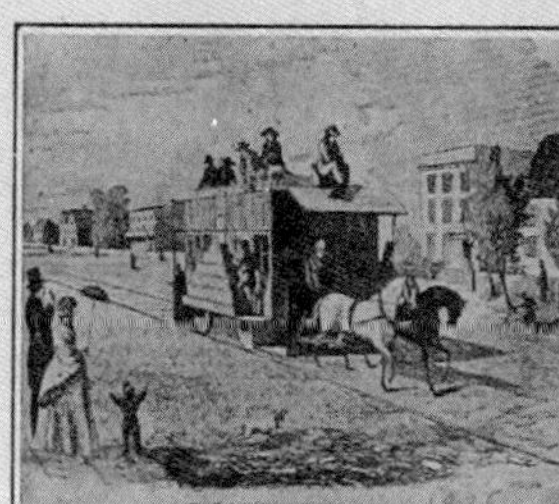

STREET RAILROAD CAR IN 1838.

Financial Crisis, 1836-'37. The downfall of the United States Bank, establishment of multitudes of poorly capitalized banks, and wild speculation in land caused a terrible money crisis throughout the United States. There were few banks in New Orleans; with a little over $2,500,000 in their vaults, they had $7,000,000 in circulation, and were purported to have a capital of $37,000,000. Their failure prostrated the city. So strong a sentiment against banks arose that the Constitutional Convention, then in session, provided that no banking

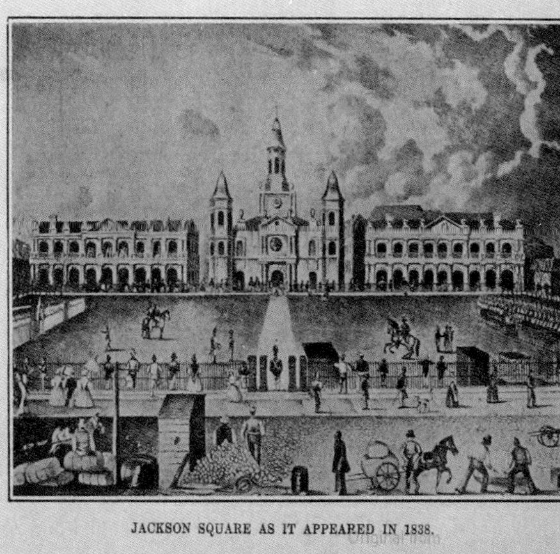

JACKSON SQUARE AS IT APPEARED IN 1838.

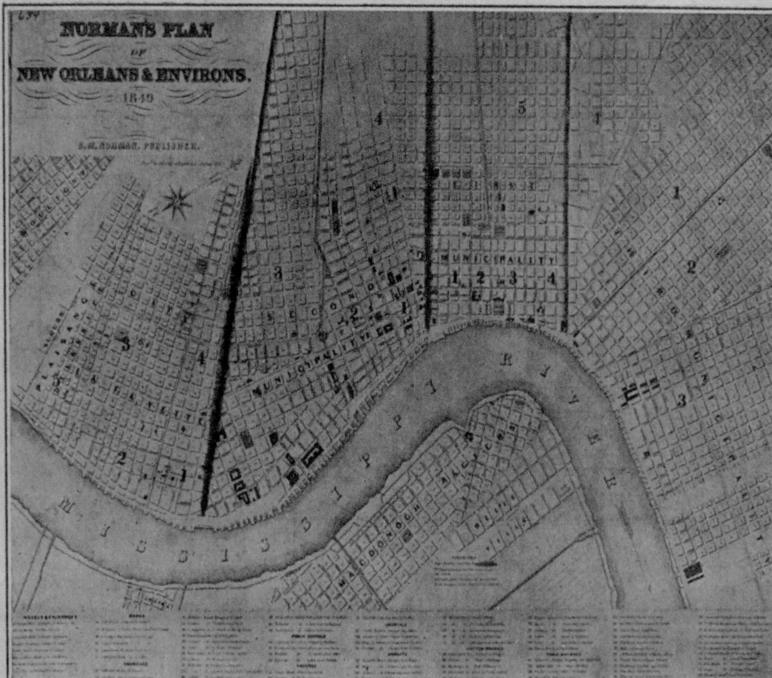

MAP OF LOUISIANA, 1849.

both enterprises, and by 1855 the first and by 1857 the second extended eighty miles from the city.

City Expansion. The ancient fortifications disappeared about 1808. The city spread out above and below along the river bank. New streets were cut; they were wider than the old ones, especially those in the American quarter, and, after 1820, paved with brick or stone. Even the batture being formed by the river in front of the Faubourg Ste. Marie was taken and built up for business purposes. Before the eighties, the expansion was entirely along the river, following the line of commerce. The little town of Algiers, on the river, opposite the second municipality, began to develop its marine workshops.

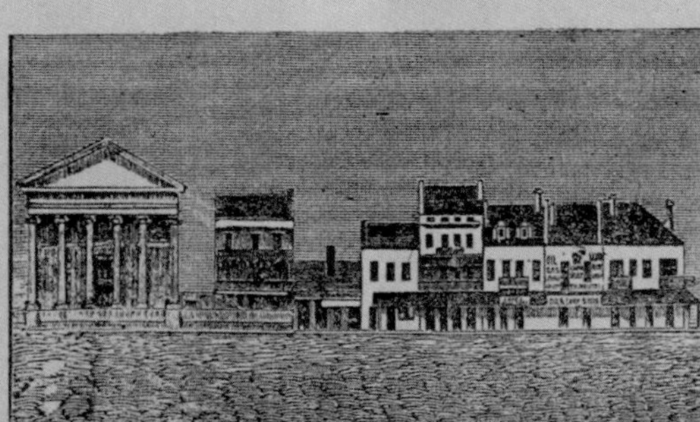

THE TOURO BLOCK, CANAL STREET, IN 1846.

The view in Canal street is from Royal to Bourbon on the north side, where the great Touro Block now stands. The edifice with the colonnade in front was the original Christ Church, which was then situated on Canal street, on the east corner of Bourbon. It was subsequently removed to the corner of Canal and Dauphine. Nothing in the picture is recognizable to-day. Everything on that side of the street was long ago demolished to make way for the great block of splendid stores now to be seen there. They, like the Picayune of to-day as compared with its early beginnings, emphasize the vast changes that have taken place in New Orleans in fifty years.

The population of the city in 1837 was about 65,000 souls. The arrivals of cotton for the year were 567,355 bales, and of Louisiana sugar, 63,000 hhds. The total tonnage of seagoing shipping was 81,710 tons. The imports amounted to $15-117,000. The exports were $37,179,000. It was a common thing to see from forty to fifty steamboats lying at the levee. There were no railroads, except a short line from the city to Lake Pontchartrain, at Milneburg. There were in the city sixteen banks, with an aggregate capital of $40,000,000. Such was New Orleans when the Picayune was born.

CANAL STREET, ROYAL TO BOURBON.

European Immigration. New Orleans shared with New York the influx of European immigrants to western lands; between 1845 and 1850, they averaged 30,000 per year.

Modern Improvements. Gas was first used in 1833 (Chap. XVI.). Water Supply and Drainage, (Chap. III.). Telegraph, (Chap. V.). Railway, (Chap. V.). Paving, (Chap. XVI.).

Union of Municipalities. The union of three municipalities and the City of Lafayette soon followed. The city was governed by a mayor and two chambers, aldermen and assistant aldermen; there were a

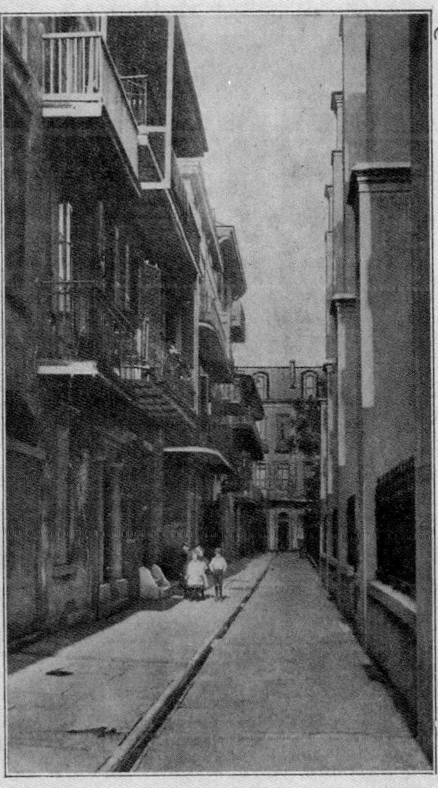

ORLEANS ALLEY.

as nothing to those in New York, which recorded 1,321, and in Boston, 376. Imports and exports were reduced $36,000,000.

Education. The Public School system was established in 1841; then occurred a period of Library development, (Chap. XII.).

Homes. The homes of this period varied from the slave's cabin to the palatial mansion in the Vieux Carré. The homes of the Americans provided the comforts afforded by the times, but were devoid of luxuries. French mirrors, beautiful carpets, handsome furniture, fine china and silverware were found in wealthy houses in the old city. The Americans, more frugal than their neighbors, were more engrossed in making money than in money spending. The houses were lighted of an evening by candles and oil lamps; the former were often supported in handsome candelabra (girondoles) trimmed with scintillating crystal drops; the oil lamp was ever on the center table. Young ladies dressed by the light of candles held by the slave girls at different needful angles. The furniture was covered with haircloth meant to withstand the ravages of time. Of all famed pieces of furniture of those days, the most noted is the four-posted bed, sometimes piled so high with mattresses as to call for a miniature step-ladder with which to scale its sides; the "tester," to quote Mrs. Ripley, "was ornamented with a wall

comptroller, surveyor, and street commissioner. By April 1, 1853, this government had paid off over $4,000,000 of the city debt. The rotunda of the St. Charles Hotel took the position formerly held by the St. Louis Bourse and became the city's unofficial guild hall.

Commerce, 1840-'60. In 1842, receipts from the interior were valued at $45,700,000; they increased rapidly, and in 1851 were estimated to be worth $107,000,000. The tobacco trade was given new life. One-tenth of the arrivals by sea were steamships. This trade was carried on, despite the danger facing vessels entering the river. In the space of a few weeks in 1852, forty ships went aground at the entrance to the river. The terrible yellow fever scourges of 1853-'55 reduced the volume of the trade. This was regained, and a high-water mark reached in 1857. The financial crash followed. Fifty-eight mercantile houses failed, and in the course of the next year forty-five more. But the failures in New Orleans were

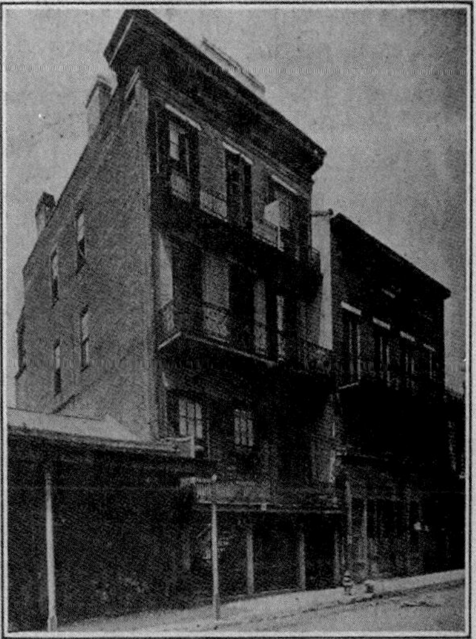

TYPICAL HOMES IN THE VIEUX CARRE, ERECTED DURING THE FIRST HALF OF THE NINETEENTH CENTURY.

Note the handsome wrought-iron balustrades.

paper stuff, a wreath of impossible red and yellow roses, big as saucers, stamped on it, and four strands of same roses reaching to the four corners of the monstrosity"; some "swells had testers covered with silk." Open fire-places with a crane served in the kitchen until about 1840, when stoves began to be used. The households were very busy; all sewing was done at home; there were no ready-to-wear garments then; even the men's shirts, elaborately tucked and beruffled affairs, collars and cuffs were made at home. The cast-off clothes of the larger were turned out as the Sunday best of the smaller members of the family.

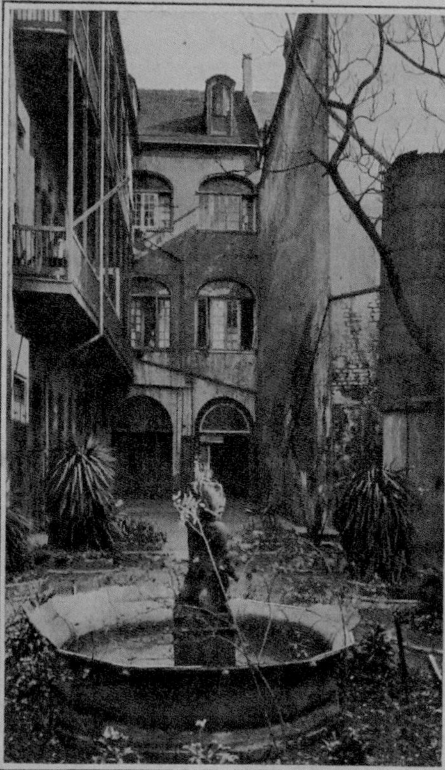

COURTYARD IN VIEUX CARRE.

Hotels. An important feature of New Orleans in ante-bellum days, was the brilliant hotel life. The habit of the planters in bringing their families to the city for the festivities of the winter season developed this mode of living. This life centered about the St. Charles Hotel, in the Second Municipality, and in the St. Louis Hotel in the old town. These were the first of the great American hotels and became mercantile and political, as well as social centers. Noted travelers praised the St. Charles enthusiastically. Oakey Hall wrote of it: "Put the St. Charles down in St. Petersburg and you would think it a palace; in Boston, and ten to one you would christen it a college; in London, and it would marvelously remind you of an exchange; in New Orleans, it is all three." Lady Wortley, an English literateur and traveler, declared she had not found a finer piece of architecture in the new world than its wonderful dome and Corinthian portico. The St. Charles was destroyed by fire in 1851, but immediately rebuilt, though on a lesser scale; the famed dome, which was second in size in the United States only to that of the Capitol in Washington was omitted from the new edifice. This rotunda had been the great center of the city's life. Parlor P. was one of the great political centers outside of Washington. The Old St. Louis, like the Old St. Charles, was grander than its successor; Canova had decorated the splendid rotunda. It was burned ten years before its rival, and was immediately rebuilt. Society gath-

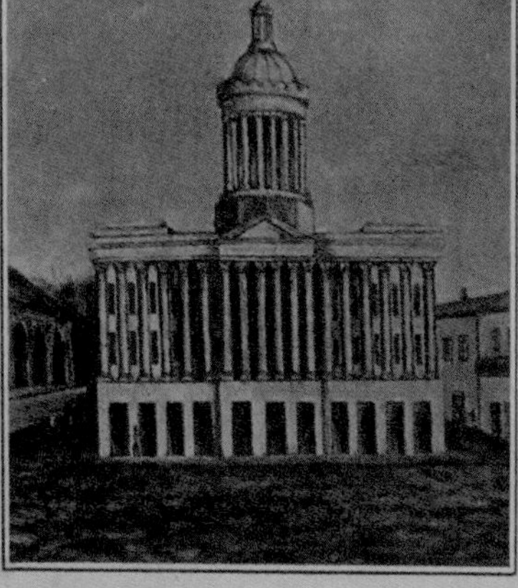

FIRST ST. CHARLES HOTEL.

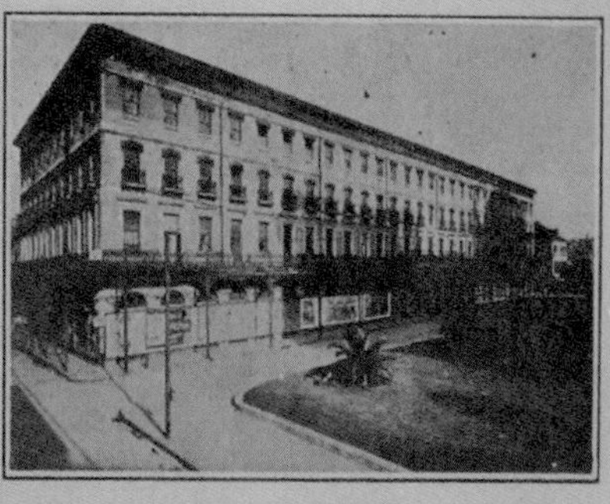

SECOND ST. LOUIS HOTEL.

ered here for some of the most famed balls in its history. Here, in the winter of 1842-'43, was given the wonderful subscription ball in honor of Henry Clay, when 200 guests were entertained at a ball and supper at a cost of $20,000.

Lake Resorts. Three lake resorts were opened up during this period, namely, Milneburg, Spanish Fort, and one a few miles above West End. Hotels and restaurants flourished at all. Spanish Fort occupied the site of the old fort erected by Governor Carondelet for the defense of the entrance to Bayou St. John. It was at Milneburg that friends and admirers of the great English novelist, William Makepeace Thackeray, entertained him at a sumptuous dinner.

Clubs. Club life began in New Orleans in 1832 with the organization of the Elkin Club. Its headquarters were in a hostelry at the mouth of Bayou St. John. The aristocratic Old Pelican Club, with its rival, the Orleans Club, succeeded the Elkin Club. To-day club organizations like the Boston, Pickwick, etc., finance the famous Carnival pageants for which New Orleans is celebrated; and the Elks and others father many worthy charitable enterprises.

Steamboats on the River. As travel to New Orleans was possible only by water, and that required a fair amount of time, steamboats became commodious, elegant. They were large and airy and had huge saloons extending their full length, with highly polished floors for the enjoyment of the dancers. The cuisines were of the best; the skill of the chefs being widely known. Visitors to New Orleans, when possible, boarded on the boat on which they had made the trip, instead of taking up a residence in the city; especially was this true at Carnival time. The building of the railroads drove the palatial river boats out of existence.

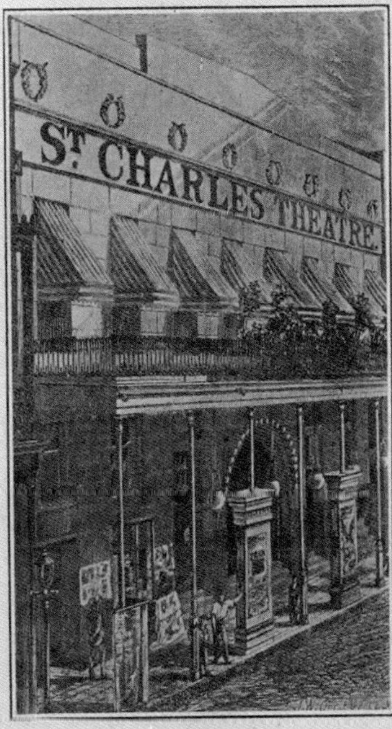

OLD ST. CHARLES THEATRE.

Theatres. The Orleans Theatre, on Orleans, between Royal and Bourbon Streets, was the home of the opera. It was built by subscription in 1817;. John McDonogh having acquired it later on, willed it to the City of Baltimore. It was destroyed by fire in 1868, but the famous ballroom that adjoined it was saved and used as a criminal courtroom from 1872 until the court's removal to St. Patrick's Hall. Opera of the first order was sung to large and appreciative audiences. Not to have a box or seats at the opera was a cause of social ostracism. Operas were given on four nights in the

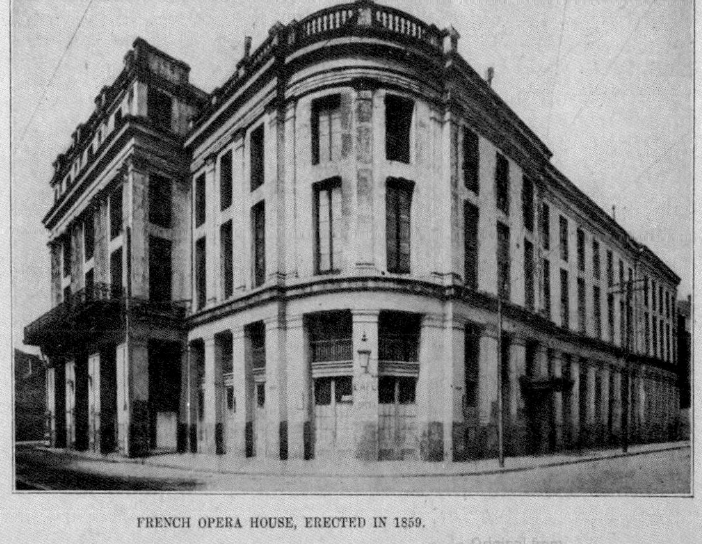
FRENCH OPERA HOUSE, ERECTED IN 1859.

week, the fashionable evenings being Tuesday and Saturday; nights when there was no opera, the drama held the boards. Ludlow introduced English plays the very first year of the theatre's existence, but English drama did not flourish until 1820, when James H. Caldwell took charge of the St. Philip Street theatre. Caldwell was the personal exponent of the most progressive spirit of the city; he was an Englishman of handsome and charming manners, brilliant, clever, able; in England he had mingled with such noted actors as the Kembels, Keans, Cooper, Booth, and the like. He organized a theatrical troupe of known talent (Booth, Barret, Russel among the members), and came to the United States. They tried Richmond, Virginia, then came to New Orleans. Booth was the leading actor and, with Mrs. Caldwell, played in French as well as in English. In 1823, Caldwell erected a theatre in Camp Street, able to accommodate 1,100 people; to this, he moved his troupe from the Orleans Theatre. He met with great financial and dramatic success. In 1824, he lighted this theatre by means of gas. Edwin Forrest began his great theatrical career in the Camp Street theatre. In 1835, Caldwell had the St. Charles Theatre built, at a cost of $350,000; it was then the largest in the United States; the building was noted for the wonderful chandelier, over two tons in weight and supporting two hundred gas-lights, that was suspended from the center of the building. Four years later, the Camp Street theatre was closed. Mr. Caldwell was not only a promoter of theatres and the highest form of English drama, but also of other city improvements; he was the founder of the St. Charles Hotel and the gas works.

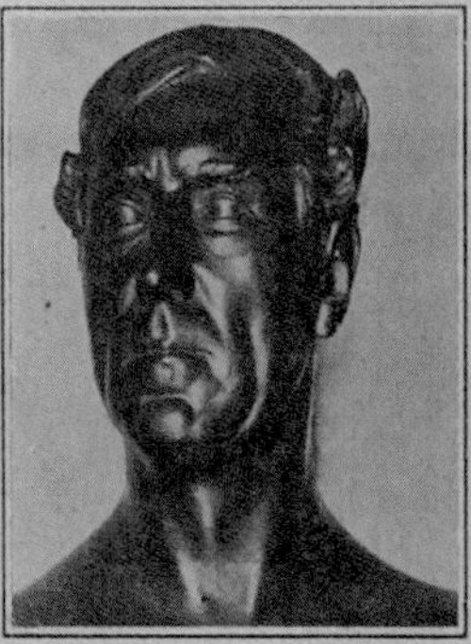

JAMES H. CALDWELL.
From bronze bust in Louisiana State Museum.

3. WAR TIME AND RECONSTRUCTION DAYS.

Outbreak of Civil War. The Republican party had won in the presidential election, and thereupon South Carolina passed an ordinance of secession. Casting her lot with the other Southern States, Louisiana seceded January 26, 1861, and sent her ablest sons to the front.

New Orleans as a Strategic Point. New Orleans sent over 5,000 of her best soldiers to the defense of the northern line of the Confederacy. The southern government seemed oblivious of the city's location; not so, the Washington authorities. Two expeditions were set afoot for securing the Mississippi to the Union; one under Grant, to descend the river, the other under Farragut and Butler to ascend it.

Capture of New Orleans, April 25, 1862. Grant was slowly but surely pushing his way down stream. Farragut, with a fleet of forty-three vessels, was entering the river from the Gulf. In vain, General Lovell asked for assistance; none could be given him. He did his best to obstruct the passage of the Federal fleet by having cables put across the river below the city; old vessels were linked together and set ablaze. Farragut succeeded in passing the two poorly armed forts and making his way up to the city, which, because of the high water, he was able to sweep with his guns. General Lovell, recognizing the uselessness of fighting, retreated. The city front blazed with the fire from the thousands of bales of cotton and hogsheads of sugar and molasses which the citizens burned to prevent the Federals obtaining.

Military Rule. General Butler, with 15,000 soldiers, took charge of the city on May 1, 1862. Mayor Monroe was put out of office and a military commandant appointed in his place. The City Council was replaced by the Bureau of Finance and the Bureau of Streets and Landings. Butler's rule in New Orleans has ever been execrated by the people of the city and condemned by the outside world as disgraceful; he was removed before the year expired. The city's commerce had been reduced by the war to a diminutive trade in war supplies with the neighboring territory. Cotton sold in 1864 at $1.63 per pound, and sugar at 26 cents. The end of the war caused the immediate renewal of commercial intercourse with other parts.

Reconstruction Acts. The Republican Congress decided that the Southern States should be regarded as conquered territory, reconstructed, and readmitted into the Union. First of all, the new freemen were to be secured in the enjoyment of their citizenship and suffrage. The white men of the state were virtually deprived of the use of the ballot by all the restrictions placed upon its exercise.

Misrule. As is the case after most wars, a host of undesirable individuals, seeking to make fortunes by easy means, followed in the wake of the victorious northern army. They became known as "carpetbaggers," as the southern people of a like class received the appellation of "scalawags." In New Orleans, they became the leaders of the voting populace—largely composed of the newly enfranchised negroes—and thus gained control of the government. The city's property was literally stolen. By 1872, the extravagant expenditures had reached $6,961,381 and the bonded debt $21,000,000, on some of which ten per cent. interest was being paid. The city issued an enormous amount of valueless "city currency" with which the officers and Public School teachers were paid. Taxation rose to 2$\frac{75}{100}$ per cent. in 1871. This government maintained itself by means of the "Metropolitan Police," especially organized for the protection of the officials, and a rigid system of espionage conducted against those opposed to their rule.

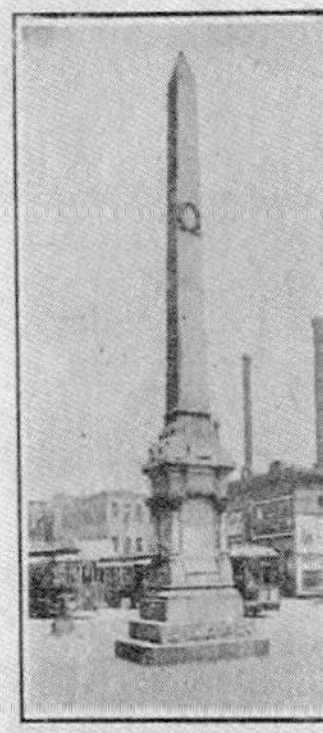

MONUMENT IN MEMORY OF THE MEMBERS OF THE WHITE LEAGUE.
Who Fell in Conflict September 14, 1874.

September 14, 1874. The citizens of New Orleans had formed the "White League" for the expulsion of the carpet-bag government. To frustrate their plans, an order was issued that forbade a citizen to keep a firearm even in his home, a thing permitted by constitutional right. It was learned that a ship with a cargo of ammunition for the League was to arrive on September 14th. The Metropolitan Police formed at the foot of Canal Street and the levee with mounted cannon to prevent the citizens from reaching the vessel. The "White League" moved out Poydras Street to the levee until they faced the Metropolitans. A skirmish followed, with the result that the Metropolitans fled, suffering the loss of many of their members. The "White League" lost sixteen. In memory of the citizens who lost their lives, a monument was erected at the foot of Canal Street, where had stood the Metropolitans' cannon. The "White League," by gradual successes, finally restored the citizens to the control of their city.

Improvements. It was impossible for any progress to be made under the prevailing conditions. The city undertook the operation of the water works in 1869. Paving the streets with wood was tried and, as it proved a failure, abandoned. A drainage system was projected in 1871, but because of its costliness and the ruinous condition of the city's finances, was shortly after given up. The Board of New Orleans Park Commissioners bought the Upper City Park, now Audubon Park, in 1871, at a cost of $80,000.

Population. From 168,755 in 1860, the population increased to 191,418 in 1870. This was due in great measure to the incoming of freed negroes from the country districts.

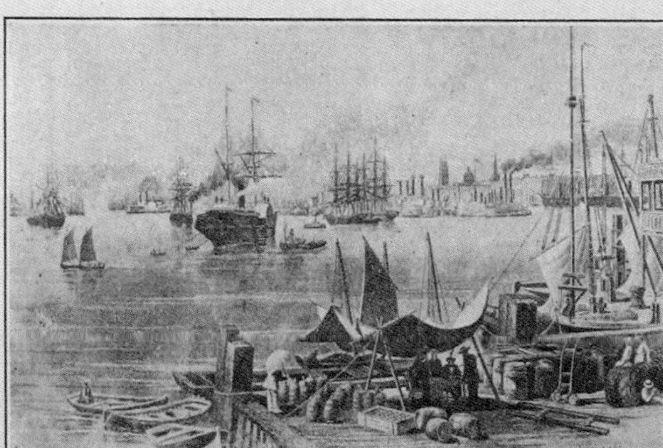

HARBOR OF NEW ORLEANS, 1873.

Expansion of City Limits. In 1870, two districts, the Fifth and Sixth, were added by the annexation of the town of Algiers, on the opposite side of the river, and of Jefferson City, a town adjoining the Fourth District, the former City of Lafayette. By the addition of Carrollton, in 1874, as the Seventh Municipal District, the city attained its present limits.

4. MODERN PERIOD, 1874-1919.

Premium Bonds. With the victory of the Regular Democracy in electing Charles Leeds as mayor in 1874, the carpetbag government may be said to have been ended. The bonded debts reached $20,000,000 in 1875. Real estate had depreciated; business in general had greatly declined. A crisis had come in the city's affairs. Edward Pilsbury was administrator of the Department of Finance; he formed the Premium Bond plan; by this, all the city bonds were funded into bonds of $20, bearing five per cent. interest when drawn by lots. By this system the annual interest was reduced from $1,416,000 to $307,500. Pilsbury succeeded Leeds as Mayor in 1876.

Board of Liquidation. In 1880, the Legislature created a board to see to the liquidation, reduction, and consolidation of the city's debt. Thus the payment of the city debt was taken out of the hands of the city officials.

Improvements Before the Exposition. The telephone was introduced in 1876, and two years later the first line was constructed. A little later, the various lines in operation were joined into the New Orleans Telephone Exchange for the purpose of intercommunication. The Carrollton Railroad was franchised and the New Orleans and Pacific Railroad was granted the batture in front of the Audubon Park. With money derived from the gambling houses of the city, an almshouse was erected at a cost of $100,000 and named in honor of Mayor Shakespeare. The greatest of all improvements was that at the mouth of the river. In 1879, Captain Eads completed the jetties in South Pass, begun June 2, 1875; from seventeen and a half feet, the water on the bar was deepened to thirty feet. The benefits to commerce were innumerable. According to the United States census of 1880, the population had increased to 217,140.

Return to Aldermanic Government. The people became dissatisfied with the Bureau system, said it was too expensive, and demanded a return to the old aldermanic form of government. So, in 1882, the Legislature passed an act changing the city's form of government. Under the new charter, the executive officers were Mayor, Treasurer, Comptroller, Commissioner of Police, and Commissioner of Public Works, each receiving a salary of $3,500. The Council was composed of thirty members.

Cotton Centennial Exposition, 1884. An exposition was held in New Orleans to celebrate the hundredth anniversary of the first exportation of cotton; in 1784, a few bags had been sent to England from Charleston, South Carolina. The Fair Grounds were in the Sixth District and comprised seventy-five acres. The main building was larger than any that had yet been erected at an exposition. The Horticultural Hall, which had been left standing, was entirely destroyed by a hurricane in September, 1915. The exposition was one of the causes of the opening of the Sixth District.

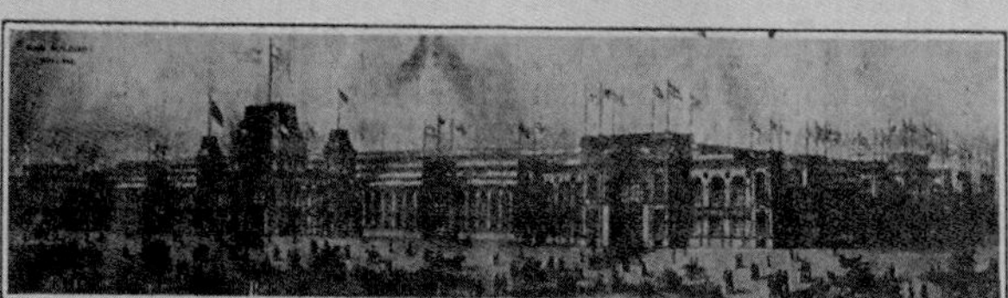

CENTRAL BUILDING, COTTON CENTENNIAL EXPOSITION.

Principal Improvements Before 1900. Electricity for street lighting was introduced in 1884; Royal Street from Canal to Esplanade was thus lighted. St. Charles street was paved with asphalt in 1884. Four years later, the erection of the present Criminal Court House and parish prison was begun; St. Patrick's Hall, the former domicile of the Criminal Court, was some years later made to serve as a Public Library by the removal of the Fisk and Public Libraries to it. The Orleans Levee Board was organized, as well as the Public Library Board. A paid Fire Department replaced the Volunteer Corps in 1891. In this year, the New Orleans and Louisiana Construction and Improvement Company undertook the management of the city wharves for ten years, but their excessive charges caused the state to purchase their rights in 1896; the Legislature created a Board of Commissioners of the Port of New Orleans to manage the wharves. Two railroads received grants along the river front, the Illinois Central and the Louisville and Nashville. The former received a grant in the Sixth District and soon erected the Stuyvesant Docks and large grain elevators; the latter was allowed to run their tracks on the levee below

Canal Street and build a depot at the foot of Canal. In return for these privileges, the corporations had to maintain the levees within the limits of their grants. The present drainage system was begun in 1899 and put into operation in 1900, in which year, also, an ordinance was passed providing for a City Public Belt Railroad. The neutral ground on Canal Street was paved. In the centennial year, the city took another step toward municipal ownership of public works by taking over the control of the markets.

Public Works. The city's present policy tends towards municipal ownership of public works, so as to operate them at cost for the benefit of the citizens. For light and paving, see Chapter XVI.; for water and drainage, see Chapter III.

Realty Improvements. The Cotton Centennial Exposition inaugurated the development of the city's real estate by drawing attention to the desirability of sites in the Sixth District; extension of the street car system, street lighting, and paving have united to open up the outlying sections. Modern development was then first begun in the Sixth and Seventh Districts. The Second District then came to the front; all the land between the cemeteries and the lake was cleared, drained, paved, and lighted; trees and palms were planted along the streets; and now Lakeview is a rapidly growing and pretty suburb. Extending northeast from City Park, really a continuation of Metairie Ridge, is Gentilly Terrace, one of the most beautiful of New Orleans' many garden spots. The tract of land beyond Gentilly and along Lake Pontchartrain to slightly east of Little Woods was developed by the New Orleans Lake Shore Land Company; between this and Chef Menteur is the Michaud Tract, which is being improved in like manner, by drainage and splendid shell roads, so that lots now sell at the former price of acres. The United States Government, by the erection of the Naval and Immigration Stations, has contributed to the development of the Fifth District. A great plan is now in progress for the improvement of the Jefferson Plaquemines Drainage District; 11,500 acres are within the limits of Algiers. Bayou Barataria is the natural drain of this district, and, with Harvey Canal, almost makes an island out of the land in the river's bend. A dam has been constructed across Bayou Barataria, where it is joined by Harvey Canal; huge pumps erected

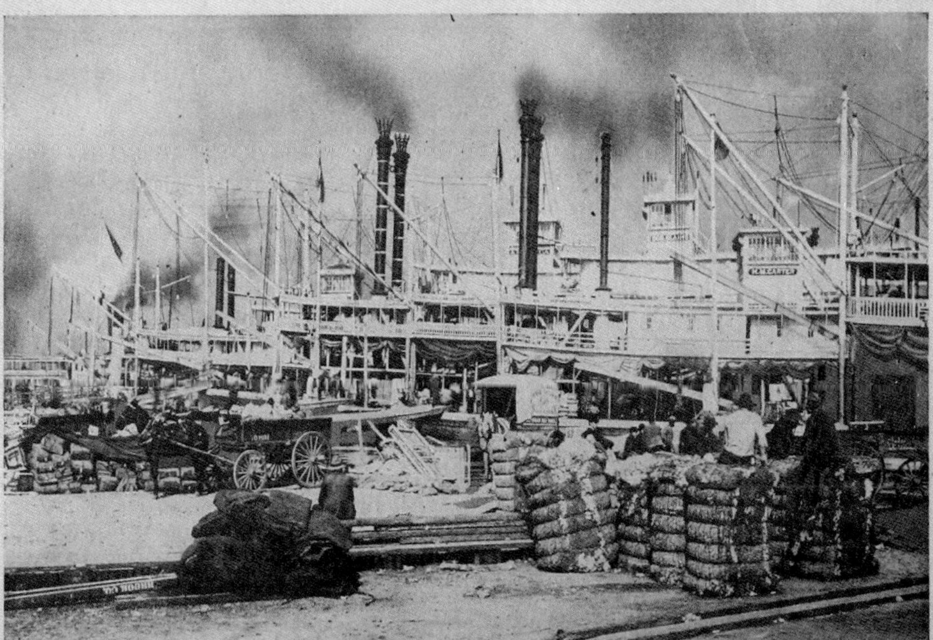

OLD STYLE STEAMBOAT LANDING.

at this point are to lift the water across the dam into the bayou. New Orleanians may enjoy farm life on the banks of Bayou Barataria and yet be within twenty or thirty minutes of the heart of the business section, by way of the road alongside the New Orleans Southern and Grand Isle Railroad, the Jackson Avenue ferry and car line. Metairie Ridge is a delightful suburb outside the city limits, in Jefferson Parish.

Commission Form of Government. In 1912, by special act of the Legislature, the city's government was changed, a modified form of the Commission Plan of Municipal Government being adopted. (See Chapter XV.)

Present Financial Condition of the City. The city's bonded debt increased to $37,937,568.50 in 1913. This increase is due to the city's undertaking the operation of her own sewerage and water system and the Public Belt Railroad; the former added between $16,000,000 and $17,000,000 and the latter $2,000,000 or $3,000,000 to the city's debt. The tax receipts for 1918 were $7,315,805.70 on an assessment of $332,536,623.00.

Federal Bank Established. The Federal Reserve Act of December, 1913, separated the United States into districts in each of which one city was to be designated as a Federal Reserve City because of the establishment therein of a Federal Reserve Bank. Atlanta received the apportionment of the district in which New Orleans was located. As the convenience and customary course of business of the Crescent City was thus interfered with, the district was readjusted and a Federal Bank was established in New Orleans.

Centennial Celebration of the Battle of New Orleans. January 8, 1915, the hundredth anniversary of the Battle of New Orleans, marked also a century of peace between the two great English-speaking nations of the world, Great Britain and the United States. With characteristic hospitality, New Orleans entertained representatives of King George V. of England, the Canadian Government, and distinguished Americans. The walls of the old Cathedral re-echoed the chant of the solemn Te Deum as they had one hundred years before, military and civic parades recalled the spirit of Jackson and his followers, and the ladies of 1815, as well as the heroes of battle, seemed to live again in the "tableaux vivants," presented as a fitting climax to the celebration.

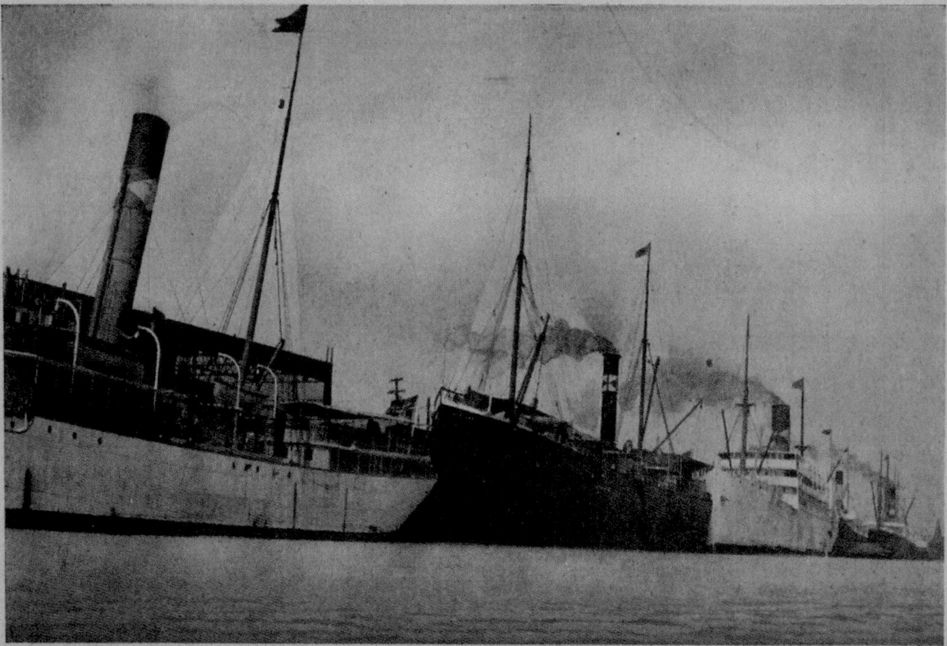

SHIPS AT THE WHARVES.

TOPICS: **Section 1,** French Domination: 1. Louisiana before 1718; 2. Proprietorship of the Company of the West; 3. New Orleans, 1731-1763. **Section 2,** Spanish Domination: 1. Manifestation of the Spirit of Liberty; 2. Establishment of Spanish Control; 3. Spanish Development of New Orleans; 4. New Orleans in 1800. **Section 3,** Transition Period. **Section 4,** American Domination: 1. New Orleans, 1803-'15; 2. From 1815-'60; 3. War Time and Reconstruction Days; 4. Modern Period.

REFERENCES: Bossu, Travels through that part of North America formerly called Louisiana (translated by John Reinhold Forster); Charlevoix, History and General Description of New France (edited by John Gilmary Shea); La Harpe, Journal Historique de l'Etablissement des Francais à la Louisiane, Nouvelle-Orléans, 1831; Le Page du Pratz, Histoire de la Louisiane; Reuben Gold Thwaites, The Jesuit Relations and Allied Documents; King and Ficklen, Stories from Louisiana History; Claiborne, "Mississippi"; Bunner, History of Louisiana, 1841; Early Voyages Up and Down the Mississippi, Albany, 1861; B. M. Norman, New Orleans and Environs, 1844; A. Oakey Hall, The Manhattaner in New Orleans, 1851; Jewell's Crescent City, 1873; Waring and Cable, History and Present Conditions of New Orleans, 1880; Guide and Sketch Book to New Orleans, 1885; Andrew Morrison, New Orleans and the New South; F. X. Martin, History of Louisiana; Phelps, Louisiana; Charles Gayarre, History of Louisiana; Alcée Fortier, History of Louisiana; Walter Fleming, Documentary History of Reconstruction, etc.; The South in the Building of the Nation; Rightor (editor), Standard History of New Orleans; T. W. Campbell, Manual of the City of New Orleans, 1900; Grace King, New Orleans—The Place and the People; Eliza Ripley, Social Life in Old New Orleans; Publications of the Louisiana Historical Society, De Bow's Review, 1846-'59 and 1867 to '68; Stanley C. Arthur, The Battle of New Orleans, published by the Louisiana Historical Society; New Orleans Directories; Newspaper files of the Bee, Picayune, and Times-Democrat.

MAYORS OF NEW ORLEANS.

1803—Etienne Boré.
1804—James Pitot.
1805—John Watkins.
1807—Joseph Mather.
1812—Nicholas Girod.
1815—Aug. McCarthy.
1820—J. Rouffignac.
1828—Dennis Prieur.
1838—Charles Genois.
1840—Wm. Freret.
1844—Edgar Montegut.
1846—A. D. Crossman.
1854—John L. Lewis.
1856—C. M. Waterman.
1858—Gerard Stith.
1860—John T. Monroe.
May, 1862—G. F. Shepley.
July, 1862—G. Weitzel.
Aug., 1862—J. H. French.
Sept., 1862—H. C. Deming.
Nov., 1862—J. F. Miller.
July, 1864—Stephen Hoyt.
May, 1865—Hugh Kennedy.
March, 1865—S. M. Quincy.
June, 1865—Glendy Burke.
1865—Hugh Kennedy.
1866—John T. Monroe.
1866—E. Heath.
1868—J. R. Conway.
1870—B. F. Flanders.
1872—L. A. Wiltz.
1874—C. J. Leeds.
1876—Edward Pilsbury.
1878—I. W. Patton.
1880—Jos. A. Shakespeare.
1882—W. J. Behan.
1884—J. V. Guillotte.
1888—Jos. A. Shakespeare.
1892—John Fitzpatrick.
1896—W. C. Flower.
1900—Paul Capdevielle.
1904—Martin Behrman.

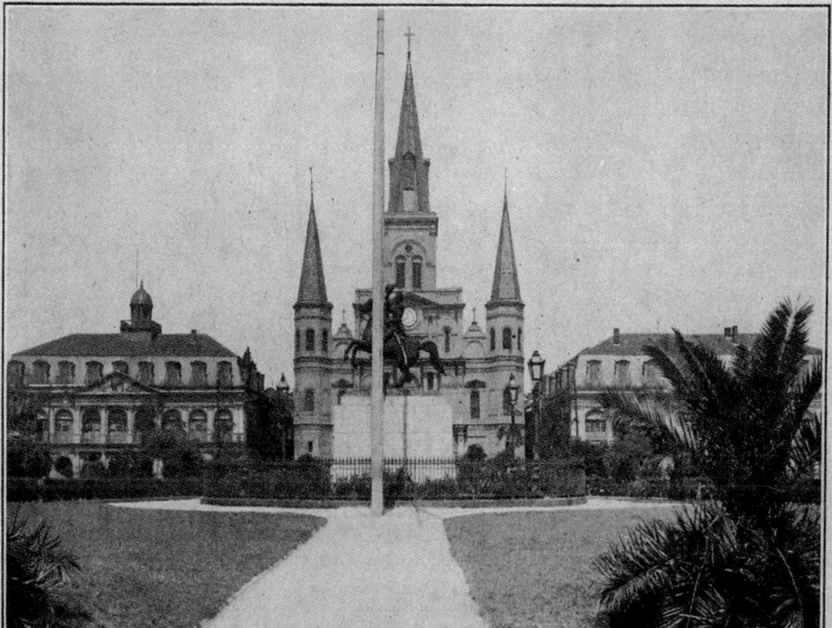

JACKSON SQUARE AS IT IS TODAY.

CHAPTER III.

Drainage—Sewerage—Filter Plant.

1919

Sanitary improvements are of vital importance in progress, and the three great systems of sewerage, water, and drainage have helped New Orleans in the race for civic advancement.

New Orleans' Problem. In the construction of these works, New Orleans, owing to the flat surface, faced its greatest municipal problem. High water in the river is above the highest land in the city. The natural drainage is away from the banks of the river, and generally towards the lakes to the north. The level of Lake Pontchartrain is the level of the sea, but the accumulation of waters along its south shores, owing to the influence of continued north and northeast winds, often reached several feet above that level. Without artificial aid, New Orleans would always be flooded by the rains falling upon it and running to it from the river slope, and also by the high lake tides backing into the low part of the inhabited area.

Early Attempts at Drainage. In the early colonial days, Governor Perrier found it necessary to construct a levee in front of the city. Some attempts at drainage were made by the governors, Vaudreuil and Carondelet. The Carondelet Canal, (Old Basin) after its completion to the Bayou St. John, drained a great part of the old city limits. By 1838, a natural drain in the rear of the Second Municipality had been broadened and deepened into the Melpomene Canal, giving some relief to the then new portion of the city. From 1871-73, considerable work was done in the excavation of drainage canals. In 1880, the city depended for its drainage upon a rude form of pumping machines similar to those used in Holland. These machines were solely for the purpose of removing surface water from the streets and the house lots. The gutters were deep channels from two to three feet wide, but were more or less filled with tidal water from the Lakes and helped little in the drainage. By 1895, enough construction work had been carried out by private drainage companies to demonstrate the practicability and the cost of drainage and sewerage.

Inception of the Present Development in Drainage and Sewerage Systems. It was not until 1895, that the city took upon itself to design an effective drainage system. Construction work was begun in 1897 but no adequate financial provision had been made to complete it. The people of the city were beginning to believe that they must have a sewerage and a water works system as well as drainage. This sentiment grew because the epidemics of 1897, 1898 and 1899 were vital in their effect on trade and growth. Finally, in 1899, after a campaign in which the Era Club did a vast amount of educational work, a law was passed providing for a bond issue. Property holders voted for a tax to meet the payment of these bonds. Women property owners voted for the first time. This law also created a board for the execution and the subsequent management of the three systems.

Effects of Improved Drainage. About 1900, the work had proceeded far enough in the construction of a main drainage system to remove as rapidly as it fell a rainfall of moderate intensity, thus preventing the supersaturation of the soil and giving it a chance to dry out. Lands before worthless became at once available for agricultural or city development. Mosquitoes decreased, and gutters—if only cleaned out—drained to their bottoms. The death rate dropped from 27.2 per 1,000 to 22 per 1,000. The area now drained is from the Mississippi River to Lake Pontchartrain, and from the upper to the lower Protection Levee. The drainage of New Orleans has convinced the world that the millions of acres of marsh land surrounding the city can easily be reclaimed and put under cultivation.

The Capacity of the Drainage System. The drainage system consists of about 38 miles of masonry lined and covered main drains and 300 miles of covered lateral drains connected therewith and of 50 miles of open canals from all of which the water is pumped; and of about 20 miles of high level outfall canals into which the water is pumped, the latter discharging either into Lake Pontchartrain or into Lake Borgne. The system is constructed and operated so as to produce **artificially** the **necessary slope.** Seven great pumping stations cause the water to flow into and through the canals. The total drainage pumping capacity is over 7,000,000,000 gallons per day. The drainage system is designed to send all dry weather and small storm flow into Lake Borgne, and only the flow from great storms into Lake Pontchartrain.

Reasons for Separating the Sewerage and Drainage. It was considered undesirable to discharge the sewage of the city into tidal or lake waters. A small flow of sewage in the large storm water drains would not move rapidly enough to reach the outlets without fermentation, which would cause objectionable conditions in the drains. Owing to the great amount of work required and the cost, the construction of one system of sewerage and drainage would have taken many years. It was desired within the shortest possible time to sewer the five hundred miles of inhabited streets.

Operation of the Sewerage System. In order to accomplish the desired results, a system of sewers was designed composed of main, submain, and lateral sewers. These lead to ten separate pumping stations with good **slopes** or **falls** from the higher end of the sewers to the pumping stations. The largest portion of the sewers drain directly **by gravity** to the principal pumping station. Remote ones drain to other pumping stations, and some of the sewage passes through two pumping stations before it reaches the principal station, from which it is discharged into the river. Seven of the intermediate lift stations are operated by electricity from the main station, automatically starting and stopping their pumps as the sewage flows into them. These stations raise the sewage from a low level sewer on the suction side to a higher level sewer on the discharge side; and the flow of sewage to and from them is just as much

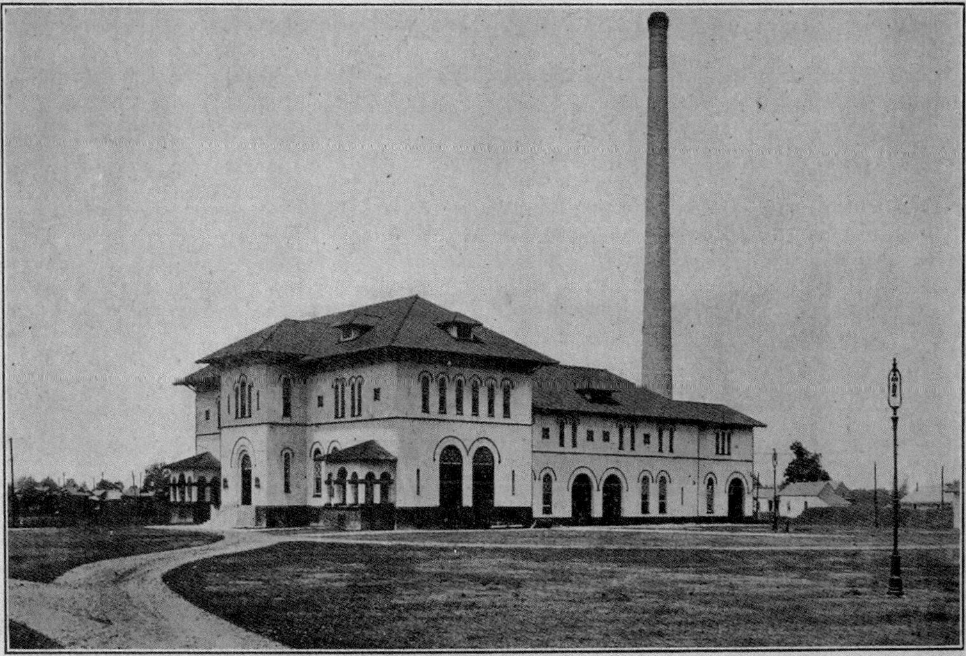

MAIN WATERWORKS PUMPING STATION AND DRAINAGE POWER HOUSE No. 2.

by gravity as if the sewers had the usual **gravity** outlet.

Time Taken for the Construction of Sewers. The construction of the sewers was begun in June, 1903, and they were ready for operation in October, 1907. Practically the entire populated area of the city is now sewered and nearly all premises on the line of a sewer are connected.

The Water Supply. In 1810, an attempt was made to establish water works, which were of the most primitive character. The pipes were hollowed cypress logs and the water supply was obtained from the river by slave labor. The slaves pumped the water into a large reservoir from which it was distributed through the hollow logs to such citizens as had subscribed. The majority of the people depended upon cisterns or wells. In 1833, the Commercial Bank was organized, its purpose being to establish water works in New Orleans. The cypress log pipes were replaced by iron ones. A few cement pipes were used but proved unsatisfactory. The charter of this company expired in 1869, and the city bought the water works, issuing bonds for that purpose. Owing to bad management and lack of funds, the city, in 1877, gave the monopoly to the New Orleans Water Works Company for fifty years.

The Water Supply Problem. The water supplied by the New Orleans Water Works Company was pumped directly from the Mississippi River without any purification and was so muddy as to be entirely unfit for most uses. A filter plant built for said company in 1892 was not successful, was not accepted, and was never put into regular use. Coincident with the design of the sewerage system a study was begun of the water problem. Many held that the purification of the Mississippi River water, so as to convert it into a safe and acceptable water supply, was an impossibility; and that the only solution was to go north of Lake Pontchartrain for a water supply. Others believed that a sufficient and satisfactory artesian supply could be found.

Experimental Purification Tests. The Mississippi River is very muddy and moderately hard; its chemical and sanitary conditions are excellent. Between 1892 and 1900, the methods of treatment which were applicable to the economical purification of very muddy, clay-bearing waters were greatly developed. In 1900, the Sewerage and Water Board made a thorough

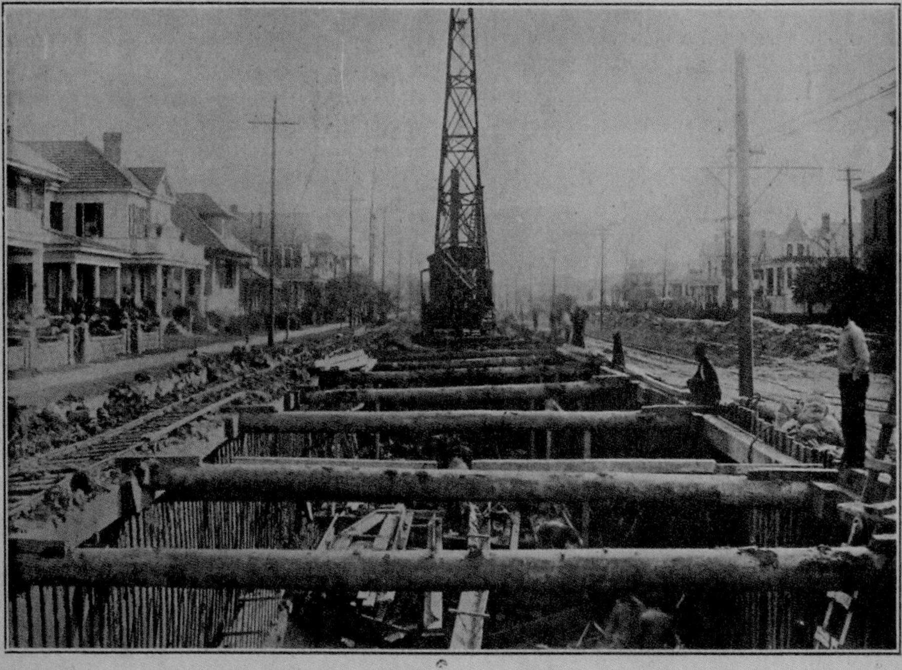

VIEW SHOWING NAPOLEON AVENUE DRAINAGE CANAL IN COURSE OF CONSTRUCTION

study of these methods at an experimental plant, built at Audubon Park. Here the proper methods to be applied to the Mississippi River water at New Orleans were fully determined.

Water Works Plant. The water works plant, covering about seventy acres or twenty-six city blocks, was begun in 1905 and put into operation in 1908. The water works intake is at the extreme upper end of the city. The system of purification is sedimentation, coagulation (the coagulants being lime and sulphate of iron) and filtration. The water is first pumped from the river into the grit reservoirs where the coarser suspended matter, mostly sand, is removed by sedimentation. From here, the water passes into the lime-mixing reservoirs; then into the coagulating reservoirs where the process of sedimentation is completed, and the water is softened and prepared for filtration. The filters are merely gravity sand filters designed to handle large quantities of water, and to be easily and cheaply cleaned. The entire cost of treating and filtering the water, and pumping it into the distribution system is not over two cents per thousand gallons, and the cost of water delivered through meters is less than the prices paid in other metered cities.

Methods of Water Distribution. New Orleans being almost flat, there is no possibility of a reservoir at high elevations into which water can be pumped, and from which the supply can be drawn. The pumps of this plant can be adjusted to maintain whatever pressure is desired; and will automatically increase and decrease their output to maintain the pressure for which they are set, and to deliver the quantity of water which is being drawn from the mains. Pressure, maintained in this way, is as satisfactory as if it were supplied from a high level reservoir. The distribution system consists of four-inch pipes to forty-eight-inch mains and covers 600 miles of streets. There are 5,500 fire hydrants. The pressure is sixty-five pounds per square inch, which is ample for first class fire protection. The present capacity of the pumping system, including Algiers, is 100,000,000 gallons per day; the present daily consumption averages about 32,000,000 gallons.

The Cost and Effect of the Three Systems. The three systems combined have cost about $32,000,000. Malarial infection has ceased to exist; the city has improved conditions of living and provided adequate fire protection; useless tide-level swamps have been developed into beautiful city suburbs. The world realizes that New Orleans is now a healthful city, in no manner handicapped by unsanitary conditions.

TOPICS: The New Orleans Problem; Inception of the Present Development in Drainage and Sewerage Systems; Effects of Improved Drainage; Capacity of the Drainage System; Operation of the Sewerage System; The Water Supply Problem; The General Operation of the Plant.

REFERENCES: Reports of the Sewerage and Water Board.

CHAPTER IV.

Health Conditions.

New Orleans offers many advantages to those seeking health or longevity. Chief among these is its delightful climate, which does not only favor, but actually fosters, outdoor living. However, before the city could become healthful, the surrounding swamps had to be drained and mosquitoes destroyed. By installing an artificial system of drainage and reclaiming the swamp lands, the disadvantages of a low altitude were overcome. These achievements were so notable as to attract the attention of the whole country.

SECTION 1. EARLY HISTORY OF SANITATION IN NEW ORLEANS.

First Sanitary Measures. One of the earliest sanitary measures was the cutting of the trees between the river and the lake by order of Governor Perrier, so that the fresh lake breezes might sweep the settlement. This work was not finally completed until during the Civil War. It was Governor Perrier, also, who caused the first levee to be built before the city, thus saving it from annual overflow and greatly advancing the work of sanitation.

Drainage. In the early days of the history of New Orleans, there were open ditches along some of the streets and a wide ditch surrounding the city. But this form of drainage proved unsatisfactory.

Carondelet Canal. The Spanish Governor, Carondelet, strove to improve conditions by constructing a canal from the city to the lake. Work was begun in 1794 and completed in two years. The government sought to interest the people in land improvement. To this end, lots along the canal were offered at very low rental to all who would drain them and keep the property in good condition.

Vaccination. The colony, in common with all places, was frequently visited by small pox. In the latter part of the eighteenth century, Dr. Jenner, an English physician, discovered that, by inoculating people with the virus of cow-pox, they would be protected against the dread disease. This was called vaccination, and its use began in Louisiana in 1802. Since then small pox is no longer a menace.

SECTION 2. EPIDEMICS.

Yellow Fever. It is not exactly known when yellow fever first made its appearance on the continent. Before the coming of the white man, the Indian tribes were decimated by a malignant fever, thought by those familiar with their traditions to have been yellow fever. French settlers from the West Indies brought this fever into Louisiana in 1701, and again in 1704, the year in which the famous Tonti fell victim to its ravages. Though it was present in the colony from time to time after that, no record of cases of deaths was kept until 1796, when the first real epidemic occurred. There were serious epidemics in 1853 and 1878; and there were years when there were not even slight recurrences of the disease.

Ignorance of the fact that mosquitoes carry the disease prevented the use of proper remedial measures. Besides, facilities for a good system of quarantine were lacking. In those days the Federal Government had not yet evolved the system now carried out by the Public Health Service and was, therefore, not prepared to meet its responsibility in protecting the port of New Orleans, and indirectly the whole country, from this scourge.

The Mosquito Theory. It is now an established fact that diseases are transmitted by certain insects: typhoid fever by the fly, bubonic plague by the flea, malaria and yellow fevers by the mosquito. This does not mean that these insects are the originators of the disease; they are merely carriers of the germ which must have been obtained from some infected source. All this has been proven beyond the possibility of a doubt, by investigations and tests costing vast sums of money, and even life.

During the Spanish-American War, more men were carried off by fevers than by actual conflict. This high death rate caused the United States Government to appoint a commission, in 1900, to investigate the causes of yellow fever and to give exhaustive tests to the different theories of its origin and transmission, particularly the mosquito theory which had been experimentally proved by Dr. Carlos Finlay of Cuba, in 1882. This commission was headed by Major Walter Reed. Experiments were made on volunteer human subjects, one of whom was Dr. Lazear, a member of the commission. Unfortunately, Dr. Lazear succumbed to the disease. The result of the study of these scientists is the knowledge that yellow fever is transmitted by the striped-legged, cistern-bred mosquito and that the only practical means for exterminating it is to prevent breeding by removal of the stagnant water in which the eggs are laid or by oiling water and preventing the larvæ, wiggle-tails, from securing a supply of air.

Health Measures. Within recent times, the installation of a sub-surface drainage, reclamation of outlying swamp land, abolishment of the cistern, improved maritime quarantine, and the fumigation of ships which, incidentally, destroys the full grown mosquito have reduced the number of mosquitoes and made the recurrence of a yellow fever epidemic impossible.

Epidemic of 1905. During the epidemic of 1905, the plan of attack of the New Orleans Board of Health under the leadership of Dr. Kohnke followed the lines indicated above. An Isolation Hospital was established and the campaign of eradication turned over to Dr. Joseph H. White of the United States Public Health and Marine Hospital Service. This was done because of the greater resource of this Service and the experience of its sanitary engineers in yellow fever districts of the tropics. Four-fifths of a fund of $320,000 contributed from the state, city treasurer, and by private citizens was placed at the disposal of the Federal Officer. The improved method of handling the epidemic brought the total number of deaths down to 452, ten per cent. of which were imported from outlying infected districts.

This epidemic gave a great impetus to the sanitation of the city and the completion of the sewerage and drainage systems; it also taught the people many facts in disease prevention and hygiene.

Cholera. Located near the Gulf of Mexico and accessible to tropical countries in which fevers are endemic, it is not surprising that the city, back in 1832, was visited by an epidemic of Asiatic cholera. To-day, there is no possibility of a repetition of this scourge, as wells and cess-pools have been abolished and sanitary water, drainage, and sewerage installed.

Bubonic Plague. In the summer of 1914, an unknown Scandinavian was taken ill at the home of the Volunteers of America, and, after several days, removed to the Charity Hospital, where his malady was pronounced bubonic plague. There had been cases of plague in Havana for several years, but careful quarantine had kept it out of New Orleans, this being the first case on record. No concealment was practiced. The facts in the case were published, other States notified, and citizens instructed in eradication of it. The confidence of other cities was retained and business suffered no interruption.

Campaign Against Rats. In plague epidemics elsewhere, scientists learned that rat-fleas transmit the disease to human beings. Therefore, there was need of a war on rats. Taking the Home of the Volunteers of America as a focus, a district of the radius of four squares was marked off as the infected area, where rat-extermination was to begin. The inmates of the Home were isolated in a perfectly rat-proof building until the time required for the disease to develop had passed. A large rat-catching force was set to work in the district marked off; those caught were immersed in kerosene to kill the fleas, and then sent to the Board of Health laboratories for bacteriological examination to determine if they were, or were not, infected. In this way, sanitary measures could be applied where needed, and an epidemic prevented.

Ratproofing. As the matter was of vital importance not only to the City of New Orleans but to the entire nation, it was deemed expedient to turn the campaign over to Surgeon General Rupert Blue of the United States Public Health Service, who had made an extended study of the plague and successfully combatted it in Honolulu and San Francisco. An ordinance was passed by the Commission Council requiring all premises to be ratproofed; that is, all buildings must be so constructed that rats cannot live in the walls or floors, and all rubbish where they might find shelter must be destroyed. The enforcement of the ordinance was left to the Federal Officers. The total number of deaths from plague was ten, and the last case was reported September 10, 1915. Thus the efficacy of modern sanitary and preventive measures was demonstrated. The war on rats continued through 1916-1917 and the number was diminished by hundreds of thousands.

Influenza Epidemic. In the fall of 1918, several cases of influenza were imported into Boston. From there the disease rapidly spread over the United States, assuming proportions of an epidemic. In New Orleans it raged during the last months of this year and the beginning of the next. Strenuous measures were adopted to combat it, among them the closing of schools, churches, and amusement places. The Elks opened an Emergency Bureau, from which physicians, nurses, medicine, and food were sent to afflicted people. The Orleans Parish Medical Society established an Emergency Bureau for physicians and nurses. An Emergency Hospital was opened in the Touro Almshouse to care for the overflow from other hospitals. The work here was directed by the Red Cross. The Knights of Columbus opened their hall to convalescents and all philanthropic and charitable agencies co-operated in alleviating distress.

SECTION 3. MARITIME QUARANTINE.

Establishment of the Quarantine Station. The Quarantine Station was first established at English Turn in 1821, but the system was very lax, as was evident from the frequent visitations of yellow fever and other tropical diseases foreign to this country. In fact, at times there was no quarantine at all. Alarmed by the experience of 1853 and 1854, the Legislature in 1855 appropriated $50,000 for a new Quarantine Station about seventy miles below the city. But even then the enforcement was lax or altogether nil. It was not until 1885 that a thorough system of maritime sanitation was inaugurated by Dr. Joseph Holt, President of the Board of Health. This was improved by his successor in office, Dr. Clement P. Wilkinson. Other state and local health authorities hastened to inaugurate this system.

Station Sold to the Federal Government. In 1906, the Quarantine Station was sold to the United States for $100,000, and is now controlled by the United States Public Health Service under the Treasury Department. The station forms one of a series of bulwarks against the enemies of public health, more important than forts or outposts, for the invasion of an armed force is seldom threatened, but disease is always a menace.

How the Federal Government Guards Against the Importation of Disease. The United States Public Health Service has officers in all foreign ports. These officers send to Washington, D. C., complete records of health conditions in the localities where they are stationed, with special reference to quarantinable diseases, namely, yellow fever, small-pox, Asiatic cholera, bubonic plague, and typhus fever. The Treasury Department issues weekly bulletins containing these reports, besides which, telegraphic notices of any special danger are sent to all Maritime

Quarantine Stations in the United States. A ship arriving from an infected or suspected port is thoroughly fumigated and detained long enough for any possible cases to develop. The time of detention varies according to the disease quarantined against. If there is no manifestation of disease, after the required number of days has elapsed, the ship is allowed to make port and disembark passengers and cargo.

Time and Money Saved by the Modern Method of Quarantine. Careful fumigation of ships subject to quarantine and examination of passengers is all that is now necessary if there are no suspicious cases on board. Sometimes even the fumigation is dispensed with, when the authorities have sufficient assurance that neither crew nor passengers have been exposed to infection. Thus there is very little delay or expense to shipping since the new plan was inaugurated, and commerce is not diverted to other ports unnecessarily.

Vigilance Against Yellow Fever. Any ship coming from the tropics or yellow fever zone during the months when that disease is prevalent must be detained six days after fumigation. Yellow fever symptoms become evident within six days after a person has been exposed to the disease. In order to save as much time as possible, the United States officer in the foreign port often fumigates the vessel at the hour of leaving. That plan reduces the time of detention by the number of days spent at sea. Of course vessels out at sea more than six days do not have to be detained at all. Fruit vessels, on account of their perishable cargo, are not fumigated, but are required to carry physicians, who are responsible for the health of all on board, and for the enforcement of all quarantine regulations.

Other Cities Adopt the New Orleans Method. New Orleans was the first city to adopt this system, based on the scientific fact that certain diseases take a specific time to develop. San Francisco was second in its use and was soon followed by New York.

SECTION 4. SANITARY IMPROVEMENTS SINCE 1803.

Sanitary Improvements. As early as 1817, Governor Claiborne suggested quarantine. He was forced to abandon his plan because public opinion was so bitterly opposed to it. Many eminent physicians of the day did not believe in the importation of disease, and considered quarantine ridiculous. Governor Villeré was, however, more successful, establishing a Quarantine Station and a Board of Health in 1821. Both enjoyed a very checkered career, being dissolved and re-established many times. The work of the Board of Health has been more or less continuous since 1855.

Dr. C. B. White, who was President of the Board of Health in the seventies, inaugurated a sanitary campaign in New Orleans and introduced the disinfection of premises with carbolic acid. The Auxiliary Sanitary Association was organized after the epidemic of 1878. They established a system of flushing the gutters, all open at that time, with water from public hydrants and with water lifted by a steam pump erected for that purpose. They also furnished the city with boats for the removal of garbage. From that time on there has been a steady improvement in sanitation, as is evidenced by the gradual reduction of the rate of mortality.

Potent Factors in Sanitation. The most powerful factors in attaining and maintaining the salubrity of New Orleans have been:

1. Drainage of adjacent swamps.
2. Sewerage and Drainage Systems.
3. Water supply.
4. Paving of streets.
5. Cleaning of city and removal of waste.
6. Effective quarantine.
7. Health legislation by State and City Boards of Health.
8. Enlightenment of the masses in the matter of sanitation and personal hygiene.
9. Rat-proofing.

(4 is considered in Chapter XVI.)

SECTION 5. STATE BOARD OF HEALTH.

State Board of Health. With the wonderful progress of medical science and with the realization that most diseases are preventable, epidemics of tropical diseases have become a matter of history in all modernized communities. Always conservative, Louisiana was slow to adopt preventive measures until the weight of public opinion and the pressure of neighboring states forced the adoption of effective quarantine and organized health work. A State Board of Health was organized in 1855, but reorganized in 1898; since then, with limited resources, it has steadily labored to improve conditions in Louisiana. The last five years, 1910 to 1915, have marked a wonderful advance in sanitation, relieving Louisiana of the stigma of insalubrity and unprogressiveness. People do not live in unhealthful surroundings through preference, but through ignorance. The Louisiana State Board of Health Laboratory Car with its assemblage of sanitary objects and appliances, pathological specimens, motoes, and working models, is a concrete embodiment of the best ideals for which medicine stands. It aims to give ocular proof of the conclusions of science and to impart facts in hygiene and preventive medicine. This educational work of the Board is supplemented by medical lectures given to schools and organizations and by copious free publications for use by school children and the general public. The State Board of Health shapes legislation to the end of promoting the physical well-being of all residents of the State. There are many excellent regulations to their credit, among them being those in regard to public drinking cups, common towels, habit-forming drugs, barber shops, etc.

Sanitary Inspection. In order that all sanitary regulations may be properly enforced, the Board has a regular system of inspection. Score cards containing questions which may vary according to the nature of the place to be visited are furnished the inspector. This officer fills out the blanks, points out violations of regulations, takes samples, and makes seizures. All cards are sent to the head office where they are graded and filed. Notices are then sent to owners and managers with a time limit set for improvement, after which, if the regulations are still violated, vigorous prosecution follows. In the City of New Orleans, the City and State Boards co-operate in these inspections. Many places have been temporarily closed until the regulations have been complied with.

This rigid inspection has caused great improvement in the dairies of the suburbs. The small top milk pail has been introduced. The campaign against insanitary markets has resulted in the screening ordinance and the erection of several model markets, such as the Dryades. The inspection is extended to eating establishments and places for storage and sale of foods. The regulations here aim to insure clean and safe foods to the consumer.

All public buildings, including prisons, are inspected once a year or oftener and health regulations enforced through the proper controlling body.

Rural sanitation is looked after with the same zest as urban, with the result that health standards have been materially raised over the State.

Food and Drug Laws and Regulations, and Net Weight and Measure Laws. In 1906, the State Legislature passed the first food and drug law, authorizing the State Board to make rules governing the manufacture, sale, and inspection of foods, drugs, liquors, and waters, insofar as they might affect the public health. Further laws have since been enacted against the misbranding of foods, drugs, etc., and also requiring all foods sold in package-form to bear the net weight of the measure or contents.

The Food and Drug Department of the State Board of Health, therefore, looks into food adulteration and misbranding, and regulates the sale of habit-forming drugs. Foods are adulterated if any substance has been substituted for the article, if any valuable constituent has been taken out, if any substance has been added to reduce or lower or injuriously affect its quality or strength, if any poisonous or deleterious ingredient has been added or if it consists in whole or in part of filthy, decomposed animal or vegetable matter. For example, milk may be adulterated by watering, by skimming, by having added to it a chemical to preserve it, or by becoming sour. All canned goods having puffed or swelled ends are adulterated, since the contents are nearly always spoiled. Foods and drugs are misbranded if the label contains any statement regarding the ingredients which is false or misleading in any particular. For example, cotton seed oil labelled "olive oil," patent medicines bearing false curative claims, or any packages labelled with incorrect weight or measure are misbranded.

Habit-forming drugs, such as morphine, opium, cocaine, and their compounds, cannot be sold except under the prescription of a physician. The sale of poisonous drugs is also regulated. The State Board has secured the co-operation of the Times-Picayune and the New Orleans Item in the matter of permitting it to censor all drug advertisements.

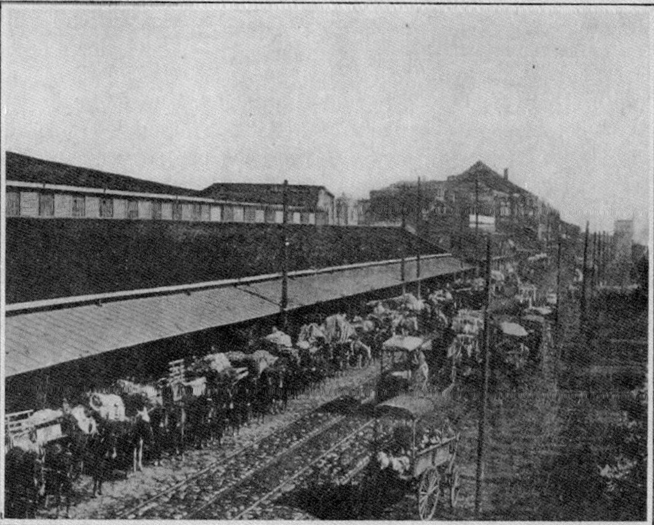

FRENCH MARKET BEFORE RENOVATION.

The food and drug department has an inspection force, a laboratory, and analysts. It makes a specialty of the analysis of water supplies for schools and communities, and, on application, sends a sanitary engineer to any community contemplating the installation of a sewerage and water system.

The State Board of Health conducts a bacteriological department where examination of specimens for consumption, malaria, hookworm, diphtheria, and typhoid fever are made. The department sends free anti-typhoid vaccine when called for by physicians.

The Department of Vital Statistics is under the control of the Board of Health and is conducted by the State Registrar. This Department keeps a record of births, deaths, and all cases of illness reported. In 1918 the State was admitted into the registration area for deaths.

Besides these varied activities, there is a force of men for the inspection of oils, which, by explosion or combustion, might endanger life or property. No fuel or illuminating oil that would ignite below 125° Fahrenheit can be sold in Louisiana, and all receptacles containing oil to be sold must bear the signature of a Board of Health Inspector.

The Department of Child Hygiene, one of the most important in the State health organization, is equally active. It co-operates with the Children's Bureau of the United States and local agencies in matters pertaining to the health and physical welfare of children and initiates independent measures for their care and protection.

Indirectly through the work of physicians, the State Board of Health controls all health work in the State by exercising a supervisory and restrictive jurisdiction. This it does by determining the qualifications of physicians and by granting and withdrawing licenses to practice. For mal-practice or quackery, a physician's license may be revoked at any time.

SECTION 6. CITY BOARD OF HEALTH.

Organization. The City Board of Health was established by the Legislature in 1898, making it distinct from the State Board. The act establishing the commission form of government for the City of New Orleans provides for a Board of Health consisting of five members, one to be the Mayor, one the Commissioner of Public Safety, and three other members at large to be chosen by the Commission Council, at least one of whom shall be a physician licensed to practice medicine in the Parish of Orleans.

Maintenance. This board is maintained by appropriations amounting in 1916 to about $89,000, and revenues obtained from fees, fines, etc., amounting in the same year to about $45,900.

Prevention of Contagion. One of the most important activities of the guardians of public health is the care of communicable diseases. Physicians are required by law to report all such cases to the Board of Health, where, by a carefully planned system, the exact city block infected is watched, and the progress of the case is noted. The house occupied by a patient suffering from a contagious disease is posted, and quarantine maintained until the premises are fumigated by officers of the Board of Health. During the period of contagion, health inspectors visit the premises to ascertain that all requirements as to disinfection are observed. A house to house inspection of the nine blocks surrounding the point of infection is made. All Board of Health inspectors are empowered to arrest those who violate the sanitary ordinances.

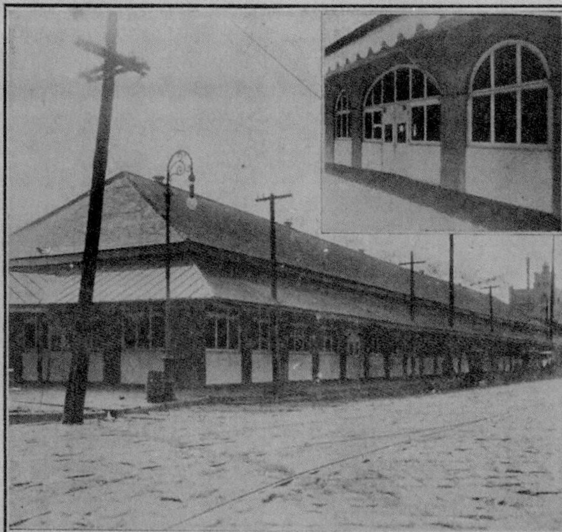

FRENCH MARKET AFTER RENOVATION.

Food Inspection. As a large proportion of sickness is caused by poor or tainted food, the duty of inspecting food supplies devolves upon health officers. Dairies, bakeries, confectioneries, abattoirs, markets, restaurants, and hotels, come under special supervision. Numerous and detailed ordinances requiring a high standard of sanitation are enforced in New Orleans. As an illustration some of those regulating the operation of a dairy will be given. Before a dairy may be opened, a permit must be obtained from the Board of Health, whose duty it is to see that sanitary requirements are met and that the water supply is pure and adequate. Veterinarians examine the cows. Samples of milk and other dairy products, taken at irregular intervals, are subjected to chemical tests to ascertain the presence of adulterants, preservatives, or impurities. (See Chapter IX for meat inspection.)

All restaurants, hotels, and other eating or refreshment places are subject to inspection without notice. Kitchens, store-rooms, refrigerators undergo a thorough examination, and, unless they meet the required standard, the places are closed until they receive a cleaning satisfactory to the health authorities. The owners are fined for violation of health ordinances.

Bacteriological Department. Besides a chemist, the board employs the services of an expert bacteriologist, a doctor who has made the study of germs a specialty. Sometimes, a physician is doubtful of the nature of a disease, for many germ diseases are similar in their early stages. Suppose he suspects a case to be diphtheria; he takes a culture from the patient's throat, that is, wipes it out with a little swab. This is sent to the bacteriologist, who, by a microscopic examination, proves or disproves the presence of the disease. The doctor is then enabled to proceed with the treatment, instead of waiting for more pronounced symptoms.

Department of Vital Statistics. This department may be justly regarded as the barometer of public health, whereby we may compare conditions of past years with the present. Louisiana has been admitted to the registration area for deaths. This puts her in the class of progressive states and helps in her material advance, because these statistics are relied upon by prospective settlers. Birth registration has been stimulated by the activities of the Child Welfare Association. This function of civil life has been promoted in the interest of better supervision and protection of children. Records in the books of the Board of Health are also used in establishing parentage and claims to inheritance. The statistical work is made complete by recording all deaths and their causes.

Curve of Death Rate from Malaria in City of New Orleans Covering 32 Years, 1880-1911, Based on Estimated Population from United States Census, Adding Each Year 10% of Ten Years' Increase. J. B. Guthrie.

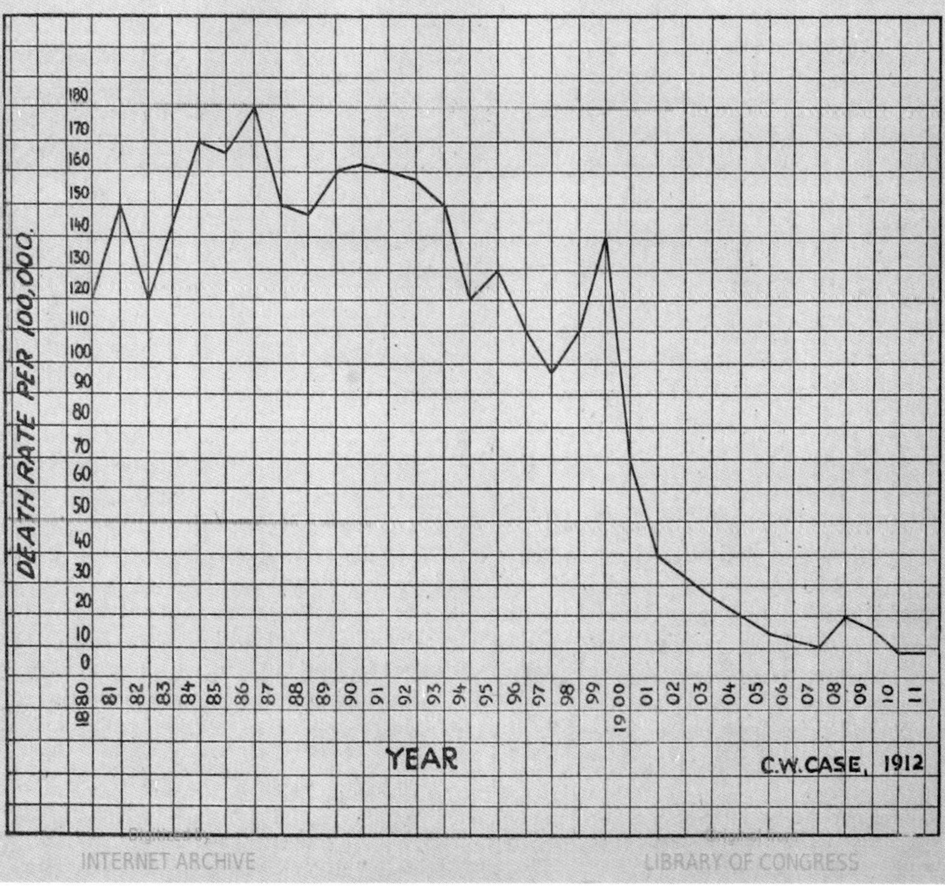

MORTALITY RATE,

Showing the High Death Rate Years Ago, the Improved Conditions of the Past Decade, and the Constant Decline in Rate in Each Decade.

GENERAL DEATH RATE PER THOUSAND OF POPULATION.

1809-'19	52.95	1860-'69	40.22
1820-'29	48.55	1870-'79	37.77
1830-'39	63.55	1880-'89	27.62
1840-'49	51.59	1890-'99	27.05
1850-'59	60.49	1900-'09	21.04
		1913	19.8

DEATH RATE OF 1916 (LOWEST ON RECORD).

		Non-residents Excluded.
White	14.13	12.53
Colored	28.87	24.72
White and Colored	18.11	15.82

Deaths From Prominent Causes—1908-1917.

CAUSES OF DEATHS.	No. of Deaths.	Percentage of Total Deaths.
Heart Diseases	12,263	.17
Tuberculosis	9,809	.135
Bright's Disease	5,769	.08
Diarrhœal Diseases	4,733	.065
Pneumonia	4,124	.055
Cancer	3,200	.044
Senility	1,116	.015
Typhoid Fever	857	.011
Diphtheria and Croup	598	.008
Malarial Fever	330	.004
Whooping Cough	276	.0038
Measles	245	.0034
Scarlet Fever	138	.0019
Smallpox	24	.0003
Total Deaths From These Causes	43,482	
Total Death From All Causes	72,097	

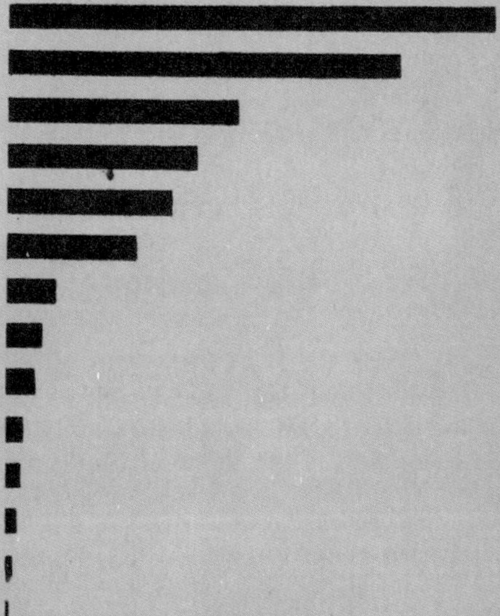

Biennial Report of Board of Health for the Parish of Orleans and City of New Orleans.

SECTION 7. REMOVAL OF GARBAGE.

Old System. The proper disposal of waste matter can hardly be over-rated as to its effects on the sanitary condition of a community. The old method practiced in New Orleans, of hauling all garbage to the river front to be loaded on boats, which carried it to a point below the city, there to be dumped into the river, has been done away with by national legislation.

System in Use. The system adopted, and at present in operation, is that of dumping such refuse into the outlying lowlands. All garbage must be kept in tightly closed cans which are placed out upon the sidewalk early each morning, except Sundays. A train of carts carries it from individual premises to the Public Belt Railroad, by which it is transferred to cars running out into the swamps and deposited in the vicinity of Bayou Bienvenu.

The High Temperature Destructor. Such a system is necessarily only temporary, as the lands are gradually being drained and occupied by the surplus population of a growing city. This was duly recognized by the city authorities who made a careful study of the subject. Having arrived at the conclusion that the use of the high temperature destructor is the most economical and effective method of disposal, after the necessary legislation, they contracted for the installation of the Cobwell system of dehydrator and reducer. The apparatus consists of a huge receptacle for the garbage, where, by forced draughts, the temperature, averaging from 1800° to 2000° Fahrenheit, destroys everything, and reduces all glass and metals to clinkers. All obnoxious odors are consumed, so that it might be constructed in the heart of the city without causing discomfort to the residents. By the high temperature, enormous steam power, easily converted into electrical energy, can be produced. Now that the close of the war has released labor and material and there is no longer an injunction against the establishment of large-scale improvements, the work is forging ahead.

Street cleaning is done under direction of the Department of Public Property. A force of street cleaners, in white uniforms, works during the hours of least traffic. On paved streets, the flush system is used and is followed up by the sweeping of debris into piles near the curb, where it is picked up and carted away. On unpaved streets it is proposed to have oiling after resurfacing with gravel if taxpayers on the street concerned unanimously consent to the expense.

SECTION 8. HOSPITALS AND CLINICS.

Charity Hospital. One of the oldest institutions in the United States is the Charity Hospital, in charge of the Sisters of Charity since 1834. Now, the management is in charge of a Superintendent, although the Sisters still train the lay nurses and care for the sick.

The ambulance service was added in 1885, but, since then, has been modernized. Two internes always accompany the ambulance to do first aid work. By this rapid relief many lives have been saved.

The Charity Hospital is open to the medical students of Tulane University for observation and clinical work. This exceptional opportunity for study has attracted many students to this department of the University. All indigent people are treated gratuitously. There are wards for the colored people and the care of the best physicians and nurses is bestowed upon all. Cases of small pox are not admitted, as there is a special hospital for that disease.

Connected with the Charity Hospital is one of the best equipped and most complete hospitals for children in the United States. It was donated by Mrs. Deborah Milliken at a cost of $100,000.

Eye, Ear, Nose, and Throat Hospital. As the science of medicine progresses, there is a tendency among physicians to specialize in some particular branch. In order that those who can ill afford treatment by a specialist may not be debarred from such advantages, the Eye, Ear, Nose, and Throat Hospital was opened in 1889, where free treatment is given. The numbers who grasp this opportunity are large and increase from year to year, as so many children are found suffering from adenoids, the removal of which greatly improves their condition.

Hotel Dieu. The nucleus of the present Hotel Dieu was the Maison de Santé, opened in 1852 by four Sisters of Charity from Emmitsburg, Maryland, at the clinic of Doctor Warren Stone. He befriended these Sisters during his lifetime and left them in possession of his property at death. The increasing demand upon the services of the gentle Sisters made the need for larger accommodations imperative, which resulted in their removal, in 1858, to the present site of the Hotel Dieu. With the growth of the institution and advance in medical science, they have steadily enlarged their opportunities for service to suffering humanity. Here, besides caring for the sick, they conduct a most successful training school for nurses.

Touro Infirmary. Judah Touro, who died in 1854, was a Jewish merchant and philanthropist. The bulk of his fortune was left for charitable purposes. One bequest was $80,000 for an almshouse. Touro also left a building, on Levee and Gaiennie Streets, then rented out as a private hospital. This gift was to be used in organizing a charitable institution for the relief of indigent sick. This section of Touro's will was not attended to until 1867, when, during the yellow fever epidemic, the need of a Jewish Hospital was keenly felt. About $30,000 was raised by the Hebrew Benevolent Association, and, in 1868, using some of this money, the Infirmary left by Touro was fitted out for its proper mission. In the course of time, the old building having proven inadequate, it was raffled, a large sum realized through its sale, and the site of the present hospital was purchased. This was in 1882.

Touro Infirmary now has accommodations for 265 patients and a free clinic which serves 260 sufferers daily. In 1917, 7,000 patients were taken into the wards and nearly 96,000 treatments were given in the free clinic. A training school for nurses was organized in 1896. The last improvement made was the building of porch wards for diseases where open air and sunshine are imperative. A home, donated by Julius Weis, for the aged and infirm is run in connection with the Infirmary.

Touro Infirmary is supported by donations from benevolent people, by fees from patients who occupy pay wards, and by an appropriation from the Commission Council.

Presbyterian Hospital. The New Orleans Sanitarium, now the Presbyterian Hospital, was opened in 1886 as a training school for nurses, the first in the South.

Isolation Hospital. In order to further protect the public health, the city opened on December 21, 1916, an Isolation Hospital. It is equipped with all the safeguards, comforts, and conveniences known to modern science. Smallpox patients are admitted. The recoveries thus far have been one hundred per cent.

New Orleans Hospital and Dispensary for Women and Children. This was established in 1905 by a group of women physicians who wished to insure treatment to patients who were reluctant to offer themselves for observation and study by medical students. With the help of public and private funds the work has been considerably extended.

Through the generosity of Mrs. John Dibert, New Orleans received a donation of $300,000 with which to erect a Tuberculosis Hospital. This is intended as a memorial to Mrs. Dibert's husband. The hospital will be located at the intersection of Tulane and Carrollton Avenues and will be equipped with every appliance and convenience known to medical science. The City of New Orleans will maintain it with the help of a fund given by the donor for this purpose. This beneficence meets a long felt need and is highly appreciated by the citizens of New Orleans.

The United Sates Marine Hospital. In 1802, the United States government established a hospital for sailors in New Orleans. No building was provided, and the sick, by special arrangement, were cared for in the Charity Hospital. The present location on Henry Clay Avenue and Tchoupitoulas Street was secured by authorization of Congress in 1882. There is a group of buildings comprising the wards, office building, houses for the surgeons, and laundry, etc. Any American seaman in need of treatment is received at the hospital, as is also any foreign seaman bringing a request from his consul. The hospital belongs to the Federal government and is managed by the United States Public Health Service.

Clinics. The Touro Infirmary and the Charity Hospital maintain an elaborate system of free clinics. All the usual types of disease treated in this way are represented in the patients who visit them. The good done by the clinics in removing defects and improving the physical efficiency of the poor is incalculable.

The Tulane Free Dental Clinic is under the auspices of Tulane University. Services are given free to people unable to pay, to others a nominal charge is made. The clinic is equipped to treat one hundred cases daily. During the late draft eleven thousand cases among soldiers were treated, the cost of the material being paid by the Red Cross.

SECTION 9. HEALTH AGENCIES.

The Child Welfare Association. This Association was organized May, 1913. It divides the city into districts of approximately ten blocks square and in each of these districts opens an infant welfare center in charge of a trained nurse. At this center, physicians hold conferences for mothers and children, and nurses instruct the mothers in the care of well and sick children. The nurses visit the homes once every ten days, and, in case of illness, several times, if necessary. Especial attention is given to the children of pre-school age, who are thoroughly examined and relieved of physical defects before beginning school.

In the five years of its existence the Association has established twenty milk stations and a staff of thirty nurses in as many centers with full time service of a baby specialist. There are over eight thousand children receiving the medical and supervisory care of the Association.

So successful has this work been, that, while the city was losing one out of every ten children, the Association, working in the most destitute sections, was losing only one out of every two hundred on roll. This record shows the effect of scientific care.

Medical Inspection in the Public Schools. The Health Department of the public schools is provided with three physicians and a nurse who exercise health supervision over the children. The physicians make examination of the children if the school locality becomes infected or if special cases are referred to them by the principal; they also exercise supervision over the buildings and grounds and co-operate with the City Board of Health in stamping out communicable diseases. They made free vaccinations of children applying for admission and formulate rules for the guidance of school people in health matters.

TOPICS: 1, Early History of Sanitation in New Orleans; 2, Epidemics; 3, Maritime Quarantine; 4, Sanitary Improvements Since 1803; 5, State Board of Health; 6, City Board of Health; 7, Removal of Garbage; 8, Hospitals and Clinics; 9, Health Agencies.

REFERENCES: Waring & Cable, History and Present Condition of New Orleans, 1880; Rightor (editor), Standard History of New Orleans; Augustin, History of Yellow Fever; Biennial Reports of the Louisiana State Board of Health; Biennial Reports of the Board of Health of the City of New Orleans; Sanitary Code of the State of Louisiana; Laws and Ordinances Relating to Health and Sanitation of the City of New Orleans; Kohnke, The Problem of Mosquito Destruction in New Orleans.

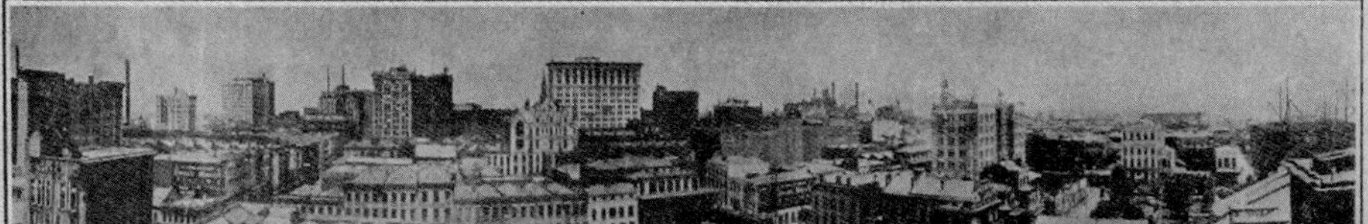

PANORAMA OF COMMERCIAL SECTION, VIEWED FROM TOP OF CITY HALL.

CHAPTER V.

Systems of Communication.

SECTION 1. POSTAL SYSTEM—POST OFFICE.

The post office is a Federal government service for the dispatch of letters, parcels, etc. The prototype of the modern postal system existed at an early date among the Persians, Romans, Aztecs, Chinese, and other peoples, in the form of an organized establishment of state carriers. In America, the first step in the organization of a postal system was the appointment in 1639, in the Massachusetts colony, of an official to take charge of the delivery of letters. The American Congress, in July, 1775, appointed Benjamin Franklin as the first postmaster-general.

Beginning of the Mail System in New Orleans. Previous to the introduction of the mail system, post riders, stage coaches, and steamboats carried the mail to all parts of the United States. A mail coach, owned by two Orleanians, ran in 1804-1805 from New Orleans to Manchac Church twice a week. A post office was established in New Orleans by the United States soon after its acquisition of Louisiana. Blaise Cenas was the first postmaster, his commission being dated October, 1803. In 1804, the postmaster made the announcement that the mail would arrive in New Orleans every Monday and leave every Tuesday. In September, 1810, the mails began to arrive and depart more frequently. By May, 1811, New Orleans boasted of the fast time made by the mails. It took twenty days for a letter to reach New Orleans from Washington City; to-day, it takes about thirty-four hours.

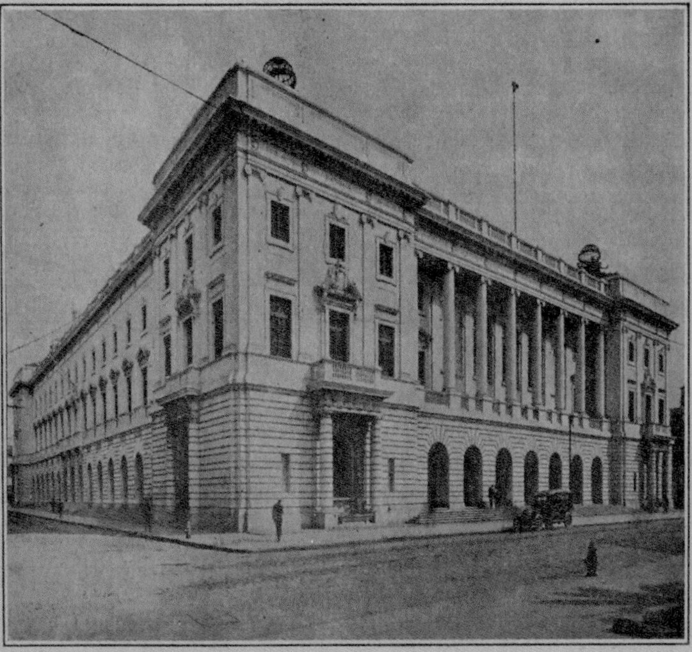

UNITED STATES POST OFFICE.

The railway mail service was inaugurated in 1864, after a successful experiment upon a few large railroad lines. It has reached a perfection attainable only in a country of great extent. This service is one of the earliest exponents of classified civil service. The government is contemplating aerial mail service between the large cities, but up to February, 1919, no definite plans have been formed.

Postage. Originally, postage was charged according to the distance that a letter had to be carried. At first, there were no postage stamps, and the cost was marked across the face of the letter, to be paid by the person receiving it. Some letters cost only six cents, while others cost as much as twenty cents. Heavy letters often cost three or four times that amount. The use of adhesive stamps was authorized by Congress in March, 1847. In 1856, prepayment by stamps was made compulsory. In 1863, postage on letters was three cents per half ounce, but, then, was reduced to two cents per ounce. During the period of the World War postage was increased one cent. A bill providing for the return to the former rate, by June 1, 1919, has been passed by Congress.

The system of registry, adopted in 1855, did not attain any degree of excellence until after 1860. The money-order system was established in 1864. Money-orders are exchanged with most of the important countries of the world which have money-order systems of their own. The introduction of the parcel post, January, 1913, was the result of many years of agitation for the admission to the mail of parcels of merchandise of greater weight than four pounds, and for a lower rate on this class of matter. This was the first time the Post Office Department inaugurated a new service and put it into immediate operation without trying it on a small scale.

Under an order issued at Washington, October 1, 1914, the postmasters of New Orleans and fourteen other cities are directed to assist in building up the farm-to-table business of the parcel post. The way is thus opened for direct dealing between consumers and producers. The only middleman in the transaction will be the post office and the only tolls will be the cost of the stamps. In one or two cities where the plan has been tried, newspaper accounts have indicated its partial failure. Whether it will succeed in New Orleans, with its numerous suburban truck farms, public markets, and wagon peddlers, remains to be seen. The wider competition it makes possible ought to discourage any tendency to excessive prices in the local markets, just as "water competition" discourages unreasonably high rail rates.

Postal Savings. The Postal Savings Department was established in 1911. The deposits for the year ending May, 1919, amounted to nearly $248,407, credited to 850 depositors.

Establishment of Sub-stations. There are three sub-stations,—Station A in Algiers, Station B at Napoleon Avenue and Prytania Street, Station D at 3214 Dauphine Street,—and every neighborhood has a convenient numbered station within its boundaries.

The free delivery system has been extended to the suburbs of the city to those who have provided the requirements of paved sidewalks, extending from the former line of delivery service to their residences, of house numbers, and of mail boxes. The business districts now have five deliveries a day.

The Special Delivery system was put into operation in 1895. The collection carts were introduced in 1899. Since 1860, the post office had occupied a part of the lower floor of the Custom House. This department was moved into the handsome building in Camp Street, opposite Lafayette Square, in March, 1915.

TOPICS: Early History of the Postal System; The Beginning of the Mail System of New Orleans; Postage.

REFERENCES: Nelson's Encyclopedia; Newspaper Files.

SECTION 2. ELECTRIC TELEGRAPH.

Early Modes of Communication. The savage, who lights a fire so that the smoke may be seen from afar by his comrades, is using a telegraph such as all men used once upon a time. The soldier who waves two flags about in a peculiar manner is also telegraphing. The heliograph, a mirror reflecting the rays of the sun, flashes messages to those who can read the signals. This latter method is used to-day in some parts of California. Electricity, one of nature's most powerful forces, carefully kept its secret for ages. Now, that its use is known, man is able to achieve wonders.

No one is absolutely certain as to the name of the man who first suggested the electric telegraph. Many clever inventors prepared the way. Among these are Volta, Humphrey Davy, Michael Faraday, Francis Ronald, Sir Charles

Wheatstone, and Sir William Cooke. The last two mentioned made, in 1838, the first practical telegraph used in England, and from that beginning her whole national system of telegraphic communication has sprung.

In America, when there arises a demand for something vital which shall play an important part in national development, science comes forward to meet the need. When a swifter mode of communication between commercial centers became necessary, Professor Morse was able to transform into a messenger boy of commerce that mysterious force which Benjamin Franklin had captured from the clouds. Morse's alphabet and method of telegraphing are used throughout America.

The Growth of the Telegraph System. At the beginning of the nineteenth century, there was not a line of electric telegraph in the United States. To-day, there is a vast mileage traversing all lands and all seas. "God and man have linked the nations together." The growth of the system is bounded by less than seventy-five years, most of it by the last thirty-five years. Edison invented the quadruplex system and also a means of sending six telegrams simultaneously.

First Line Into New Orleans. The Washington and New Orleans Telegraph Company was operated in 1848, and became one of the most important lines in the country. Four other companies operated lines into New Orleans between 1856 and 1866. The Western Union, organized in Rochester, New York, in 1851, had absorbed all lines South and Southwest, by 1866. Its only formidable rival is the Postal Telegraph, which was organized in 1883.

Telegraph Offices in New Orleans. In former years, the gravity "bluestone" batteries were exclusively used and are still used in small towns, but in New Orleans, as in all other large cities, these have been replaced by the dynamos. There are about one hundred wires from different parts of the country entering the Western Union office in New Orleans. Single lines are used along the railroad routes, but trunk lines are employed between large cities. The wires are duplexed and quadruplexed, hence, two or four messages can be sent in opposite directions at the same time. The duplex system consists of a receiving and sending apparatus at each end, which are worked simultaneously without interference with each other. For example, New Orleans sends a message to Memphis and Memphis to New Orleans at the same time without mixing the signals. The quadruplex is a combination of two duplexes of different designs on which New Orleans can have two operators sending messages to Memphis, and Memphis to New Orleans; while Memphis can connect St. Louis or Chicago by the automatic repeating apparatus on one side, and can send messages to New Orleans, while St. Louis or Chicago is using the wire. The wires come into the office by a switchboard, an apparatus by which the chief can locate trouble on the wires between stations, and give the necessary instructions.

Ocean Cables. We owe this remarkable means of communication to Cyrus Field, who, after several failures, succeeded in putting the New World on conversational terms with the Old. New Orleans sends her cable messages for Europe to the Western Union and Postal Telegraph offices in New York, where they are transferred to the Atlantic Cable companies for transmission to Liverpool and then by land, in most cases, to their destination. Dispatches for eastern Asia, Australia, and the Pacific Ocean points are sent for transmission to the Pacific Cable Company in San Francisco. The Mexican and South American cable service is handled from Galveston, Texas, but Mexico can also be reached by land lines via El Paso and Laredo, Texas. The West Indian business is done through Tampa and Key West.

Wireless Telegraph. Marconi's patent was applied for in England, in 1896, and obtained in 1897. Wireless stations are now operated in all seaports. The first one in New Orleans was erected by the United Fruit Company. There are now three wireless stations in New Orleans; one, on Metairie Ridge, operated by the Marconi Company; another, at the Naval Station in Algiers; and the third, near City Park, operated by the United Fruit Company.

Note.—By Act of Congress, August 1, 1918, all telegraph, telephone, and cable companies of the United States passed under the control of the government. This control, unless repealed by Act of Congress, will continue until the Treaty of Peace is ratified by the Senate.

Note for Teacher.—Discuss wireless telephone.

TOPICS: Early Modes of Communication; The First Telegraphic Lines into New Orleans; Ocean Cables; Wireless.

REFERENCES: Archives of Cabildo.

SECTION 3. THE TELEPHONE.

History tells us that, as early as 1667, Robert Hooke made sound travel along a stretched wire. Philip Reis of Frankfort, Germany, produced an electric telephone in 1861. In 1876, two telephones were patented; one by Elisha Gray, the other, by Alexander Graham Bell. These two men, unknown to each other, applied on the same day at the Washington office for their patents. Bell's proved the better instrument, and with many improvements is still in use. Thomas Edison has given us one of the most important things in the telephone—the carbon transmitter.

How the Sound Carries. We use the telephone to change the air waves into electric waves, which travel along the wire quicker than sound travels from the tongue to the ear. The words strike one disc and become electric waves; the waves strike another disc and become words again, because both discs are in tune and give off the same sound when the wave strikes them.

The First Telephone in New Orleans. The first telephone put into service in New Orleans was brought from the Philadelphia Exposition, 1876, by a member of the firm of Horter and Fenner, manufacturers of saddlery and harness. This firm connected their salesroom on Magazine and Gravier with their factory on Poydras and Church Streets. Shortly after this introduction, the Louisiana Telephone Company fitted up an exchange on the top floor of the Denegre Building. Their system was known as the Magneto System. They employed boys seventeen to twenty years of age as operators. The switchboards were different from the ones used at the present time, and the connections complicated and difficult to complete. Both persons, when wishing to disconnect their lines, would signal the operator with a short ring. If, after the termination of a conversation, they failed to notify the operator, the connection would remain on the switchboard until some one went to a neighboring telephone and asked the operator to disconnect the lines. The first conversation held over the telephones of this company was in the nature of a concert. One instrument was installed at Camp and Gravier Streets and the other at the Magazine Market. Singers were engaged to sing into the receivers, entertaining those at the other end of the line. This company soon had about 1100 subscribers.

Great Southern Telephone and Telegraph Company. In 1883, the Louisiana Telephone Company was sold to the Great Southern Telephone and Telegraph Company. This company removed the telephone circuits from the housetops and placed them upon cross-arms on poles. On January 20, 1883, the boy operators were replaced by girls, with the exception of the chief night operator and one assistant. The style of equipment was changed and the first Western Multiple Switchboard installed, with a capacity for 1,800 subscribers. The demand for service became so great that the modern building now known as the Main Exchange was constructed. The first private branch exchange was installed for the Cotton Centennial Exposition of 1884.

In 1897, the Cumberland Telephone and Telegraph Company acquired the Great Southern. The New Orleans operators handle, every twenty-four hours, four hundred and fifty-five thousand local calls and seventeen hundred long distance calls, through seven exchanges known as Main, Hemlock, Galvez, Uptown, Walnut, Jackson, and Algiers.

Description of an Exchange. The exchange is a wonderful sight. The walls are lined with switchboards, which enable one to talk any distance. These boards are covered with tiny holes like a bee's honeycomb, each having a number. On them are dull glass knobs no larger than a shoe button, also having numbers. In front of these boards are the clerks, generally women. At their ears they have receivers, the part of the telephone which gives the message, and under the lips a transmitter which sends the message. Both are fitted so as to leave the hands free. The moment a man lifts his telephone, one of the knobs of dull glass on the switchboard lights up. The clerk sees the light, looks at the number under it, and puts a plug in the hole in the honeycomb having the same number. As soon as this plug is put in, the telephone is connected with exchange and he tells the clerk he wants to speak to Main 179. Quickly, she lifts another plug joined to the first one and puts it into the hole having the number the man wants. When she does this, a bell rings at Main 179; the owner of that office takes up his telephone and talks to the man who has called him. When they have finished talking, they hang up the receiver, the little light goes out, the clerk removes the plugs, and the wires are disconnected.

The volume of telegraphic communication has been enormously lessened by the telephone. This reduction in telegraphic business results from the substitution of long-distance calls. The telegraph remains superior for long distances, if the message is taken as a unit, but on the base of the number of words and time for exchange of messages, the telegraph is at a disadvantage. The rates for the two methods differ little for medium distances.

TOPICS: The Invention of the Telephone; The Telephone in New Orleans; Description of an Exchange; Rates of Telephone and Telegraph.

REFERENCES: City Archives; Pamphlets of Telephone Company.

SECTION 4. STREET RAILWAYS.

Early History of Street Car Line. As a means of public conveyance, the omnibus was first used. The first line of street cars in the United States was the one established by the New Orleans and Carrollton Company, September 26, 1835. It ran from the corner of Canal and Baronne Streets to Carrollton, the same route now traversed by the St. Charles Belt. The charter given this company authorized it to lay one single track between the above named points. It stated that if the majority of the inhabitants, through whose property it passed, complained of it as a nuisance, this company, after receiving thirty days' notice from the mayor, had to remove the track and put the street in the same order as before. In 1845, steam dummies were placed on this road from Carrollton to Lake Pontchartrain. From Lee Circle the cars were brought down by means of animal power. Rope cables were tried as a means of propelling the cars, but, owing to the shrinking of the rope with the changes of the barometer, they had to be given up. The fare was 50 cents from Lee Circle to Carrollton.

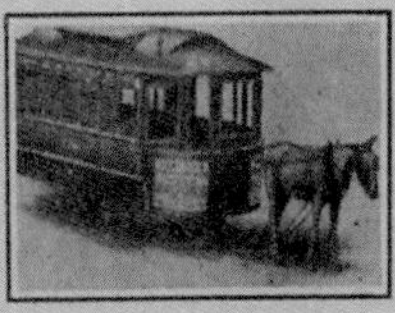
MULE TRACTION.

In February, 1893, electricity was adopted on this road. In 1899, the track was rebuilt and the Canal and Claiborne line was purchased by it. The City Railroad Company, formed in June, 1860, commenced to run cars in June, 1861, from Canal and Rampart via Esplanade to Bayou Bridge. These cars were built in omnibus style. By June, 1864, this company ran the Magazine and Prytania lines to Pleasant Street; the Rampart and Dauphine lines to the Barracks; and the Canal Street line to the City Park and the Cemeteries. The Levee and Barracks line was opened in 1866. This same company purchased the New Orleans City and Lake, and the Crescent City Railroad Companies. The St. Charles Street Railroad Company, organized in 1866, built the Carondelet, Dryades and Clio lines. It was the first company to issue transfers. The Orleans Railroad Company was organized in 1869, with three lines—Bayou St. John, Broad Street, and French Market. Electricity was used on all the main lines by 1895.

Present System. The New Orleans Railway and Light Company, organized in 1905, now operates every street railway in New Orleans, besides an electric light plant and a gas plant. It controls twenty-nine distinct lines, reaching every portion of the city. The nominal far is six cents and a limited system of transfers enables passengers to reach long distances and outlying districts without additional cost. There are 218.41 miles of single track, 548 motor and passenger cars, besides work cars, wreckers, sprinklers, etc. This plant has three generating stations for electricity; twenty-three generators with a capacity for 60,000 kilowatts. The passenger traffic in 1918 was 123,932,220 revenue and 26,666,129 transfers, making a total of 150,598,349 passengers. It furnishes the electrical current for lighting and power purposes. The gas mains run everywhere, gas being used for fuel and heating as well as for lighting. The company is now in the hands of a receiver.

TOPICS: Early History of the Car Lines; The Present System.

REFERENCES: Rightor's History; City Hall Archives.

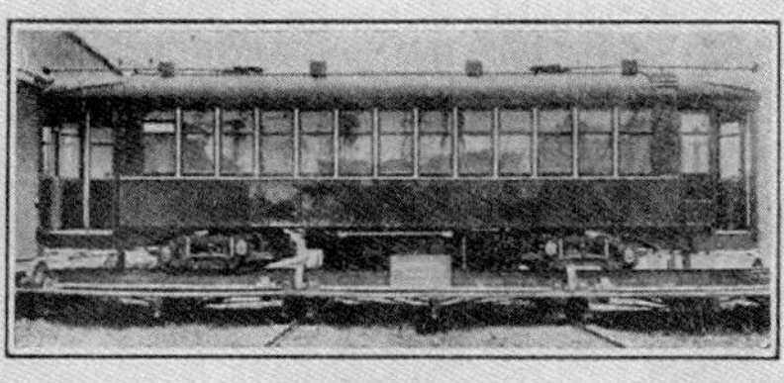

LATEST TYPE OF ELECTRIC CAR IN USE IN NEW ORLEANS.

CHAPTER VI.

Trade.

SECTION 1. SHIPPING.

Port. The word "port" comes from a Latin word, meaning "gate." The term is used to designate a place where goods brought to it on land are placed on boats to be carried over water, or taken from boats to be carried by land.

Tonnage. The amount of freight a ship can carry is called "tonnage." Her freight-carrying capacity is spoken of as so many "tons register." This is because every ship is required to have a home port, where she is registered; the number of tons she can carry is part of her description; this number is found out by ascertaining how many cubic feet of space she contains. A tonnage tax is collected on her arrival in a new country.

International Regulations. The rules were originally made for sailing vessels. When steamships were built, space had to be allowed for boilers, engines, and fuel, which space could not be used for freight. These deductions are by agreement among nations practically the same everywhere, and amount to much more than the actual space occupied by the machinery, etc. This lessens the tonnage, and so makes the running of the ship cheaper, which is a benefit to commerce. The freight on a ship is called "cargo." As a matter of fact, ships can usually take cargo equal to nearly twice their registered tonnage. Ordinarily, a 3,000-ton ship will take 5,600 tons of cargo.

Control by United States Government. In the United States, all laws and rules with regard to registration, measurement, tonnage dues, and navigation are passed by Congress and are under its authority. All navigable waters are controlled by the United States Government.

Control of Wharves. All laws and rules affecting the wharves and landings are passed by the Board of Commissioners of the Port of New Orleans, an agency of the State of Louisiana.

Wharves can be constructed only after obtaining permission of the Dock Board, under provision of the Constitution.

Wharves. A ship cannot lie alongside the natural shore, because when she has cargo on board she sinks deep into the water. For this reason, in some places, wharves are built straight out, so that, when a ship is alongside, her bow is toward the shore. These are called piers. Where piers can be built, much less "water front" is needed for the same number of ships than where piers are impracticable or impossible. The river current is too swift at New Orleans for piers, so there are wharves on the levees along the river.

SECTION 2. SEAPORT AND RIVERPORT.

Combined Seaport and Riverport. New Orleans has direct water communication as far as Pittsburg on the east, Chicago on the north, and Kansas City on the west, and deep-sea trade routes to all the principal ports of the world.

Jetties. Though about 110 miles from the Gulf of Mexico, New Orleans is rightly considered a seaport, for the largest ship afloat can enter the Mississippi and ascend beyond New Orleans. Until the second half of the nineteenth century, sea trade was interrupted by the formation of sand bars at the mouth of the River. Silt, carried seaward by the strong current, was dropped when the waters of the Gulf retarded those of the river. Constant dredging was necessary to maintain a channel. This was expensive and inadequate. The commercial prosperity of the Mississippi Valley was hampered by this hindrance to navigation and several disasters occasioned actual loss.

To improve these conditions the jetties were constructed by Captain James B. Eads in the mouth of the River, called the South Pass. Congress appropriated $1,000,000 for the work, which was begun in 1875 and completed in 1879. The jetties are walls of willow mattresses weighted with stones and held in place by piling. Debris and silt, brought down by the River, gradually filled in all crevices, making firm, tight walls. These walls are connected with the River banks by dams and run parallel with each other 1,000 feet apart. The current of the mighty River, thus reduced to a much narrower channel, becomes swifter, and, instead of depositing sediment across the mouth of the River, carries it far into the deep waters of the Gulf. The force of the waters scours and continually deepens the channel, making dredging unnecessary. Like improvements are being made at Southwest Pass.

SECTION 3. HARBOR.

Size of Harbor. When vessels arrive at New Orleans, they can discharge their cargoes directly upon the wharves, as the depth of the water ranges from twenty to seventy feet alongside of the wharves and up to 150 feet at low water, in mid-stream. The narrowest portion of the River opposite New Orleans has a width of 2,000 feet. The distance of New Orleans from the open sea is an added protection to ships in the harbor, for the severe storms of the Gulf do not reach so far inland.

Fresh Water. New Orleans possesses an advantage over most seaports in the fact that it has a fresh-water harbor. In salt water, the hulls of ships become covered with barnacles, which injure the ship and retard navigation. As the barnacles die and fall off in fresh water, a trip to such a harbor saves the expense of having the hull cleaned.

Naval Station. The United States Government maintains a Naval Station on the west

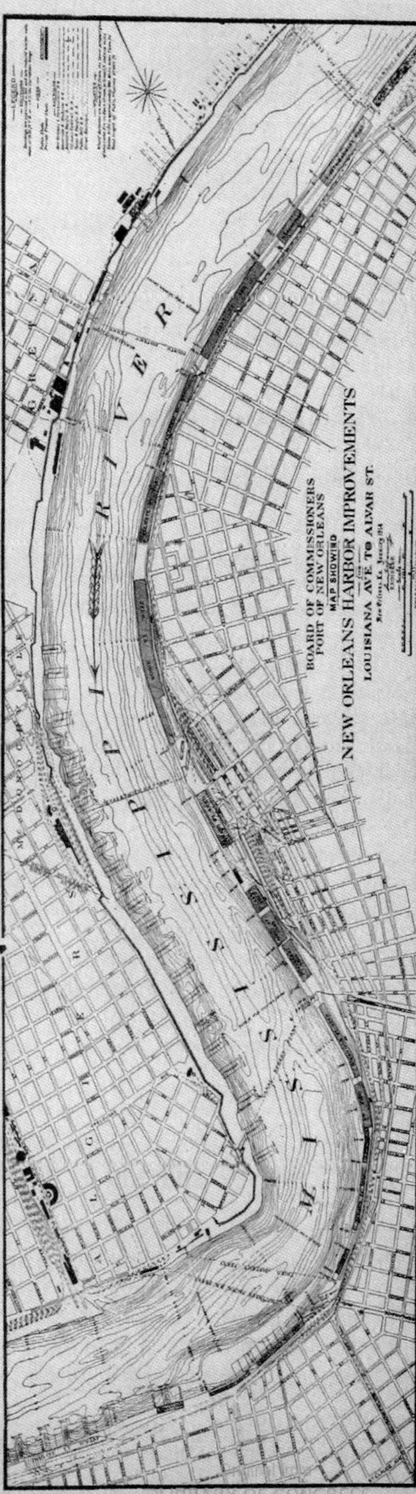

MAP OF NEW ORLEANS HARBOR, LOUISIANA AVENUE TO ALVAR STREET.

bank of the River below Algiers. Political differences led to the abandonment and subsequent re-establishment of this station. The common opinion is that New Orleans, the nearest United States port to the Panama Canal and the first city from the mouth of the Mississippi River, is the most favorable location for a naval base in the southern part of the United States. The Naval Station is a place of deposit for supplies, a coaling station, and a repair plant. Since the entrance of the United States into the World War, the Naval Station has become an important base for general military and industrial supplies, a training camp for sailors, and a Marine Barracks. When the hull of a vessel has to be painted or repaired, the vessel must be raised out of the water. This is done by means of a dry dock. A dry dock is a large floating platform with walls along two sides, but open at either end. These walls contain compartments into which water is pumped to lower the platform below the water surface. The ship enters the dry dock when there is sufficient depth of water. The compartments are then emptied and the platform rises, lifting the vessel out of the water. The United States Government dry dock at the Naval Station is capable of raising out of the water a vessel of 18,000 tons displacement.

Immigration Station. Below the Naval Station is the United States Immigration Station, which is the largest south of Philadelphia. Its purpose is to exclude from the country undesirable aliens. Hence, all immigrants are subjected to physical and mental examinations, and are required to furnish proof of good character and means of support. An immigrant, who would probably become a burden to the community, is returned to the country from which he came.

Factories. As a result of transportation facilities to be had near the River, factories have been established along both sides of the harbor. Numerous canning factories, breweries, rice mills, cotton mills, oil and fertilizing plants are situated on or near the River.

SECTION 4. PUBLICLY OWNED WHARVES.

State Ownership. The wharves at New Orleans have, for the most part, always been public property, as, by the Constitution, are all landings in the state. Formerly, the wharves were under the control of the city and were leased out, but this plan was not successful, because the lessees did not keep them in good condition, and charged so exorbitantly for their use that business went elsewhere.

The Board of Commissioners of the Port of New Orleans. When it was determined to stop the leasing system, all of the wharves were in very bad condition and much money was needed to make them fit for use. The City, restricted by the State Constitution, was in debt for the full amount allowed by law. For this and other reasons, a new body was formed, called legally the "Board of Commissioners of the Port of New Orleans," but spoken of always as "The Dock Board."

Power of the Dock Board. To this Board was given by amendment to the Constitution and by act of the Legislature (Act No. 70 of 1896) complete control of the wharves and harbor. It passes all ordinances for harbor purposes just as the City Council does for the city at large.

Work of the Dock Board. The Dock Board took charge May 29, 1901. The members are appointed by the Governor and report to him. They serve without pay and elect all their officers. The financing has been very successful, and there have been built nearly eight miles of excellent wharves, most of which are covered by steel sheds.

Terminal Stations. In addition to these public wharves, there are several terminal stations controlled by different railroad lines. At Westwego, on the west side of the River, the Texas and Pacific Railroad has two grain elevators and about three-quarters of a mile of wharfage. On the east side, at Stuyvesant Docks, the Illinois Central Railroad has 4,800 feet of river front occupied by wharf, covering the distance from Napoleon Avenue to Louisiana Avenue. This provides berth-room for ten ships at once. There are two grain elevators back of the wharf. The Louisville and Nashville Railroad has a berth for one ship at St. Joseph and Calliope Streets. At the American Sugar Refinery, there is room for three ships at once.

Port Chalmette. The New Orleans Terminal Company, which is owned by the Southern Railway Company, has Port Chalmette about six miles below Canal Street, where a grain elevator is located, and about a half mile of wharf. Below this wharf, there is berth room for steamships handling, through pumping plants located there, bulk cargoes of creosote oil and crude petroleum.

Chalmette Slip. This Company owns between Port Chalmette and the American Sugar Refinery what is known as "Chalmette Slip," a novel departure from the ordinary construction of wharves and berths at this port. The Slip, which is enclosed in immense concrete walls, extends from the River back into the land—a distance of 1,680 feet—along the sides of which are fire-proof freight sheds built of steel and concrete construction which provide storage room aggregating 548,600 square feet, or nearly thirteen acres.

A sufficient depth of water is maintained in the Slip to accommodate the largest steamships discharging or unloading cargoes at the freight sheds. There is berth and wharf room within the Slip for six steamships at one time.

During the World War, at times there were stored in these freight sheds, and in the railroad yards adjoining them, as much as 70,000 tons of food stuffs, munitions and other war material.

"Pumping Stations." In addition to these wharves, there are numerous "pumping stations," where petroleum, oil (both crude and refined), creosote, and molasses are handled both in and out.

Power of the Dock Board Over Private Terminals. Under the law, the Dock Board can take possession and control of any of these so-called "private terminals" at any time it thinks the public interest so requires, by paying the appraised value for the improvements at the time of their being taken over.

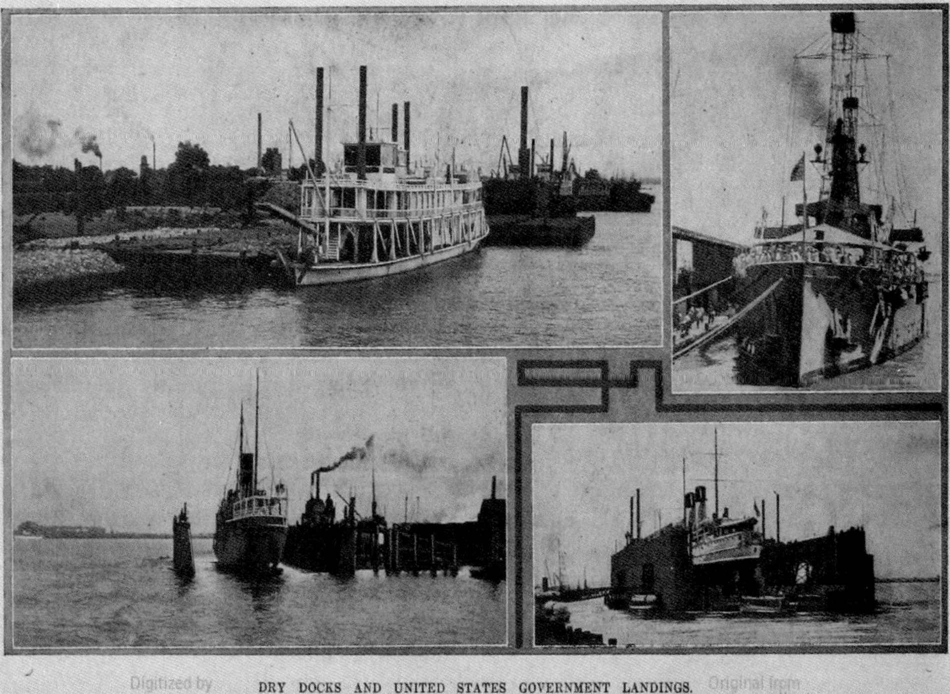

DRY DOCKS AND UNITED STATES GOVERNMENT LANDINGS.

SECTION 5. HANDLING CARGO.

Laborers. The men, who make contracts with ships to load and unload them, are called stevedores. The laborers, who actually do the work, are called longshoremen. One of the advantages of New Orleans as a port is that the longshoremen do their work better than at any other port. They load more cargo on a ship and store it better than elsewhere, so that voyages from New Orleans are more profitable to the ship.

Liquid Cargoes. The various pumping stations handle bulk cargoes of liquid freight with great economy and speed, especially oils, creosote, and molasses. A tank ship bringing a million and a quarter gallons of molasses has been discharged in sixty hours.

Grain Elevators. The grain elevators are large structures, where quantities of grain are stored. By mechanical devices, the grain is rapidly and economically loaded upon ships.

Banana Cargoes. The handling of banana cargoes can hardly be improved upon. The system of mechanical conveyors, taking bananas out of the ship and delivering them on the wharf, works so that nearly ten thousand bunches an hour can be taken out of a ship working four hatches. Cars are loaded at an average rate of one every four or five minutes.

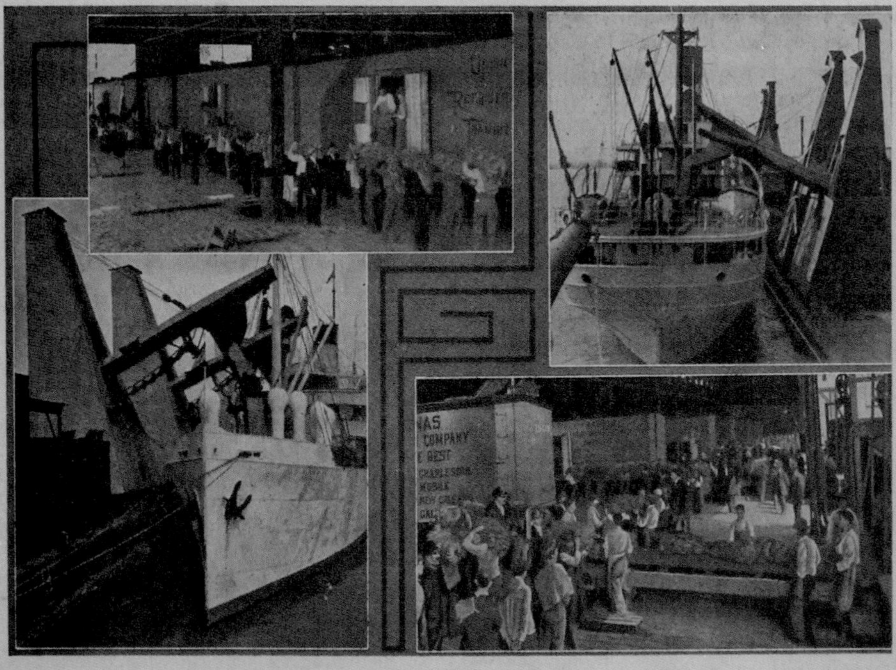

BANANA CONVEYORS.

SECTION 6. PUBLIC BELT.

Size of Modern Cargo. Not very many years ago, when ships were built of wood and a 1,000-ton ship was a large one, the wharf could easily hold all the cargo of a ship. Now, when a 3,000-ton ship is a small one, there is not room on any wharf for a whole cargo. Consequently, it has become necessary for the freight to be moved to and from the wharf quickly to prevent congestion when the ship is discharging, and loss of time when the ship is loading.

Need for Promptness in Moving Cargo. As a comparatively small ship costs $500 a day, she loses money very rapidly if idle. If the ship owner is not to lose, the cost of her idle time has to be added to her freight charges. To overcome this disadvantage, it is necessary to have abundant means for moving cargo quickly to and from the wharves on the land side.

The Public Belt Railroad. The municipally owned Public Belt Railroad, which has been in operation since 1908, meets this necessity. The Public Belt tracks make a complete circuit of the city, connecting all trunk lines, all wharves and landings, and all important industries. Before the operation of this system, switching charges ranged from eight dollars to twenty-two dollars per car. Now, engines, owned by the Public Belt Commission, carry goods from railroad to railroad, from ship to railroad, from factory to ship or railroad, for the nominal sum of two dollars a car. This includes the hauling of the empty car before loading or after unloading, for the Public Belt does not own the cars. Over 15,000 cars a month are handled by the Public Belt, and its business is constantly increasing.

The route of the Public Belt is shown on the present-day map of the city. (Shown in back of Book.)

Necessity for Co-operation Between Dock Board and Public Belt. The necessity will be understood when it is remembered that a ship a little over 300 feet long, will carry, in round figures, about 6,000 tons of cargo, while one 500 feet long will carry 15,000 tons. Six thousand tons of cargo are, on an average, 400 car loads, while 15,000 tons are 1,000 car loads. No wharf at a ship's berth can hold much over 150 car loads at one time. The need, then, of having cars conveniently placed and rapidly handled is absolute, if the ship is not to wait or be carried to another berth for part of her cargo. The expense of moving is several hundred dollars. Therefore, it will be a very great advantage when the ship can discharge and receive her cargo at one berth without any idle time.

Necessity for Many Miles of Trackage to One Mile of River Front. As a freight car is about forty feet long, the thousand cars needed to carry a 15,000-ton cargo will occupy 40,000 feet of railroad track, or seven and one-half miles. The Illinois Central Railroad, at Stuyvesant Docks, has twenty miles of trackage for one mile of wharfage, and is finding it necessary to put in additional tracks. To enable the Dock Board to get the greatest use out of its wharves, it is not only necessary to have perfect co-operation with the Public Belt Railroad, but it is also necessary for that organization to greatly increase its trackage.

SECTION 7. WATERWAYS.

Water Route of Mississippi River System. One of the greatest advantages enjoyed by New Orleans is that the Mississippi River and its tributaries furnish more than 16,000 miles of navigable waterway, extending into twenty-two of the forty-eight states of the Union, included between the Alleghanies on the east, the Rockies on the west, and Canada on the north.

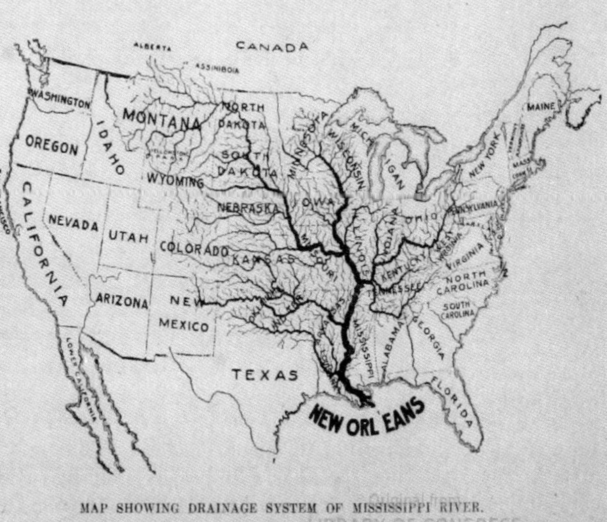

MAP SHOWING DRAINAGE SYSTEM OF MISSISSIPPI RIVER.

These are:

Louisiana	Wisconsin
Mississippi	Minnesota
Alabama	North Dakota
Tennessee	South Dakota
Kentucky	Montana
West Virginia	Nebraska
Pennsylvania	Iowa
Ohio	Missouri
Indiana	Arkansas
Illinois	Oklahoma
Kansas	Northern Texas

The new impetus given to water-borne commerce by the improvement of waterways, by the construction of modern inland water craft, and by the provision of suitable terminals, will make New Orleans a port of deposit and distribution for all the states in the Mississippi Valley.

Volume of Mississippi Valley Trade. The commerce originating in these states is more than half the commerce of the Union. Notwithstanding their continual expansion, the railroads cannot always handle it entirely. The history of railroad transportation shows that the volume doubles about every ten years. It is a matter of absolute necessity that the waterways shall soon come into general use. Already the movement is on foot to build and operate economical barges and boats, so that freight can be handled to advantage and profit on these waterways.

Barge Line. At present there are weekly trips between St. Louis and New Orleans. The permanence and success of this aid to the Valley's transportation problem depends upon the tonnage given the New Government River Line.

River Traffic. The volume of river traffic is not realized, because so few people see it. One towboat, now on the Mississippi, can bring from Pittsburg, Pennsylvania, in thirty days, twenty barges of coal of 1,000 tons each. This is equal to eighty trains of fifty cars each; nearly four miles of train. Such a large quantity of coal would not come as quickly by rail.

Much sugar, cotton, rice and general produce are brought by river boats now. There are at present within the State of Louisiana nearly 5,000 miles of navigable streams and canals connected with the port of New Orleans.

During 1918 the arrivals were:

Steamboats	1,139
Luggers and gasoline boats	1,590
Miscellaneous	502
Total	3,231

Steamboat Landing. Just below Canal Street is the steamboat landing, where river boats of every size and description may be seen unloading their cargoes of sugar, rice, cotton, molasses, and general produce. On their return trips, miscellaneous cargoes are carried to different points at which the boats touch.

Lake Trade. The trade on Lake Pontchartrain, while small in comparison with the railroad or sea trade, is by no means insignificant, either in volume or in its effect upon the cost of many necessities. Small boats, schooners, luggers, gasoline boats, and barges bring lumber, shingles, staves, cordwood, lathes, rosin, charcoal, sand, gravel, and shells, besides numerous other products of the country around the Lakes. There are, altogether, about 4,000 arrivals during the year, and the number is steadily increasing. When Lake Pontchartrain is connected with the Intercoastal Canal system, the volume and variety of the business will very greatly increase. The Lake trade finds its way into the commercial part of the city by Spanish Fort through Bayou St. John, which joins the Carondelet or Old Basin Canal, and by West End through the New Basin Canal.

The Old Basin Canal. The Carondelet or Old Basin Canal was cut in colonial times (See Chapter II). It came under the control of the railroad companies and, as its efficiency was thereby greatly impaired, the state is suing for its control. The Old Basin enjoys a monopoly of the Lake oyster trade because of its nearness to the markets.

The New Basin Canal. In 1831, the New Orleans Canal and Banking Company was chartered for the purpose of constructing a navigation canal above Poydras Street from the city to Lake Pontchartrain. The work progressed rapidly, being completed at a much less cost than had been estimated. The Canal and Banking Company was eventually separated. The canal, known as the New Basin Canal, was turned over to the state in 1838. The bank, however, has continued in business until the present day. The New Basin Canal is operated by a board and superintendent appointed by the Governor. This canal is in a prosperous condition, doing about three times as much business as the old; the plan to deepen the New Basin to eleven feet will, if carried out, further increase this advantage. Along the bank of the canal, the board maintains a shell road, which has long been noted as one of the finest driveways in the country.

Lake to the River Canals. Below New Orleans, the Lake Borgne Canal extends from Lake Borgne to the Mississippi River. While very useful, it has two disadvantages: it can be used only by small vessels and it is not under public control.

Navigation Canal—Inner Harbor. The con-construction of a Navigation Canal and Inner Harbor, near the commercial center of the City, was rendered necessary by the demand for shipbuilding, industrial, and wharf and warehouse sites upon a fixed water level. This demand is being met by the Dock Board, and many millions are being expended upon the canal, its locks, bridges and appurtenances. The largest steamships will be able to use the canal, which will connect the Mississippi River with Lake Pontchartrain. The Lake now has a fourteen and a half foot channel. The deepening of this channel to 30 feet, which should result from the building of the seawall, which the Orleans Levee Board is authorized by the Constitution to dig along the lakeshore, will ultimately enable the largest and deepest draft steamships to reach the Gulf of Mexico through the Lake, and result in the development of the Port upon the Lake front. The distance from the Gulf to the City via the Lake is about fifty miles shorter than by the River route.

The Canal and Inner Harbor will provide sub-aqueous storage for coal from the Alabama fields, and enable the delivery of iron, steel and coal from the same fields to be made in the heart of the City over an all-water route.

Intercoastal Canal. The Intercoastal Canal, now under construction by the United States Government, will furnish an inland waterway from the Rio Grande to Boston. It will eliminate much of the loss from storms encountered by ships in the open gulf or sea. A plan has been approved for the Intercoastal Canal to join the Mississippi River at a point opposite New Orleans. The canals now leaving the Mississippi near New Orleans will likely become parts of the system, as, wherever possible, lakes, streams, and existing canals are being utilized. This linking together of the waterways into one connected system will inevitably stimulate water-borne commerce.

SECTION 8. PORT IMPROVEMENT.

Port Improvement. Realizing the necessity for the rapid and economical handling of freight and of providing up-to-date facilities for the purpose, the Dock Board keeps constantly in touch with all commercial organizations, shippers and others, who are called upon to make known their needs and offer suggestions. The result is a continuous development along modern lines of port growth and the creation of a model port.

Mechanical Devices. The Dock Board has begun extensive experiments to test and try out all kinds of machinery for the handling of various kinds of goods, so as to give quick service to ships, both loading and unloading.

Warehouses. The Dock Board is having warehouses and sheds erected, where freight can be brought together for the ships or quickly transferred to the wharves to await distribution. In other words, it will make New Orleans a "port of deposit" instead of a mere transfer station. The erection of the great cotton warehouse has been the first step in this direction. Heretofore, the world's surplus has been handled and kept, for the most part, at Liverpool, and any brought back to America required the payment of double freight charges. (See Chapter VII., Section 1.)

Facilities have been provided by the Dock Board for grain, coffee, sugar, rice, and any other uniform commodity that can be brought to New Orleans, and even general merchandise can be so cared for.

Free Port. New Orleans, realizing the importance of her geographic position and also recognizing the benefits derived from a Free Port, has asked the Government to establish the Gulf Free Port or Zone at this point.

Commodity Warehouses. Upon the river front and canal, three large Commodity Warehouses are being built, one for the United States Government as a Quartermaster Supply Depot, the other two by the Dock Board for the storage of general commodities. In connection with the Navigation Canal and Inner Harbor these enormous storage warehouses will play an important part in the Latin-American trade.

Coal Handling Plant. It is proposed to erect on the Mississippi a Coal Handling Plant to be operated by the Dock Board.

SECTION 9. RAILROAD COMMUNICATION.

Western Communication. The Southern Pacific Railroad, the Texas Pacific Railroad, the Louisiana Railway and Navigation Company, and the New Orleans, Texas, and Mexico Railroad Company now furnish the medium of traffic with the west side of the Mississippi River. These give two through routes to the Pacific coast, and all the states between, besides reaching all the cities west of the Mississippi River as far as St. Louis and Omaha.

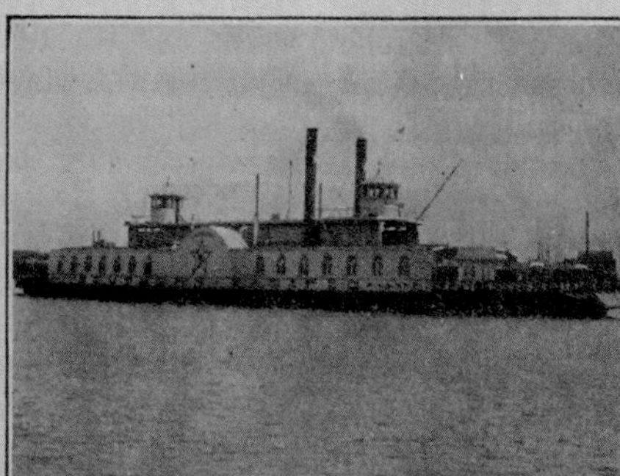

FERRYING CARS ACROSS THE RIVER.

Eastern Communication. On the east, the Louisville and Nashville, the New Orleans and North Eastern, the Illinois Central, the Yazoo and Mississippi Valley, and the New Orleans Great Northern, directly or indirectly, give railroad connection with all the United States. The Illinois Central has a double track to Chicago and reaches, with connecting branch lines, Birmingham, Louisville, Indianapolis, Omaha, and Sioux City.

Note. During the World War the Government took over the management of nearly all railroads.

Jefferson International Highway. The Highway was organized November 16, 1915, in the Chamber of Commerce at New Orleans. It extends from Winnepeg to the Crescent City, a distance of 2,400 miles, passing through seven states of the Union, one province of Canada, and connects 264 cities and towns. The road is 55% hard surface and serves the dual purpose of providing a great north and south highway and of honoring Thomas Jefferson for his part in the Louisiana Purchase. It ranks with the great Lincoln Highway in importance. Besides its value to automobile traffic, it was and will continue to be valuable to the United States as a military road and for mail service.

SECTION 10. FOREIGN TRADE.

One of the most important features of New Orleans is its foreign trade. As you approach the river any time you see the tall masts of schooners being towed up the river or turning in to the docks, and as you approach the water-front you hear the chugging of the donkey engines and the clinking of the winches as they hoist the great packages of cargo into or out of the holds of the great steam vessels. You can spend a most profitable afternoon walking along the docks observing the varied activity, for a great seaport is a most interesting place. The first thing you will see is, of course, great piles of cotton bales waiting to be sent to Europe or Asia; then there will be oats and wheat, and piles of our familiar kinds of lumber, pine, cypress, etc., awaiting export. But more interesting probably will be the mahogany logs, sisal fiber, coffee, bananas, cocoanuts, copra, etc., which have been unloaded from vessels coming from many parts of the world. You will wonder where they came from, you will examine the packages and perhaps discover just what strange island produced the vanilla beans; and if you chance to see some nitrates and make inquiry you will find that all natural nitrates outside of Germany come from Chile; and if you are curious about that very light but earthy looking substance, you will find it is copra or dried cocoanut meat being brought from Jamaica or Trinidad and going to the Southern cotton-seed mills to be made into oils and fats for cooking, soap-making, and innumerable other purposes.

As is natural, our greatest and most regular trade is with our nearest neighbors, Mexico, the West Indies and Central America, though some of the largest single items of trade are with more distant countries, as exports of cotton to European countries, imports of coffee from Brazil and of nitrate from Chile. Regular freight services (and in many instances passengers are also carried) are maintained between New Orleans and Tampico, Vera Cruz and Progreso, Mexico; Belize, British Honduras; all the principal ports of Central America, including Colon, Canal Zone; Cuba, Jamaica, Porto Rico, French West Indies, Barbadoes, Trinidad; Venezuela, Japan, Great Britain, the Scandinavian countries, Netherlands, France, Spain, and Italy. Most of these lines have been foreign, with ships under foreign registry mostly British, but an ever increasing number since the World War began are flying the American flag.

Trade With Mexico. The chief imports from Mexico are crude oil from Tampico and Tuxpam and sisal or henequin from Progreso, Yucatan. Yucatan has practically a monopoly of the world production of sisal, its climate being peculiarly adapted to the growing of that fiber. Sisal is a necessity to the American farmer, as no substitute has yet been found with which to make binder twine; a cheap fiber is required of sufficient stiffness to be automatically cut without dulling the knife-blade. Other imports from Mexico are dyewoods, coffee, chicle to make chewing gum, hides, and various minerals. We send to Mexico all kinds of manufactured goods: machinery for her industries, agricultural implements, clothing, cotton goods, canned goods, etc.

Trade With Central America and the West Indies. Most of the steamship lines running from this port to Central America and some of the West Indies are owners of immense banana plantations. The plantations are not far inland, and the steamship lines are primarily to bring their crops of bananas to New Orleans and to take back supplies needed on their own plantations, as well as supplies for the adjacent country. The largest is the United Fruit Company. New Orleans is the leading banana port of the United States. Vast quantities of raw sugar are brought from Cuba and Porto Rico and refined in New Orleans. Dyewoods are brought from Haiti and the Dominican Republic, and asphalt and cocoanuts from Trinidad. Many other tropical products are brought to New Orleans from these countries, for distribution through the Mississippi Valley; for instance coffee, cacao, cocoanuts, copra, honey, wax, citrus fruits, pineapples, gums, fibers, as ramie and kapok, vanilla, and molasses, to be used as foods or to use in the great American industries.

Exports. New Orleans is the second port of the United States, being outranked only by New York. The combined value of exports and imports for 1918-19 aggregated almost $300,000,000. Practically every state in the Mississippi Valley sends some products through the port of New Orleans. Corn, wheat, and other grains come from the Central States. The Southern States, especially Louisiana, Mississippi, and Arkansas, send cotton and cotton seed products, oil cake and meal. Oklahoma and Texas supply some cotton, but the bulk of the crop from those states is shipped from Galveston. As a lumber port, New Orleans stands first among American cities. In the heart of the cypress region, it exports both lumber and manufactured articles. The Southern yellow pine and naval stores obtained from it pass through New Orleans en route to points in Europe, Asia, Africa, and South America. Nearly all the staves used in harvesting the wine crop of Europe are supplied by this port, while quantities of oak, walnut, and poplar, as logs or lumber, are distributed to all parts of the world. Linseed products from Minnesota; tobacco from Tennessee, Kentucky, Ohio, and Indiana; iron from Alabama; farm machinery from Illinois, Indiana, Ohio, and Wisconsin; boots, shoes, and miscellaneous products from the vast area connected with New Orleans by a network of waterways and railroads swell the export trade.

Other Imports. From far-away India, British ships bring burlaps, which is fourth in value on the list of imports, and a coarser kind of bagging made from the pieces of jute unfit for burlaps. British liners carry salt, ferro-manganese, which is used in making Bessemer steel, and textiles from the world-famed looms of England, besides manufactured articles of every description. Fuller's earth, carried sometimes as ballast, is brought in great quantities; it is used for bleaching and cleaning cloth and for filtering oils. Most of it goes to the cottonseed and linseed oil mills. One of the curious paradoxes of commerce is that the same British ship that brought 8,000 sacks of salt from Liverpool carried to Liverpool on her return voyage 5,000 sacks of salt from Louisiana mines. Notwithstanding the unlimited resources for food production within the United States, many articles for table use are brought from European ports. Unexcelled wines and liquors, the secret of whose manufacture is jealously guarded; cheese, unequaled by American makes, from France, Holland, and Switzerland; olive oil from southern France, Italy, and Spain; currants from Patras, Greece; lemons and even garlic all the way from Italy are unloaded upon New Orleans wharves. Diverse minerals, such as marble from Italy, magnesite from Austria, and ferro-manganese from Luxemburg, are imported. Every kind of manufactured article—fine china, porcelains, and toilet articles from France; plate glass and baskets from Belgium—is brought to New Orleans to be distributed over many states.

Triangular South American Trade. The value of coffee far exceeds that of any other import, being over thirty-two and a half million dollars. Three British lines bring nine-tenths of the coffee imported to New Orleans from Brazil. Rio de Janeiro and Santos are the ports of origin. These same ships take cargoes from New Orleans to European ports, and there get cargoes for Argentina and Brazil, making a triangular run always in the same direction. It is a fact that great quantities of American goods

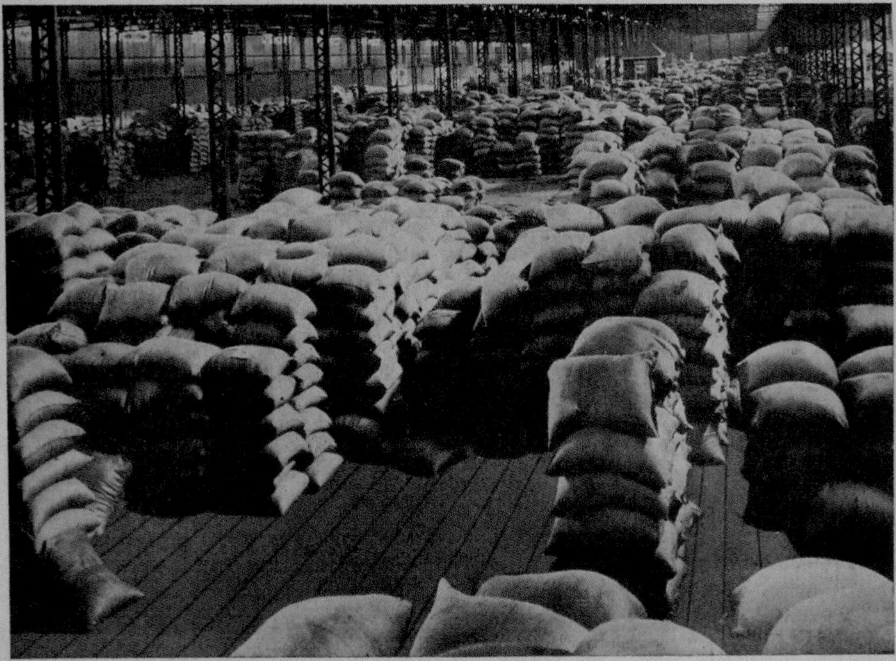

IMPORT COFFEE.

find their way to South America through European ports. Though several efforts have been made to establish direct lines from New Orleans to Brazil and Argentina, it has so far been found that the existing European lines, especially the British, were too strongly established in that trade for the new, weak lines to break into it. Lately a triangular service between Japan, Brazil, and New Orleans has been opened.

Trade With Europe. A very great trade is carried on with Europe in staples, partly by liners, but mostly by tramp steamers. The tramp steamers, (and since the World War, sailing vessels have also been used) carrying usually full cargoes of some one commodity, go from port to port searching for cargoes. For instance, a small ship may bring in copra to be crushed in our oil mills, load up with cotton for Liverpool; go to Cardiff and take on Welsh coal to unload at the British coaling station in Jamaica. Lumber is shipped to Europe mostly as deck loads, or to fill out a cargo.

Trade With The Orient. The trade with the Orient is developing wonderfully. Two Japanese lines and one British line are now running to Japan. The great spinning industry of Japan developed during the war must have American cotton; she also imports iron and steel and machinery. The Orient produces any number of materials of which we have need; hides and skins, hair, soya beans (to be crushed for oil), tea, rape seed, wood oil, camphor, cassia, egg products, etc.

Panama Canal. The Panama Canal opens the door of the Pacific Ocean to the port of New Orleans, as the nearest port of the United States to the Atlantic end of the canal. The opportunity is boundless in its possibilities. The trade of the west coast of South America, of much of the west coast of North America, a great part of the trade of Australia, Japan, and China, the Philippine Islands, and Farther India, as well as the East Indian Islands, will pass through New Orleans.

SECTION 11. THE UNITED STATES CUSTOM SERVICE.

The Custom House. The United States Government collects annually about three hundred million dollars in tariff, or what are called Customs Duties. To look after this business, as well as to attend to all the business in connection with boats and shipping, it built the Custom House in Canal Street, between Decatur and North Peters Streets. It is a noble granite structure of graceful and dignified proportions. The large hall in the center of the building, commonly called the Marble Hall, is one of the handsomest rooms in the country. The walls are of brick, faced with granite, and in parts, on the inside, with marble. They are very massive and are fastened together with heavy bars of iron built into the brickwork. The building has settled, and will probably continue to do so, but the construction is so fine and it is so well balanced that no damage has been done by what settling has taken place. It was finished about 1880. General Beauregard at one time had charge of the work as an officer of the Engineer Corps of the Army.

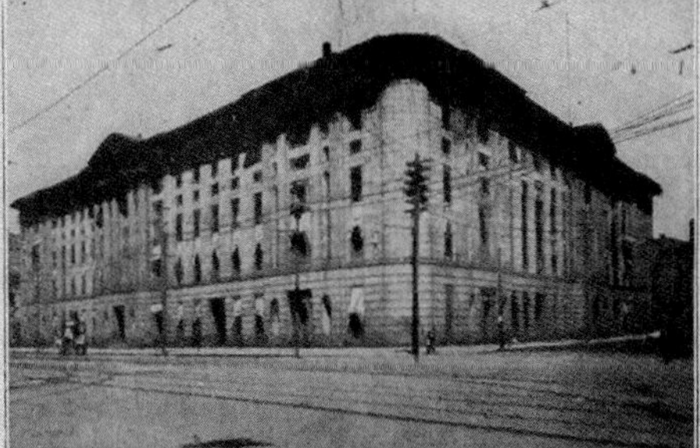

CUSTOM HOUSE.

Duties of Collector. The Custom House is in charge of the Collector of Customs, who has control not only of the port of New Orleans, but of all the State of Louisiana and western Mississippi. All ships that arrive are required to report at the Custom House to the Collector and file a list of what they have on board, called a "manifest."

This is called "entering." A ship is not allowed to leave port without filing a manifest of what she carries away, and getting permission from the Collector. This is called "clearing."

Duties of Surveyor and His Officers. The Collector has under him an officer called the Surveyor, whose duty it is to look after ships and everything pertaining to the government revenue outside the Custom House. The Surveyor has under him Inspectors, who do the actual work of executing the law and the orders of the Collector. Every ship that comes in is in charge of an Inspector, who makes a return of everything she brings in. On that return, the duties are settled and paid. No man can get his own freight until he gets a "permit" from the Collector after having deposited cash for the duties. No ship is allowed to discharge freight, unless there is an Inspector present. The Customs Inspectors also search the baggage of passengers coming from foreign countries. In fact, nothing can come lawfully from any country without passing under the supervision of a Customs Inspector. There are forty-five of these officers at New Orleans, and about twelve million dollars of duties are collected on their returns.

TOPICS: **Section 1**, Shipping; **Section 2**, Seaport and Riverport; **Section 3**, Harbor; **Section 4**, Publicly Owned Wharves; **Section 5**, Handling Cargo; **Section 6**, Public Belt; **Section 7**, Waterways; **Section 8**, Port Improvement; **Section 9**, Railroad Communication; **Section 10**, Foreign Trade; **Section 11**, The United States Customs Service.

REFERENCES: Standard History of New Orleans, Rightor; Reports of the Board of Commissioners of the Port of New Orleans.

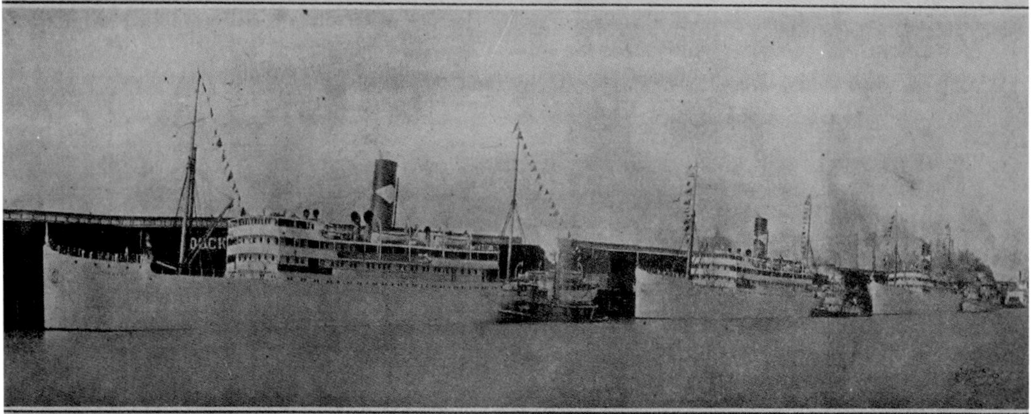

PANORAMIC VIEW OF THE HARBOR.

CHAPTER VII

Industries.

SECTION 1. COTTON.

The Cotton Plant. Cotton belongs to the mallow family, which includes not only cotton, but also okra, hollyhocks, and a number of common weeds. There are three main kinds of cotton grown in the United States, namely, short staple, long staple, and Sea Island cotton. The four leading cotton parishes of Louisiana are Tensas, Point Coupée, St. Landry, and Morehouse. Cotton, however, can be grown in every parish. By scientific methods of planting and cultivation, the farmer now makes his cotton crop in eight or nine months, where formerly it took a year.

Every nation depends largely upon the southern part of the United States for cotton. It is the crop which has a staple value in the markets of the world, its bill of lading being universally negotiable. The powerful influence it exerts on trade, its absorption both as product and manufacture, place it high in the scale of commercial economics.

The New Orleans Cotton Market. New Orleans has always been the largest market for the sale of cotton. Up to a recent date, it ranked first in point of receipts in the United States. The increase in the Texas crop and the drastic regulations of the Texas Railroad Commission have forced the bulk of the crop of that State through the port of Galveston, making that place the largest cotton receiver. The source of the cotton supply of New Orleans is principally from Arkansas, Louisiana, and Mississippi. A small part of the products of Texas, Georgia, Tennessee, and Alabama finds a market through this port. An immense cotton warehouse has been erected, and New Orleans has great prospects of becoming the center for the storage of cotton, subject to the wants of the spinners in America and abroad.

The New Orleans Cotton Exchange. The Cotton Exchange, whose membership and visiting membership embrace between 500 and 600, ranks as one of the three great contract markets in the world. Through this medium, a large percentage of the cotton crop of the United States, marketed through various ports, is controlled by the merchants of the Crescent City. The business of the membership of the New Orleans Cotton Exchange embraces the filling of orders from every state in the Cotton Belt and the cotton manufacturing centers of the North, East, and West, as well as all the great

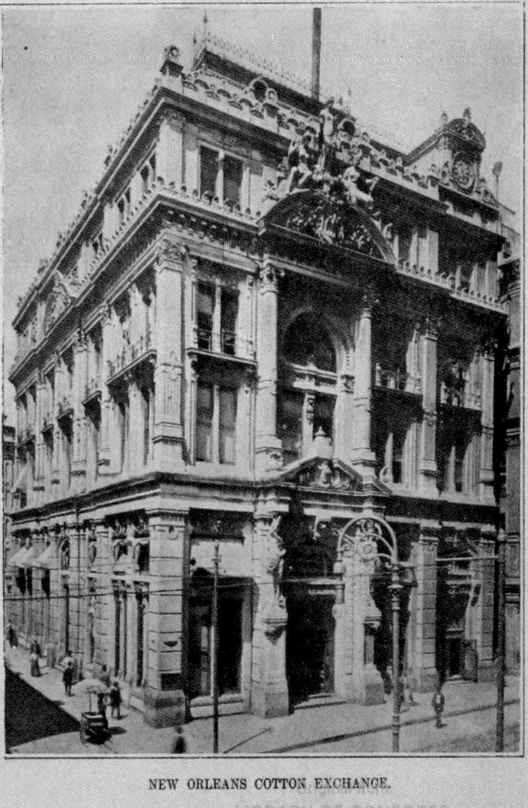

NEW ORLEANS COTTON EXCHANGE.

markets and the manufacturing centers of Europe. The daily transactions on the floor of the local Exchange reflect, and, in a great measure, govern, the world's sentiment in reference to the values of the great southern staple.

The Advantage of Cotton Futures. The system of dealing in "cotton futures" gives manufacturers of small means equal advantages with those possessing large capital in selling their product far into the future. Without the aid of the "futures" system, it is very evident that manufacturers having small or moderate capital would be at a very serious disadvantage.

Manufacture of Cotton. The first successful venture in cotton manufacturing was made in 1864, by N. L. Lane. The Lane Mills have gradually increased in size. They still retain the name of their founder, although they have passed into other hands. These mills are now equipped with modern machinery, and the most improved methods are used in the manufacture of colored cotton goods.

The Maginnis Mill No. 1 was established in 1881, and a second, called No. 2, in 1888. These mills, which were closed in 1910, and reopened July, 1914, make sheeting, drill, duck, and are specializing in cement bags.

Although there have been no large cotton mills established in New Orleans in the last twenty years, there are a number of knitting mills for the manufacture of hosiery, jerseys, knitted underwear, twine, carpet yarns, and reeler yarns.

Cotton Seed Oil—Cake. The cotton seed oil industry depends upon the state's annual production of cotton. The use of cotton seed is entering into the economic life of the people, and the by-products manufactured from cotton seed have added millions to the productive value of the cotton lands of Louisiana.

The Cotton Warehouse. Realizing the necessity of modern terminal and storage facilities, the Board of Port Commissioners has had the huge cotton warehouse erected, covering an area of 62 acres. The annual capacity of the warehouse is at present 2,000,000 bales, which will ultimately be increased to 4,000,000 bales. Fire insurance companies have agreed to a rate of fifteen cents per $100 on all cotton stored in these reinforced concrete structures. Some of the most up-to-date features of the new warehouse are three high density presses, electric trucks, internal concrete runways, and "bale-puller"; this last relieves the strain of the pile from the bale wanted, and then withdraws the bale without disturbing the pile. The warehouse will issue a receipt for a bale of cotton, which is recognized and accepted for full value anywhere in the world. Thus, New Orleans may become a point of deposit for the world's surplus cotton, as well as the point of export for a large part of the cotton crop of the United States.

In connection with this enterprise, another great piece of engineering work was the reclamation of nearly 2,000 feet from the Mississippi River in front of the cotton warehouse. This work was difficult and costly; but the acreage reclaimed and the advantage of having the warehouse along the deep water channel of the river will more than offset the work and expense.

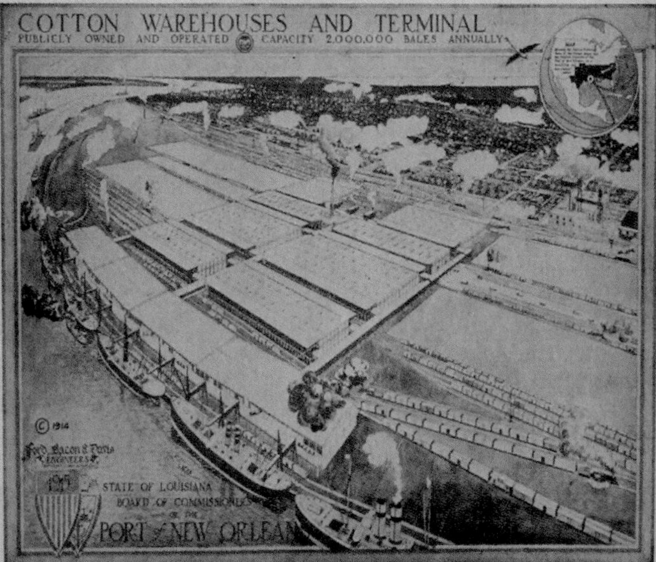

NOTE.—The Mexican boll-weevil came into Texas from Mexico about 1892, and has since spread throughout most of the cotton-growing sections of the adjoining states. The most important step in fighting the boll-weevil is to hasten the maturity of the cotton plant, so that the bolls formed early in the summer are well grown by the time weevils become very numerous, which is about the middle of July or the first of August. The boll-weevil does not do much damage to well-grown bolls, while there is an abundance of squares in which eggs have not already been laid.

Safety lies in diversified farming and intensive cotton culture. The history of the Whitney cotton gin is familiar to every boy and girl. However, few are aware that to Louisiana belongs the introduction of the first cotton gin in 1742 by M. Dubreuil.

TOPICS: The Cotton Plant; New Orleans Cotton Receipts; Financing the Cotton Crop; Manufactures.

REFERENCES: Duggar's Agriculture for Southern Schools; Leigh's Book on Cotton; United States Census Reports.

SECTION 2. CORN.

Corn belongs to the grass family. Some of the plants to which it is related are true grasses, as sugar cane and rice. Corn differs from most of its relatives, in having both a tassel and an ear, and in having these located on different parts of the plant.

Races of Corn. There are only a few races of corn, the most important being pop, sweet, dent (or common), and flint. In each race, there are many varieties. Corn is planted either in elevated ridges or beds, in depressions or water furrows, or in level ground, according to the soil and the farmer's judgment.

Corn Crop of Louisiana. Louisiana is fast taking a leading place among the leading corn states. The yield is increasing steadily, due to fertilization, deep plowing, adequate cultivation, and systematic rotation of crops. Splendid work is being accomplished by the Boys' Corn Clubs, an important branch of the Farm Demonstration Bureau, which is under the direction of the United States Department of Agriculture. Louisiana corn is harvested at a time of continued sunshine, and, if dried in a way to preclude deterioration, is preferred by the markets at home and abroad.

According to the last report of the Commissioner of Agriculture, cotton, without counting its seed, still leads, with corn a close second.

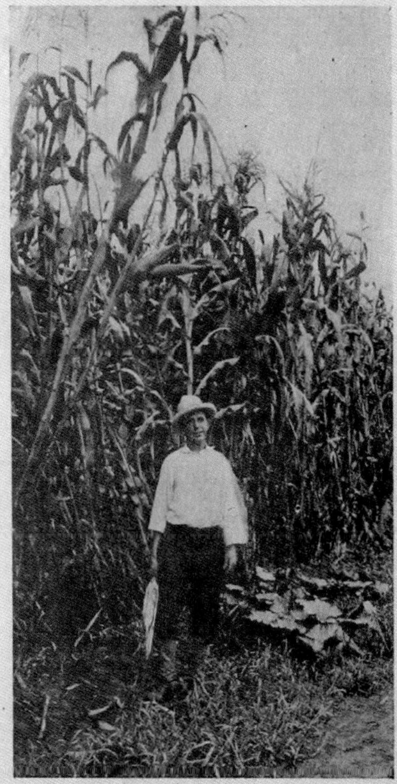

CORN CROP ON RECLAIMED LAND.

TOPICS: Corn Family; Louisiana as a Corn State.

REFERENCES: Report of the Commissioner of Agriculture for February, 1918.

SECTION 3. SUGAR.

Sugar Cane. Sugar cane belongs to the grass family. Under the tube-like lower portions of each leaf are buds, one at each joint. These serve instead of seed to multiply the plant. Sugar cane first grew in the countries warmer than the Southern States, but has greatly changed its habit of growth as it has been carried northward. In the tropics, it continues to grow fifteen months or more, before being cut.

Sugar cane was introduced into Louisiana from San Domingo in 1751, by the Jesuit Fathers. The cane grew well, but all attempts to manufacture sugar failed, until 1791, when Don Antonio Mendez succeeded in extracting sugar from cane. Four years later, Etienne de Boré made such a large crop of sugar that many were induced to go into the industry.

Preparation and Cultivation. In Louisiana, a field to be planted in cane the next year, is planted the preceding year in corn, with cow peas sown thickly among the corn. The entire growth of cow peas is turned under by the use of immense plows. This enriches the land by furnishing vegetable matter and nitrogen. Sugar cane is then grown on that field for two or three years. A good average yield in Louisiana is twenty to thirty tons of cane per acre. The tops cannot live through the winter, but the stubble and roots remain alive and furnish a supply for a second and, sometimes, for a third crop. Planting, therefore, is necessary only every second or third year. The sugar belt embraces twenty-four parishes, St. Mary leading.

Sugar Making. As the cane is cut, it is loaded by mechanical loaders into wagons of about two tons capacity. These wagons are driven to the hoisting derricks, which load the cane on the cars. At the sugar house, these discharge the cane into a patented carrier. The cane is passed through large mills which crush it, and thus separate the juice from the woody matter or bagasse. From here, the juice runs through the sulphur tanks, where sulphur dioxide is absorbed. The bagasse is carried to the furnaces. Here, it is mixed with a little crude oil and furnishes the source of fuel for operating the mill. After the juice is sulphured, it is pumped to other tanks, where lime in solution is added and the juice brought to a boil. The clear part is drawn off to settling tanks. The precipitate, or solid substance which has been deposited, is sent through the filter press, separating the juice from what is called the filter presscake or solid matter. (A filter press is a cast iron frame with heavy sheets of cloth, through which the juice is pumped.) The juice remains in the settling tank for half an hour; then all the clear juice is drawn off and mixed with juice from the filter press. The whole is passed through the evaporators, operated under vacuum, to make sugar house syrup.

This syrup is then boiled in the pan to make "massecuite," a heavy mixture of sugar crystals and molasses. This is run through the centrifugals, which separate the sugar and molasses. Generally, the sugar is washed with water before it is taken out of the centrifugals. The molasses and wash-waters are reboiled to make second sugar. The molasses in this process is used for stock-feed and is also sold to distilleries.

Refining Process. Sugar is mixed with water to make a thick magma, when it is run

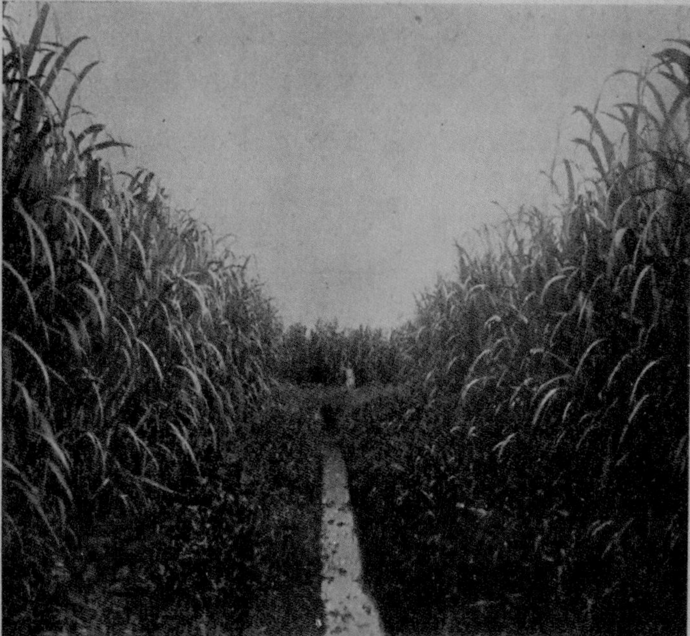

A CANE CROP ON RECLAIMED LAND.

into the centrifugals. It is again washed with water to remove the outer coating of the crystals. The remaining part of the sugar is dissolved separately, reclarified, and put through the bone black filter. The liquor is again evaporated into syrup, and finally into "massecuite." When it comes out of the centrifugals, it is put through the driers and granulators.

Louisiana Sugar Crop. Sugar made in Louisiana from the crop of cane harvested in 1918-1919, according to an enumeration just completed by the Bureau of Crop Estimates, amounted to 561,800,000 pounds. Including sugar, molasses, and syrup, the value on the plantations where produced is about $60,000,000.

The Chalmette Sugar Refinery. This refinery is a mighty tribute to the greatness of the sugar industry of Louisiana. It represents the very best in steel and concrete construction engineering. The steel docks permit three large ships to discharge their cargoes simultaneously. The shipping facilities permit the loading and unloading of fifty cars at the same time. The filtering plant has a capacity of 6,000,000 gallons a day; the huge boiler plant generates 11,000 horse-power, and is fitted with gravity coal bins of 7,000 tons capacity and with mechanical stokers. The cooperage is one of the largest in the South. The machinery is electrically driven.

The refinery has an annual capacity of 600,000 tons. More than one-third is Louisiana sugar, the remainder being imported from Cuba, Java, and the Hawaiian Islands.

The Sugar Experiment Station. The Sugar Experiment Station was moved about thirty years ago from Kenner to its present location in Audubon Park. The station experiments in the field, laboratory, and sugar house, publishing its results in bulletins. It has aided in every development of the sugar industry.

The Sugar Exchange of New Orleans is the place where buyers and sellers meet daily for the purpose of trade in sugar, syrup, and molasses.

TOPICS: Introduction into Louisiana; Preparation and Cultivation; Sugar-Making; Refining Process; Louisiana Sugar Crop.

REFERENCES: United States Census Reports; Crop Reports of 1918-1919.

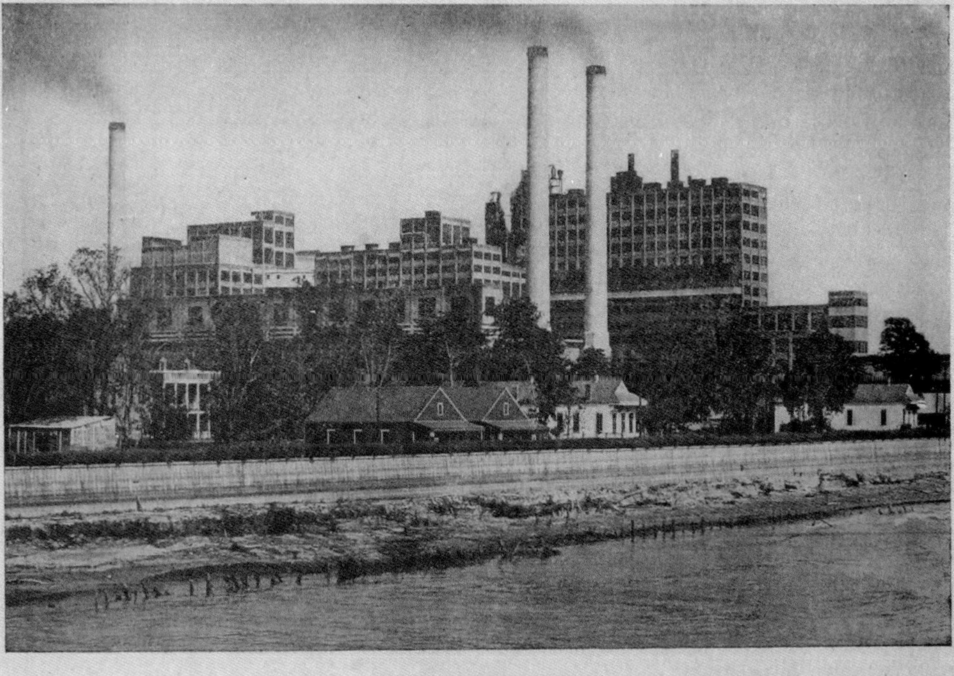

CHALMETTE SUGAR REFINERY.

SECTION 4. RICE.

The History of Rice. The history of Asia from the beginning records rice as a staple human food product. When we refer to the intrinsic value of rice as a human edible, we have the emphasis of centuries of use and the development of the Asiatic peoples, especially the Japanese, for proof. The first rice planted in the United States was in Virginia, in 1647. The experiment was a failure, this state being too far north. In 1694, a vessel from Madagascar, owing to a storm, entered Charleston Harbor. The captain gave a planter some rough rice, from which a successful crop was grown and the seed from this was distributed.

Rice in Louisiana. Rice was first raised in Louisiana in an attempt to offset the ill effects experienced by the wanton destruction of the Carolina industry. Owing to the responsive soil, rice soon became a recognized staple in Louisiana.

When rail lines were built through the prairie parishes of Southwest Louisiana, the Western farmers (about 1884) made their advent into that section. Primitive methods of sowing, binding, and threshing soon gave way to modern mechanical appliances. The most important era of the rice industry was in 1896—the year in which the irrigation canal was introduced. In commencing operations, a canal company first makes a thorough topographical survey, which makes possible the construction of the main canal and laterals in such a manner as to allow the water to go on at the higher levels and inundate by gravitation the lower levels. All the rice in Louisiana is irrigated by pumping, the exception being the alluvial sections where the water is syphoned from the river.

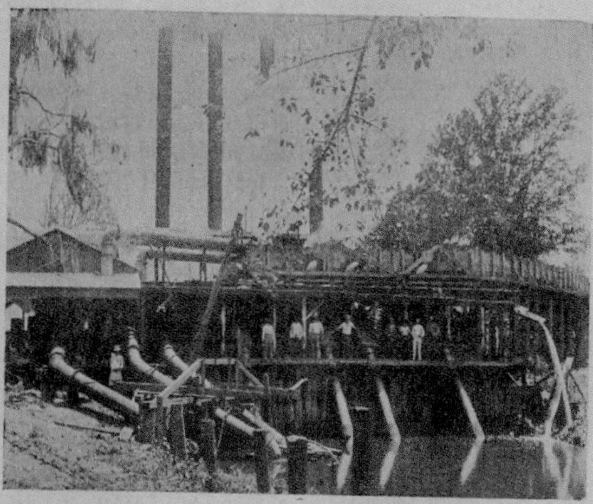

IRRIGATION PUMPING PLANT IN WEST LOUISIANA.

Rice Culture. The ground is well broken with riding plows and pulverized with large harrows. As a rule, the seed is planted by drills, although in the alluvial lands a great many growers cling to the old method of broadcasting. Unless the ground is very wet, water is turned on immediately after seeding. It is turned off again until the grain has attained a growth of four or five inches, when it is reflooded to about the same depth until a week before harvesting. This commences about the latter part of July, according to locality, and extends to about the

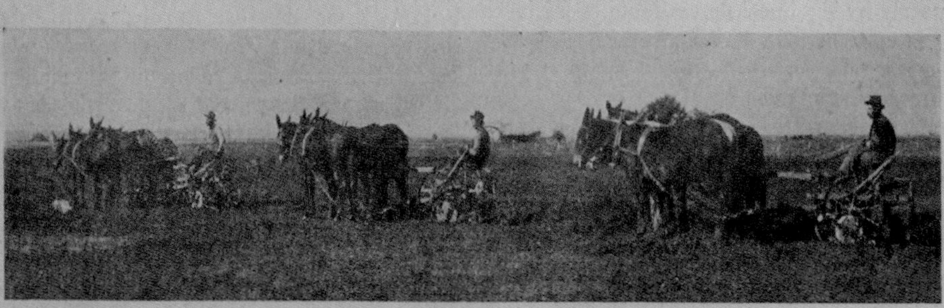

PREPARATION OF SOIL FOR RICE PLANTING IN WEST LOUISIANA.

fifteenth of November. After being threshed, the rice is either sold in the field to the agent of a mill, or consigned to one of the central rice-milling points. About one-third of the milling crop is disposed of through the factor on the floor of the New Orleans Board of Trade, which organization controls, to a great extent, the prices of rice for the entire country. Most of the rice disposed of on the Board of Trade is sold to local mills, the balance being shipped to the South Atlantic markets. Rice finds its chief use as a staple article of food. Ten per cent. of the Louisiana crop was used in the manufacture of beer.

Description of a New Orleans Rice Mill. The rice is received at the warehouse in sacks weighing 180 pounds each. These sacks are unloaded from the cars and elevated into bins by belt-conveying machinery. From the bins, the rice is run through the separators, which remove all foreign substances. It is then fed into the center of the hulling stones, where it is revolved at the rate of 250 revolutions a minute, and, through centrifugal action, the rice is forced through the perforated ends of the upper and lower stones. This process removes the hull from the grain. It is then passed through the fanning machines, which remove the hull by suction. A separator then turns back the unhulled grains to another set of stones, for about twenty-five per cent. of the rice is still unhulled. The huller is a cylinder within a metal case, which removes the oily cuticle that covers the grain. This oily cuticle is known as the rice bran. From here, the rice goes to the brushes, which are upright cylinders covered with leather. These polish the rice against a wire screen, leaving behind a white powder known as rice polish. The polishing drum, through friction, gives the highly polished appearance which is found in nearly all finished rice. The rice is then put into the clean rice separators, where the broken grains are separated from the whole grains and the various commercial grades packed.

TOPICS: The History of Rice; Rice in Louisiana; Rice Culture; A Description of a New Orleans Rice Mill.

REFERENCES: Bureau of Plant Industry of the Department of Agriculture.

SECTION 5. TOBACCO.

The crop report for the year 1918 shows that 300 acres of tobacco, producing 126,000 pounds, valued at $82,000, were planted in the parish of St. James. The same report also shows that a few acres were planted in the parish of Evangeline, and that Ouachita parish raised some tobacco for home use.

The Périque Tobacco. The Périque tobacco was first grown many years before the Civil War by an Acadian whose name the tobacco now bears. This industry has been kept up continuously by the lineal descendants of Périque, and is cultivated in the same manner as any other sun tobacco. It is sown in the early part of January, replanted in March or April, the crop being harvested in the latter part of June, or the beginning of July. After harvesting, the tobacco is hung in sheds to dry. It is then stripped and placed in presses until the following March or April, when it is ready for the market. Sometimes it is not sold until three or four years old, as it improves with age. Périque finds its chief use as a seasoner for mixtures, it being an exceedingly strong tobacco. It is shipped to all American tobacco markets, to Canada, and to England.

Manufacture of Tobacco in New Orleans. The first factory was established in 1857. New Orleans has always handled a large part of the cigarette business of the South. At present, there are two immense plants operating here. New Orleans is a meeting point of the Havana and the domestic tobacco from the tobacco-growing states of Kentucky and Ohio. The United States Weather Bureau records show that the climate of New Orleans is most favorable to the working of tobacco; its humidity is almost equable throughout the year, the changes being gradual. New Orleans, because of its very successful factories, is widely known as a cigar center.

TOPICS: Annual Production; Périque Tobacco; Manufactured Tobacco.

REFERENCES: Agricultural Report for 1917-1918; Pamphlets of the Association of Commerce.

SECTION 6. LUMBER.

Louisiana's Lumber. Louisiana is the second largest lumber-producing state in the Union (Washington, first), the annual value of the product being $100,000,000. Including by-products, the annual value exceeds $110,000,000. The state has standing timber to the amount of 120 billion feet, valued at $600,000,000. It also has over 5,500,000 acres in cut-over lands, eighty per cent. of which is now suited for agriculture. Yellow pine occurs in thirty-one parishes. In the middle and southern sections are the immense forests of long leaf pine which furnish a large industry for the adjoining states. The short leaf pine is found in the northern section, in the region of the oak uplands. Almost every known variety of oak, hickory, gum, pecan, cotton-wood, ash, magnolia, maple, and the largest variety of the elm are found. The state has about 154 species of trees within its borders.

Cypress. In Egypt, long before Abraham climbed the desert mountains that separate Chaldea from Canaan, cypress was the wood of royalty. Gopher wood, from which Noah builded the Ark, was no other than cypress. In polytheistic Greece, in pagan Rome, and in Egypt, the wood of the cypress tree was treated with religious veneration, and from it were carved the hideous faces of their heathen gods. In point of quality and value, the unparalleled forests of cypress surpass all others, and Louisiana possesses 75 per cent. of this forest product of the United States. Cypress is adaptable to many uses in building, inside and outside, having wonderful powers of duration. In all alluvial deposits of Louisiana, perfect cypress logs, hundreds of feet below the present level of the Gulf of Mexico, have been uncovered. In 1810, pipes for the water system were made of hewn cypress trees. Forces of the present Sewerage and Water Board have, in excavating, found these pipes in a splendid state of preservation.

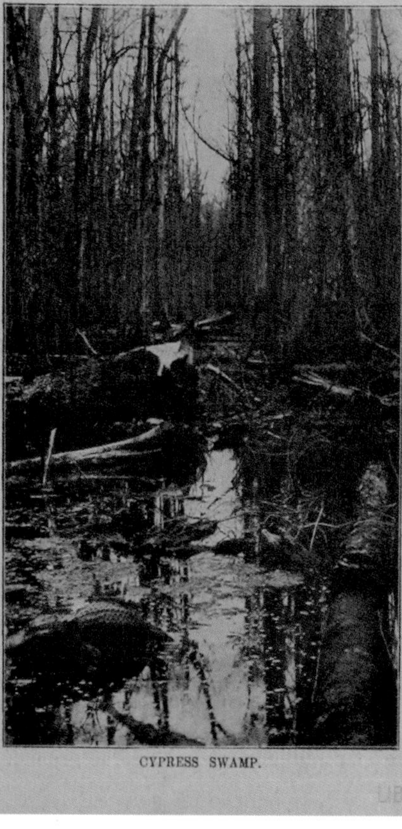

CYPRESS SWAMP.

Millions of dollars have been invested in the timber resources. The movement for the utilization of waste accumulating in the manufacture of lumber is destined to create an immense and important industry. Unregulated methods of lumbering and the turpentine industry are the chief causes of this waste, which can be used in the manufacture of charcoal and of paper.

Lumber Industry in New Orleans. A large proportion of the lumber bought and sold in the New Orleans market is used for building, by factories for making boxes, furniture, coffins, doors, sashes, blinds, and similar products. Many of these factory products are shipped to the surrounding territory and to foreign countries. The lumber that is shipped to New Orleans to be treated with creosote and other preservatives is widely distributed. The importance of New Orleans as a lumber market consists largely in its exporting to a great number of foreign countries. New Orleans is situated close to the principal lumber-producing sections. It is well supplied with railroad lines and waterways, and draws shipments for export from a wide territory.

In the export of yellow pine, New Orleans leads, with Mobile, Pensacola, and Gulfport ranking in order named. In the export of hardwoods, such as oak, gum, cotton-wood, ash, poplar, and other woods of that character, it far exceeds these three ports combined. If the shipment of logs, staves, headings, railroad ties, and miscellaneous forms of lumber partly manufactured for special uses, be added to the export of hard woods, New Orleans far exceeds any other port in the country; such export is almost as great as that of all the Atlantic ports combined. Its export of staves varies yearly, from a little under to a little over half in number of the amount exported from the entire country. Great yards are maintained, in which are stored millions of staves awaiting shipment. A large proportion of these are sent abroad in full ship loads; many of these, as parts of wine casks, have the pleasure of returning home.

The financing of the lumber industry is largely centered in New Orleans. The official figures for the year 1918-'19 show the city handled for export $12,000,000 in forest products.

Law Protecting Louisiana Forests. A law has been passed for the prevention of forest fires, making it a misdemeanor punishable by fine and imprisonment to negligently and wilfully set on fire any forest, brush, or grass land. Railroad companies, operating through forest lands, are required to keep their right of way clear of all combustible materials.

At present, there is very little reforestation in Louisiana. Acting under authority of Act 261 of 1910, the Department of Conservation entered into an agreement with the owners of denuded forest lands for the purpose of encouraging its reforestation. The Department agreed on behalf of the state to protect and supervise 28,000 acres of denuded lands, set aside for the growth of trees, for a period of forty years. This land is situated in the Parishes of La Salle, Winn, and Caldwell.

TOPICS: Louisiana Lumber; Capital Invested; Laws Protecting Forests; Reforestation.

REFERENCES: Annual Reports of Lumbermen's Association; Lumbermen's Trade Journals; Report of 1917-18 of Department of Conservation.

SECTION 7. MINERALS.

I. SULPHUR.

Nature has endowed Louisiana with many wonderful natural resources. Inexhaustible deposits of sulphur, salt, oil, natural gas, many fine kaolins, and clays can be found within its borders. Throughout the tertiary strata, there occur in varying quantities marble, sandstone, limestone, iron, gypsum, Fuller's earth, green sand, and other less important minerals. Of these, sulphur, salt, oil, and natural gas are the only ones that have been commercially developed.

Sulphur. The magnificent sulphur deposits in Calcasieu Parish were discovered in 1858, in one of the unsuccessful attempts to tap the oil deposits of Southwest Louisiana. The sulphur, covering an area of sixty-two acres, is supposed to be from a sunken volcano, several hundred feet underground, lying immediately below a quicksand. Vain attempts were made from time to time to utilize this wonderful gift of Nature.

Attempted Developments. A French syndicate leased this property from 1883 until 1885. They imported their machinery and castings from France and expended over a million and a half dollars on their project, before they abandoned what at last proved to be a fruitless undertaking. In 1889, a New York company tried to develop the mines, but failed. In 1895, Herman Frasch, a scientist, found a practical solution to the problem, which not only developed the mines of Louisiana, but revolutionized the sulphur industry of the world.

The Frasch System. The Frasch system melts the sulphur from the sulphur-bearing rock by the application of hot water and steam, and the pumping by compressed air of the consequent liquid sulphur to the surface, where it is run into wooden tanks and allowed to congeal. As each layer of sulphur congeals, the operation is repeated, until the piles have attained the height of sixty or seventy feet and become solid mountains of sulphur, which are broken up by means of explosives. The famous sulphur mines of Sicily, owned by the Italian government, are operated on the shaft and tunnel principle, the consequent loss of life being very great. By the Frasch system, a workman never goes beneath the surface, every operation being carried on above the ground.

Annual Production. The annual production of the mines is approximately 400,000 tons of sulphur, almost chemically pure, analyzing 99.8%, and valued at about $30 a ton. About 50,000 tons are exported; the remainder of the output is used in the United States, 70% in the manufacture of paper. (See Note.) Sulphur is also used in the manufacture of explosives and for agricultural purposes. It is a strong aid in the making of white sugar, without the use of bone black. Sulphuric acid is one of the most important acids known to the chemist. The actual waste of this great natural resource is estimated not to exceed one per cent. of the production.

Shipment of Sulphur. Most of the sulphur is shipped by the company's steamers from Port Sabine, Texas, to North Atlantic seaports for distribution throughout the United States and Canada. The National Sulphur Company, located in New York, is the largest sulphur refinery in the world.

NOTE.—At present, June, 1919, the mines are temporarily closed on account of the large supply of sulphur on hand.

NOTE.—In the manufacture of paper, sulphur is burned into gas and passed through a tank containing milk of lime, and then, finely chopped wood, usually spruce, is mixed with the resultant fluid, which induces the process of decomposition in the wood, and converts it into what is known as wood pulp. This industry is now confined chiefly to New York, Massachusetts, Maine, Pennsylvania, and Wisconsin.

TOPICS: The Sulphur Deposits of Louisiana; Attempted Developments; The Frasch System; Annual Production; Shipment of Sulphur.

REFERENCES: Report of Department of Conservation, 1916-18; Report of United States Geological Survey.

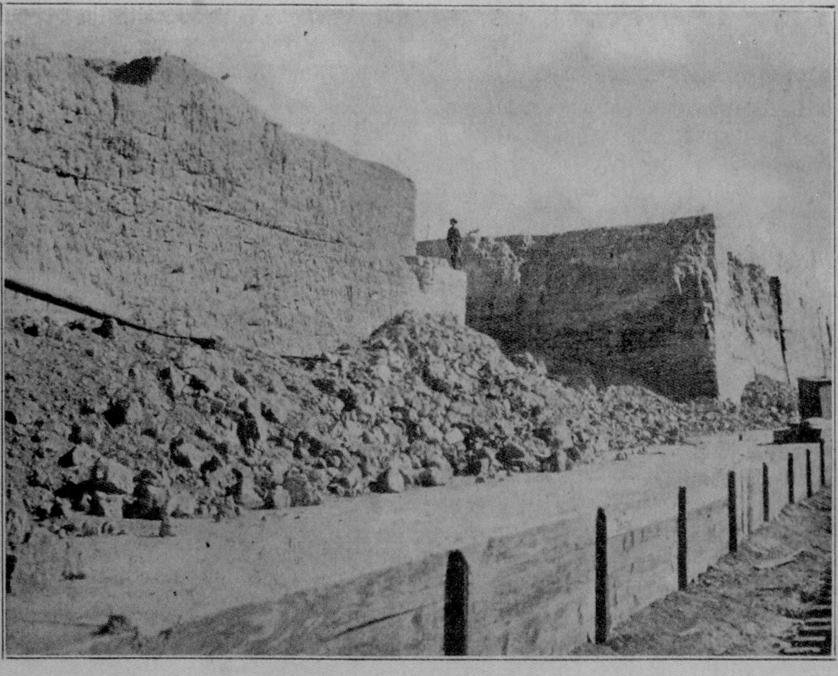

TONS OF SULPHUR READY FOR SHIPMENT.

II. SALT.

Louisiana has the greatest rock salt deposits on the Western Hemisphere. Geologists have never been able to solve the mystery of these deposits. Some claim them to be of volcanic origin; some, to the action of the wind and waves; while others say they are due to the imprisonment of an arm of the sea, through alluvial deposits, and the consequent evaporation of the salt water, so enclosed. Louisiana's rock salt mines have been confined up to the present time to Avery's Island, Weeks' Island, Jefferson's Island, and Belle Isle, the last named known as the rendezvoux of Jean Lafitte.

Louisiana Salt Industry. The production of salt is Louisiana's oldest industry, the first white settlers having reported meeting Indian salt traders. Evaporated salt made from the brine springs was quite an important industry from the time of the first settlement until after the Civil War. It was then carried on intermittently, until 1894, when it died out altogether, owing to the more economic methods of making salt.

Rock Salt Deposits. The inexhaustible rock salt deposits of Louisiana were discovered in May, 1862. Salt was very scarce at that time, and Judge John March Avery of Avery's Island determined to bore for it. A negro workman, after going down sixteen feet, told Judge Avery that he had struck a sunken log and could proceed no farther. Investigation proved that it was not a log, but the great rock salt deposits that have made Louisiana famous. Avery's Island was the only active salt mine in the state until 1903, when mining operations were commenced at Week's Island deposit. The mine at Belle Isle was worked for some time, but the shaft was destroyed by water.

Mining of Salt. Rock salt is mined in very much the same manner as all the baser minerals. The first operation is the drilling of the holes for the insertion of the dynamic charges, rock salt having the resisting power of 5,000 pounds to the square inch. This is accomplished by eleven-foot drills. The salt is cut out in tunnel form, arched columns being left to prevent a collapse. These tunnels are 750 to 1,000 feet long and 80 to 100 feet wide, and of about the same height. The blasting is sometimes done at night to prevent accident, and to allow the atmosphere to clear for the next day's work. The salt is loaded on narrow-gauge mule trains, which carry it to the foot of the shaft. There, it passes through a great forty-horse-power electric motor-driven crusher in the Myles' mine, but in the Avery's works the crushing is done at the top. After being crushed, the salt is fed by gravitation into the cage and carried to the mill, where it is fed automatically into screens and separated into the various commercial grades. If it is shipped in bulk, it is deposited by gravity into the cars, and if in small quantities, automatically fed into sacks.

Annual Output. The annual output is about 200,000 tons, valued at $400,000. Of this annual production, only 500 tons a month were actually consumed in New Orleans, this amount being sold wholesale to jobbers. The coarser quality is used in all forms of refrigerating, curing of hides, preserving of meat and fish, and the making of ice and ice cream. Salt is also used in glazing sewer pipes, as the lustrous enameling can be obtained in no other way.

The shipment of both mines originates on the Southern Pacific road, and, naturally, the volume of the business, with the exception of the Western shipments, comes through New Orleans. Some of the salt goes to the West Indies, Central, and South America, Liverpool and small shipments have been made to Copenhagen. The remainder is distributed over the United States and Canada. New York, Philadelphia, and Boston shipments are routed from New Orleans by water.

TOPICS: Louisiana's Salt Industry; The Mining of Salt; The Annual Output; The Shipment.

REFERENCES: Report of Department of Conservation of 1916-1918; Agricultural Report of 1917.

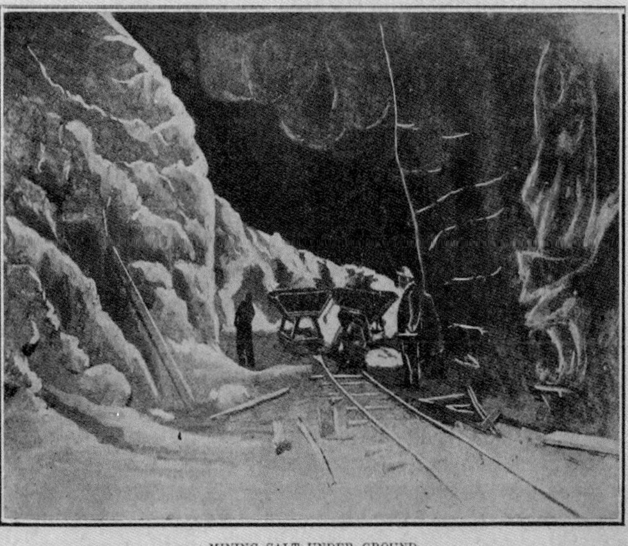

MINING SALT UNDER GROUND.

III. OIL.

This valuable substance, like sulphur and salt, occurs in proximity with the older rocks of Louisiana. Geologically, the oil is believed to be obtained from quaternary sands. Louisiana now stands sixth among the great oil-producing states of the Union. Oil was prospected for before the Civil War, but the Gulf Coast country did not attract the attention of the great oil operators until 1901, when the Spindle Top gusher in the Beaumont district caused a great rush to that section.

Annual Production. The oil output for the year 1916 in Louisiana was 14,795,220 barrels. The Caddo field, which was one of the most important oil-producing sections of Louisiana, declined in 1914, and was overtopped by the great wells discovered in the Red River section. This section produced, in 1914, nearly four million barrels of oil, valued at over three and a half million dollars. The new fields at Anse la Butte and Edgerly, in the coastal sections, helped swell Louisiana's 1916 output and put it in the fifth place among the oil-producing states of the Union, being exceeded by, in the order named, Oklahoma, California, Texas and Illinois. The 1917 increase in the Kansas fields enabled that state to surpass Louisiana and placed her fifth in the output.

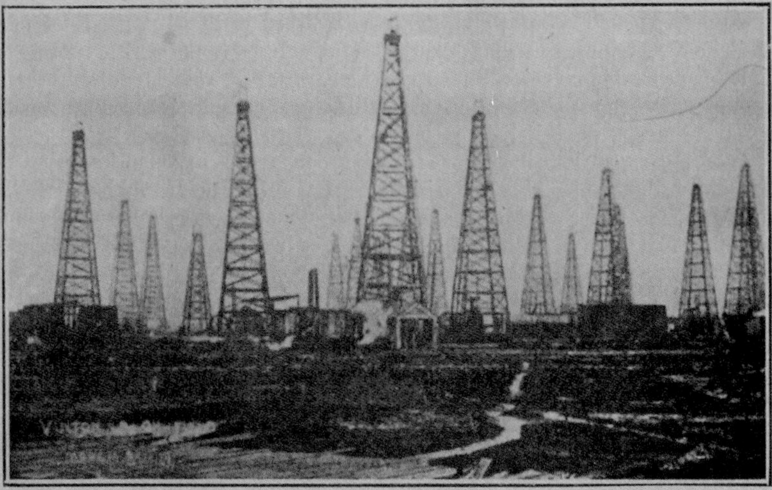

JENNINGS OIL FIELD.

IV. GAS.

The gas fields of Caddo and De Soto Parishes, according to the last Government Survey report, are among the greatest gas fields in the United States. The production from the eighty-four gas wells in the Caddo and eight in the De Soto fields is enormous.

It is believed that, through strict measures of conservation, these fields will continue to produce unlimited quantities for a great period of years. The Caddo field supplies thirty-eight surrounding cities and towns in Louisiana, Arkansas, and Texas, with gas for fuel, lighting, and manufacturing purposes.

A movement is now under way to pipe gas into New Orleans from the new gas field uncovered in Terrebonne Parish, in 1917, which has one of the largest natural gas wells in the country.

TOPICS: History of Oil and Gas; Annual Production.

REFERENCES: United States Government Survey Report of 1916-1917; Department of Conservation Report of 1916-1918.

CHAPTER VIII.

Manufactures.

Early History of This Industry. In the early French and Spanish days, New Orleans depended upon the mother countries for manufactured goods. After Louisiana became a part of the United States, there was little change in the conditions prevailing in manufacturing, because the city lacked skilled operators, and commerce was more profitable. The few factories in New Orleans owed their origin to the absolute necessities, and were for such repair work as could not be done anywhere else. The foundry, designed for the repair of machinery, led for many years in this industry, and from this business grew the manufacture of machinery, agricultural implements, boilers, etc. The development of the sugar industry proved a great stimulus to such manufactures. The iron industry of Alabama of recent years has also been an advantage. Gas was used as an illuminant here in advance of most of the Western cities; its manufacture dated back to 1833.

The census of 1850 showed the weakness of New Orleans in manufactures, and in the following decade there was a still further decline. After the close of the Civil War, manufacturing began to receive more attention. The disappearance of slavery, the enemy of free labor, had a beneficial effect, and there was a large supply of labor, though somewhat unskilled. The year 1885 marked a period of prosperity in this industry. The census of 1900 showed that New Orleans was the largest manufacturer of cotton seed oil in the world; the largest cleaner and preparer of rice and molasses, and of various canned goods. It held a high position in the refining of sugar, the manufacturing of clothing, cigars, and a number of other commodities.

New Orleans in 1918. New Orleans now ranks thirty-fifth as a manufacturing city. Government statistics show that, in the last five years, New Orleans has increased in manufactures more than any other city in the South. The center of population is now drifting southward, and the Panama Canal will increase this movement one hundredfold. At present, there are 848 factories in this city, 80,000 wage-earners, and the annual production in monetary value is $78,000,000. This is greater than the combined manufactures of Atlanta and Birmingham, or Dallas and Houston. If we include in this list the American Sugar Refinery and the various factories of St. Bernard and Jefferson Parishes, which may properly be done, since the freight movement is from New Orleans, and most of the factories have their general offices established in the city, the value of the goods manufactured in the territory would easily total $150,000,000. This is greater than Atlanta, Birmingham, and Memphis combined. Within the precise boundaries of New Orleans, the leading commodity in value is burlap and cotton bags, rice (polished) ranking second. The real strength of New Orleans as a manufacturing city is in the diversity of goods made. The number of factories is less to-day than twenty years ago, because larger factories have been installed, and many smaller ones have been amalgamated. The amount of money invested, the number of employees, and the value of the finished products are far greater.

New Orleans as a Manufacturing Center. This city is excellently located as a manufacturing center, and is the distributing point for eleven Southern States. Statistics show that 62 per cent. of the raw materials for manufacturing is found in the Mississippi Valley, and New Orleans is the gateway of the Valley. Many raw materials are shipped to and through New Orleans from Cuba, Central America, and Mexico.

Cotton, woolen goods, and tobacco products can be made to the best advantage in New Orleans, because of the equability of the humidity. The water, which is now pumped out by the modern water plant of the city, is excellent for dyeing purposes, and for that reason colored woolen and cotton goods may easily be made here. For woolen goods, the raw material can be brought from Texas, New Mexico, Arizona, and Australia, or from the Western South

American countries by means of the Panama Canal. The manufacture of pants and ready-made clothing already constitutes a large industry.

Raw Materials Now Used in New Orleans. The principal raw materials now used in New Orleans by factories are hard and soft woods, cabinet woods, metals, wool, cotton, chemicals, hides and skins, sand and glass for building, brick and tile, fresh and salt shells.

The hard and soft woods are found in the immediate vicinity of New Orleans. The lumber industry is one of the oldest, the reason being the ease with which lumber can be marketed. There are many finely equipped plants on the river front and on or near the two basins. One firm is the largest exporter of lumber in the world. The approximate figures for 1913-'14 of the lumber industry in New Orleans were about 32,000,000 feet of cypress, 3,500,000 to 5,000,000 feet of pine, and 15,000,000 feet of mahogany. The amount paid in salaries and wages in the wood-working industries, furniture excluded, was $250,000. The capital invested, furniture factories excluded, was $4,582,000. Door, sash, and blind manufactures amounted to $650,000, and the box and box shooks to about $750,000. One plant makes a specialty of the "Standard Fold-Up Box," which saves time, labor, and money, and for these reasons it has been adopted by many large factories throughout the country.

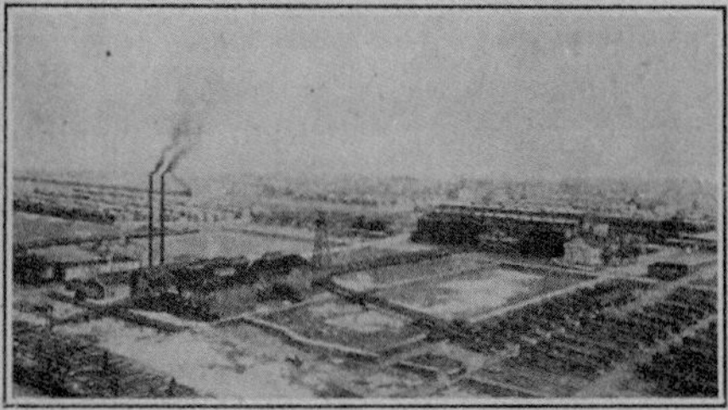

OTIS MAHOGANY PLANT.

New Orleans is well supplied with cooperages of large capacities. These plants have modern machinery for making barrels, half-barrels, and kegs of all descriptions, principally for oil, molasses, lard, liquor, sugar, produce, and fish.

Mahogany, Ebony, and Rosewood. These woods are imported from Central America, and in 1913-'14, one-third of the entire amount used in the United States, amounting to about $1,000,000, passed through New Orleans. The largest mahogany plant in the United States is located here, giving employment to several hundred men. New Orleans, because of her age, is recognized as a center of antique furniture, and several plants are turning out copies of the old styles in solid mahogany, rosewood, and walnut furniture of the highest grade. There are thirty plants making case goods, chairs of medium grade, brass and iron beds, mattresses of felt and hair, springs, etc.

Copper and Brass Works. The copper and brass works manufacture turpentine stills, an apparatus for the preparation of the South's naval stores for market, alcohol and vinegar stills, steam jackets and candy kettles. There are manufactories of tanks for all purposes, towers, stacks; in fact, all kinds of sheet metal works give employment to boiler-makers, pipe-fitters, and copper and iron workers.

Manufacture of Boots and Shoes. The manufacturers of boots and shoes obtain their raw material from the leather tanneries north of the Ohio River. As early as 1850, New Orleans manufactured nearly all the shoes used in the city and surrounding country. These shoes were then custom-made, but for many years modern machinery has been used.

Manufacture of Ice. Ice was introduced into New Orleans in 1826, and was regarded as a luxury. It came from Maine in sailing vessels, and, as a large part of the cargo was lost in the long voyage, the remainder commanded a high price. The supply was uncertain and the city was frequently without ice in the hottest months of summer. Gayarré says, "The first cargo of ice was dumped into the Mississippi River by the order of Mayor Macarty, who, backed by public opinion, declared that iced drinks would make consumptives of the people." The importation continued until 1868, when the manufactories of artificial ice drove out the New England product. The process, at first, was very expensive, but since 1898 has been improved and simplified. At present, there are many splendid ice plants, and the manufactured product is so cheap that it is within the reach of the poorest families.

Cotton Seed Oil Industry. The cotton seed oil industry owes its origin to New Orleans, because the process of manufacturing oil from the seed was discovered here. It has always been the center of this industry, and many of the mills in the surrounding country manufacture crude oil and ship it to New Orleans to be refined. Outgrowths of this industry are the soap mills, fertilizer and acid factories. Large quantities of this oil are shipped to Southern Europe. It is also used in the manufacture of lard in the Western packing houses. The mills manufacture cotton-seed cake and meal, which are excellent as a food for cattle. Thousands of tons are exported to Europe each year for feeding stock. These by-products enter into the manufacture of nearly all the commercial fertilizers now produced in the South.

Manufacture of Beer. The manufacture of beer is one of the more recent industries, the first company being organized in 1882. Since December 1, 1918, the manufacture of beer has been prohibited by act of Congress.

Canning Factories. Canning is the greatest utility industry of the age. Were it not for the canneries, our present great centers must need have been small cities—for the good reason that a great city could not be fed without the help of canned goods. It is estimated that 50 per cent. of all the fruits and vegetables in the United States would go to waste except for the canneries. It is possible to save the over-production of a good year for the famine that may come another, proving that the industry is a mighty economy and the largest conserver of foods ever discovered. The canneries in and near New Orleans buy many of their fish, vegetables, and fruits, etc., in the New Orleans markets. New Orleans, as a distributing point for the canneries, sends canned goods to all parts of the United States, Canada, and Europe. Thousands of cans of dried shrimp are sent annually to China, where they are considered a great table delicacy.

The Future of New Orleans. New Orleans, the second largest seaport in the country, is destined to become a great manufacturing center. The mighty Mississippi, on which ply many steamboats, the steamship lines, the barge lines through canals, and the eleven trunk lines that have their terminals here afford the manufacturer every facility. (See page 70.) The Public Belt Line, owned and operated by the city, has over twenty-eight miles of trackage, crossing every railroad, and covering a greater portion of the water front, giving direct touch to the steamboats and the steamships. As a center of distribution, New Orleans cannot be excelled. Previous to the World War skilled labor was plentiful, and the Immigration Station received large numbers of Europeans. Many of these were efficient laborers, anxious to secure employment. The maintenance of a factory is not expensive, as coal and fuel oil can be obtained at moderate prices. Electricity for power made by the plants in New Orleans is often used, being more economical in some cases. Wood, if necessary, can be obtained from the yellow pine and cypress mills, from waste in the furniture factories, and also from cord wood obtained in the nearby yellow pine forests. The location of New Orleans gives a delightful equability of temperature and there are few days in winter when factory doors cannot be opened.

The advancement of New Orleans in the last few years is due to the men who realize the possibilities of their city, and have succeeded in putting it in the front rank, where it rightfully belongs. To the future citizens of New Orleans will be given the task of keeping up this great work of civic advancement.

TOPICS: Early History of Manufacture; New Orleans in 1914; New Orleans as a Manufacturing Center; Mahogany, Ebony, Rosewood; Manufacture of Furniture; Copper and Brass Works; Boots and Shoes; Ice; Cotton Seed Oil Industry; Canning Factories; The Future of New Orleans.

REFERENCES: Archives of City Hall and Cabildo; Pamphlets of the Association of Commerce.

CHAPTER IX.

Foodstuffs.

SECTION 1. TRUCK FARMING.

Development of the Truck Farm in Louisiana. Because of the semi-tropical climate of the state and the varied altitudes, ranging from the high hills of northern Louisiana, the foothills of the Ozark Mountains, to the alluvial soil of the lowlands along the network of prairies and bayous, Louisiana is enabled to produce a greater variety of fruit and vegetables than any other state in the Union. Fifty years ago, there was little truck raised around New Orleans and most of it was consumed locally, because the crude methods of packing and shipping did not permit transportation to distant cities. The first shipment of truck from New Orleans to the North was about 1866, being sent by boat to Memphis and St. Louis. When the railroads and express companies furnished adequate facilities for forwarding shipments to distant markets, truck farms sprang up like mushrooms. Though the methods of handling and packing were poor, the farmers made a great deal of money, and New Orleans soon became the center of an intensive agriculture. There were no refrigerator cars, ice factories, or box factories. About thirty-five years ago, shippers began using refrigerator cars, and box factories were built to supply the containers for these products. Up to that time, many gardeners used second-hand sugar barrels, cutting holes in them for ventilation. This was unsatisfactory, as the vegetables often reached their destination in an unsalable condition. About twenty-five years ago, shippers began to use ice on vegetables packed in barrels, and this is still practiced. This business has increased to such an extent that there are now several ice companies and cooperages that supply ice and barrels to the shippers. Methods of barreling and packing are so improved that vegetables sent great distances reach their destination in perfect condition.

Change from Plantation System to Truck Farming. For many years, vast plantations were devoted to the cultivation of cotton, sugar, and rice, to the exclusion of other products. These plantations were expensive to maintain, and often an overflow would leave a rich man bankrupt. Of late years, however, conditions have changed, and many of these large plantations have been cut up into truck farms; this has so increased the trucking industry, that today it is valued at millions of dollars annually, and is growing in importance each year. The result is greater prosperity to many.

Principal Trucking Sections. The leading truck producing parishes of Louisiana are Plaquemines, St. Bernard, Orleans and Jefferson. The importance of these sections is due to the favorable winter climate and the exceptional transportation facilities available. Quick

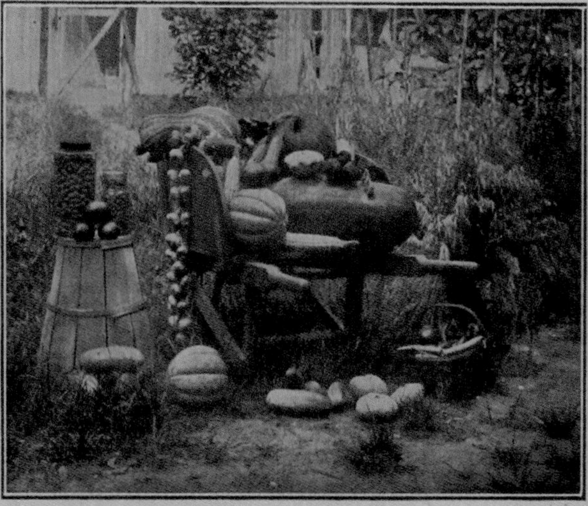

PRODUCTS OF A TRUCK FARM ON RECLAIMED LAND.

and direct transportation to big markets is the first requisite to profitable sale and distribution of fresh vegetables. Tangipahoa Parish, with Hammond as its chief shipping point, has also developed a profitable trucking business, producing a number of vegetables, including potatoes, beans, etc., but known principally for its great crops of strawberries. Onions, potatoes and garlic are the chief crops of the Lafourche trucking district, these commodities moving out of the towns of this section in car load lots. The territory immediately surrounding New Orleans, in addition to shipping in car lots, also supplies the City of New Orleans. The principal winter truck crops are lettuce, cabbage, carrots, shallots, kohlrabi, etc. Cucumbers are planted in hot-beds in the open and are matured extra early and contribute their share to the Northern movement throughout the winter months. Oats, rye, and barley make very profitable crops, while, owing to the extreme fertility of the soil, many kinds of grasses, valuable as cattle feed, may be harvested at a great profit. The cities and towns are co-operating with the country districts in a widespread movement for the improvement of farm lands, and the introduction of modern methods of farming.

School Gardening. The school garden, as well as the home garden, can direct attention to the advantages of the cultivation of the soil; for gardening is applied nature study. Economists teach that a greater production of foodstuffs is imperative. Gardens near to or within the city are a possible means of obtaining this result. If the public schools are to adapt themselves to the needs of the children, an occupation based on human welfare should be a subject of instruction. The tilling of the soil is a fundamental necessity. In 1914, The Nature Study Club of the Normal School decided to try to promote interest in gardening by conducting a school garden contest. A highly creditable exhibit was made by several schools. This so encouraged the Club that it now carries on the work in a broader way.

SECTION 2. FRUITS.

Different kinds of soil produce different kinds of fruit. Louisiana, having such a varied soil, naturally admits of the cultivation of a great variety of fruit. There are some fruits, however, which grow in all sections of the state. Among these are the strawberry, blackberry, dewberry, sand pear, and fig. The last mentioned, being so perishable, must be canned before it is shipped. On account of this, few persons outside of the fig-growing section are familiar with the delicious flavor of the fresh fruit. Many varieties of plum are raised, and the Japanese persimmon bears well. Grapes succeed best in the uplands. Bananas may be grown on Louisiana soil, but are not cultivated to any extent. New Orleans does a thriving business in importing bananas from the tropics and sending them to all parts of the Union.

The apple represents the greatest undeveloped industry in the United States. A cold storage and ice refrigerating plant has been established in New Orleans with the view of making this port the greatest distributing center for the shipment of apples to South and Central America and through the Panama Canal.

The Strawberry Industry. The strawberry farms in Tangipahoa Parish have a world-wide fame. The annual shipment of this berry amounts to over a million dollars, from a district which, thirty years ago, was an indefinable forest.

History of the Citrus Fruits. Centuries ago, there grew in the wilds of southeastern Asia and the Malay Archipelago, a ragged shrub, which produced a small berry full of seeds and bitterness. After many generations of patient cultivation and innumerable experiments, there have been evolved from this humble beginning the monarchs of the fruit kingdom, the orange, the grape-fruit, and their satellites. China is the original home of the orange.

The Citrus Fruits in Louisiana. The rich, alluvial lands of Southern Louisiana are the most favorable for the growth of the citrus fruits, which are the orange, the mandarin, the grape-fruit, the lemon, and the kumquat. It is impossible to ascertain in what year these fruits were introduced into Louisiana, but it is generally accepted that oranges were first brought to New Orleans by the Jesuit Fathers, in 1727. Later, seedling oranges became plentiful in the southern part of the State.

numerous commercial orange groves located in the district below New Orleans cover from 5,000 to 7,000 acres and afford a livelihood for a large number of people.

Life of the Citrus Tree. The citrus trees live to a great age. Trunks of large trees which have been lying for ballast in the holds of vessels have, when planted and properly tended, taken root and renewed their lives.

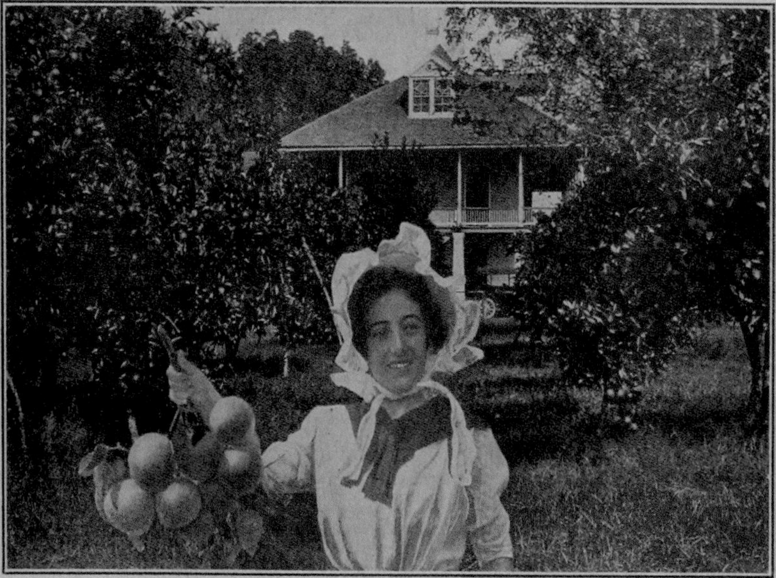

ORANGE GROVE.

First Louisiana Orange Grove. The first Louisiana orange grove, of which there is any record, was planted by Florentine Buras in 1860, and traces of this place still remain. About 1867, an orange grove of 125,000 seedling trees was planted fifty miles below New Orleans, and for some years was operated on a large scale, although modern horticultural methods were unknown. The grove is at present being cultivated in a small way. The

Medicinal Virtues. The orange has many medicinal virtues, and the Creole mothers have always recognized orange-flower water as a remedy for fevers. In recent operations in the Brooklyn Navy Hospital, the Essence of Oranges was used as an anæsthetic in conjunction with ether. This was so satisfactory that physicians predict its adoption for both Navy and Army, as it is much safer and less costly than the use of ether alone.

SECTION 3. FISH.

Fisheries. The fresh-water fish resources of the state are the spoon-bill cat, buffalo fish, and catfish, which are usually brought into New Orleans by express, packed in barrels with ice. The salt water fish such as sheephead, sea trout, pompano, Spanish mackerel, red fish, etc., are found along the Gulf Coast from the Pearl to the Sabine River, and are brought to New Orleans by schooners and luggers. New Orleans also buys salt water fish from Mississippi and Florida. All fish are bought by wholesale dealers, who sell to the markets. Some firms handle both salt and fresh water fish, while others only the former. The fresh water fisheries are valued at $2,000,000 annually. River shrimp are considered a delicacy.

Salt water shrimp are usually brought to New Orleans in the same manner as salt water fish, but some of the shrimp fishermen are now using power boats. Most of these shipments are well iced, unless the weather is such as to make this unnecessary. The annual shrimp catch is valued at not less than half a million dollars. Seventy-five per cent. of the product is canned in the canneries in New Orleans and along the Gulf Coast. There are several colonies of Chinese in Barataria Bay, whose chief occupation is the drying of shrimp. The largest platform is "Manila Village," the shrimpers, however, being a mixed population, representing almost every country of the globe.

SECTION 4. OYSTER INDUSTRY.

Oyster Resources. The oyster industry of Louisiana, at present, is dependent on 60,000 acres of natural reefs on which oysters are found growing freely without any cultivation; and on about 20,000 acres of leased bottoms, on which special methods are used by the leaseholder in order to promote the growth of oysters.

Method of Oyster Cultivation. The method of oyster cultivation is to provide a surface to which young oysters or spats may attach themselves. If such a surface is established in the neighborhood of a natural reef, the spats from the latter will become attached to the new location and grow there. Otherwise, seed oysters must be placed where the new bed or reef is to be formed, so that in the spawning season a supply of spats will be provided for the stocking of the new bed. Oyster shells and other hard substances, called "cultch," are the materials used in making a new oyster bed.

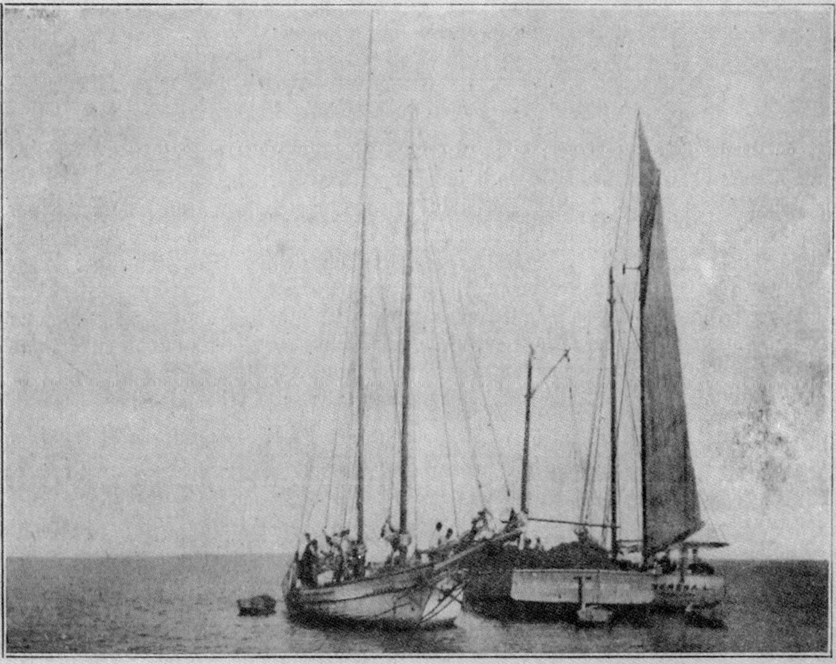

LOADING OYSTERS ON A TRANSPORT.

Value of the Oyster Industry. The oyster industry is valued at about $5,000,000. New Orleans receives annually about 250,000 barrels, worth about $560,000. Oysters are brought generally in sacks by lugger and other craft. Small shipments, however, of opened oysters in containers, are also received. Oysters are bought principally by wholesale dealers, who sell to the local markets and ship to other points.

Small shops sometimes buy from the oystermen of St. Bernard Parish. Counter oysters come from the Bayou Cook district in Plaquemines Parish, and cooking oysters from the Timbalier field in Lafourche Parish.

It is difficult to say which is the best oyster ground. Some sections are better at one season and others at another, everything depending on the condition of the water, especially the degree of salinity. The Timbalier territory promises to be one of the leading sections in a few years. Fine oysters come from Bayou Chaland, but the supply is limited, as they do not multiply rapidly on these beds.

SECTION 5. GAME-BIRDS.

Louisiana is the winter home of about 75 per cent. of the migratory wild waterfowl of the United States and Canada and its duck grounds are among the most famous in the country. About fifteen species of ducks are present in more or less abundance during the mid-winter. Only two species nest in the state, the summer mallard and the beautiful wood duck. The principal species are the mallard (better known locally as the "French Duck"); pintail, gadwall or grey duck, blue- and green-winged teals, spoonbill, canvasback, redhead, ring-necked or "black duck," the scaups or "dos-gris"; six species of wild geese, including the Canada, blue, snow, white-fronted, and Hutchin's geese are regular winter visitors. Other game birds include the coot or "poule d'eau", the gallinules, snipe, woodcock and several species of rail. The upland game birds include the wild turkey, Bob White (quail or partridge) and the mourning dove.

Up to 1918, New Orleans was noted for the game birds sold in its markets. During the season the dealers in the French and other markets received more than 200,000 ducks, geese, snipe, coots, and rails, the value of which exceeded $100,000. Now the sale of all migratory game birds is prohibited by a Federal law acting in conjunction with a treaty with Canada.

Note.—See bird exhibit at Louisiana State Museum.

SECTION 6. GAME-ANIMALS.

The state's principal game animals are the Louisiana white-tail deer which are found in our cypress swamps and other heavily wooded sections; the Louisiana black bear still inhabits the canebrakes in the southwestern portion of the state, and in a number of the river parishes from Pointe Coupee to the Arkansas line. Five species of squirrel are hunted each winter by an eager army of sportsmen, and cougars and wild cats still abound in some of the dense woodlands along the large rivers.

The sale of deer meat is prohibited by our laws, but squirrels are allowed to be sold during the open season, as are the two species of hares or rabbits that are found in almost every part of the state; southern cotton-tail and the marsh hare.

Department of Conservation. Realizing the value of the natural resources of the state, the

Legislature of 1912 established a political body called the Conservation Commission to patrol, protect, and upbuild all of these resources. In 1916, it was changed to the Department of Conservation. This department has its office in the New Orleans Court Building, and, owing to the diversity of the resources under its control, has varied duties and powers. It has an armed patrol on the boundary line between Louisiana and Mississippi, and throughout the state, to prevent violations of any of the conservation laws. Its officers, inspectors, and agents have the power to search or examine any cold storage warehouse, boat, store, conveyance, or basket when they have cause to believe that the law is being violated.

This department issues reports and bulletins dealing with its activities for the purpose of educating the people of the state as to the value of these resources.

SECTION 7. FUR-BEARING ANIMALS.

The State of Louisiana is particularly rich in fur-bearing animals, and the trapping industry has reached such proportions as to make it a resource of large revenue and means of livelihood to a considerable percentage of the population of the state. The principal fur-bearers of Louisiana, from which are taken about five million pelts a year, are otter, mink, muskrat, raccoon, opossum, skunk, fox, wolf, and wild cat. In 1918 the trappers of the state earned over one million dollars by their work.

SECTION 8. MEATS.

In no state of the Union can live stock be more easily raised than in Louisiana, and many farmers are turning their attention to this industry. Cattle are fattened, not only on ample pasturage and forage crops, but also on the cotton seed meal and hulls, rice bran, polish, and shorts from the rice mills, and cheap molasses from the sugar factories. Thousands of these cattle are shipped annually to the Northern and Western markets. Sheep-raising is carried on very profitably,—the cut-over pine lands affording splendid ranges. Hogs are easily raised, and great interest is now being manifested in this kind of farming.

The Abattoir Companies. There are two large slaughter-houses from which the people of New Orleans obtain their supply of meat. The live stock reaches the yards by rail when shipped from points in Louisiana, Mississippi, Alabama, Arkansas, and Tennessee. Stock shipped from points on the west side of the Mississippi River is transferred by boat from the railroad terminals.

How Purchased. All live stock is consigned to commission merchants, whose offices are located on the stockyard grounds, and who here sell direct to the butchers. The slaughtering is done by the abattoir companies, and the beef, veal, pork, and mutton are stored in refrigerators until called for by the butchers.

Inspection — Slaughtering. Before being slaughtered, all stock is examined by inspectors of the State Board of Health and of the United States Government. After being killed, they are dressed and are ready for the refrigerators. While they are being dressed, inspection is made by a representative of the City Board of Health and by a United States inspector. All carcasses found unfit for food are condemned and tanked for by-products—grease, tallow, and fertilizer,—which are manufactured by the company.

Refrigerators. The refrigerators are of the direct expansion system and are kept at a temperature from 30° to 35° Fahrenheit. The meat, as a rule, remains in the cooler from three to twenty days, according to the size and quality.

Means of Delivery. The meat is delivered by means of wagons and auto trucks (owned by the slaughter-house company) between the hours of 12 M and 6 A. M.

Western Packing House. Four large branches of Western packing companies are located in New Orleans, and do an immense wholesale business with markets, hotels, and steamships. The meat is sent here in refrigerator cars, having had both ante-mortem and post-mortem inspection. It is inspected here by the city and the United States inspectors. Since the advent of the Morris interests, one of the greatest packing companies, which recognized Louisiana's possibilities as a live stock state, New Orleans has become the largest live stock market in the South.

TOPICS: History of Trucking; Sources of the New Orleans Supply; Co-operation of the City and the Country Districts.

Louisiana Fruits; Strawberry Industry; History of the Citrus Fruits; Louisiana Orange Groves.

Fisheries; Oyster Resources; Oyster Cultivation; Value of the Oyster Industry.

Game-Birds and Animals; The Department of Conservation.

The Live Stock of Louisiana; The Abattoir Companies; Western Packing Houses.

REFERENCES: Agricultural Report of Department of Conservation of February, 1917-18; Newspaper Files.

CHAPTER X.

Professions—Trades.

SECTION 1. THE BENCH AND BAR.

Louisiana Laws. The Louisiana laws are all that is best of two great systems built up by the genius of man and tested by the experience of generations. Their fundamental principles approach as near the ideal as possible, for they are a texture composed of the best material from both the Common and the Roman Civil Laws. The Common Law of England inspires men with the knowledge that the power of government must never overshadow the rights of man. The Civil Law of Rome, modified by the noblest thoughts of France and Spain, teaches that the lasting foundation for right and justice is to be found in the Golden Rule. The Civil Law will always receive the homage of scholars as a singular monument of wisdom.

Early History. In the early days of American domination, it was a question whether the laws of Louisiana were the laws of France or of Spain. Until 1769, when Don O'Reilly took possession of the colony, the laws were those of France, but he issued an edict proclaiming the laws of Spain. After the cession to the United States, the question arose as to whether this edict had repealed the laws of France. This point has never been settled, but as both systems took their origin from the same source, the difference was not great.

The Courts After the Cession. For a long while after the cession of Louisiana, it was an absolute necessity for the judges to understand both the French and the English language. In every court, there was a permanently employed interpreter, who translated the evidence, and, when necessary, the charge of the judge to the jury. The juries were composed of men, some of whom did not understand one word of French, while others were equally as ignorant of English. The litigants had to employ two lawyers, one speaking French and the other English. All writs were in both languages. Trial by jury was new to the Louisianians. While the American lawyers were speaking, the French jurymen were excused. The English-speaking members were, in turn, excused to enjoy their cigars and promenade in the arcades. After the argument, the jury met in their chamber to decide the case, and in most instances came to a satisfactory agreement.

The Codes of 1808 and 1825. The original Code of 1808 was founded on the projêt of the Code Napoléon. The Code of 1825 was revised in 1870, and is the present Louisiana Civil Code. Many of its articles are but translations of that Code, but there are amendments by different legislatures to many parts of it. An Act of 1828 abolished the Roman, French, and Spanish laws that were not reprinted in the Code of 1825.

Distinguished Jurists and Lawyers. The Bench and Bar have always stood deservedly high, but it would far exceed the limits of this chapter to attempt to record the individual achievements of all the jurists and lawyers who have left the impress of their worth on every page of the statutes and in every volume of the law reports. The sons of Louisiana thrill with pride when they hear the names of Francois X. Martin, John R. Grymes, Edward Livingston, Alfred Hennen, Christian Roselius, Pierre Soulé, Etienne Mazureau, Judah P. Benjamin, Thomas J. Semmes, and Ernest B. Kruttschnitt.

Francois X. Martin. Genius such as his requires neither brass nor stone to preserve his memory, for he built for himself an imperishable monument in the jurisprudence of the state. He was the first Attorney-General and a judge of the Supreme Court for thirty-one years. The legal reputation of Louisiana was founded on the genius of Judge Martin, whose decisions were able and authoritative and read like the Code. Judge Martin left a large fortune. He became blind about eight years before his death. His will was contested on the ground that a blind man could not make a valid olographic will. The Supreme Court, however, upheld the will, which left his estate to his brother.

John R. Grymes. John Randolph Grymes came to New Orleans not long before the Battle of New Orleans, in which he served as an aide to General Jackson. In the latter's dispatches to Washington, the name of John R. Grymes was mentioned in complimentary terms. Colonel Grymes was counsel for General Jackson in the United States Bank case. He was opposed to Daniel Webster in the Gaines case. He was also attorney for the Baratarian smugglers. On one occasion he went to their lair on the Gulf Coast to collect his fee. He remained for a week, and said his stay was most enjoyable.

Edward Livingston. Edward Livingston arrived in New Orleans in 1804, just after his brother Robert had completed negotiations for the purchase of Louisiana. He was a profound jurist and an accomplished scholar. He represented Louisiana in the Senate, was Secretary of State under General Jackson, and Minister to France.

Alfred Hennen. Alfred Hennen was one of the most distinguished lawyers of the first part of the nineteenth century. He came to New Orleans in 1808. Many members of the bar received their legal education in the office of Alfred Hennen, or attended his lectures at the Law School.

Christian Roselius. Christian Roselius came to New Orleans in 1819 as a "redemptioner," that is, he hired his services for a stated period in payment for his transportation. Mr. Roselius was first a printer, but later studied law and gradually rose to prominence, becoming Attorney-General of the State. His legal reputation was so great that he was offered a partnership by Daniel Webster, which he declined. It is said he possessed a voice of immense volume and great carrying power.

Judah P. Benjamin. Judah P. Benjamin studied law in New Orleans in a notary's office and was admitted to the bar in 1832. At first, he met with small success and devoted himself to teaching, meanwhile, keeping up his legal studies by taking notes from the law reports. He finally established a good practice, and about 1847, his reputation became national. Louisiana histories tell of his brilliant career before and during the Civil War. Northern writers speak of him as the "brains of the Confederacy." After the war was over, Benjamin escaped to England through perils enough to make a romance. He read for the English bar and was admitted to practice in 1866, supporting himself, meanwhile, by newspaper writing. It was only after his "Book on Sales" appeared that his reputation as a lawyer became established. When he retired in 1883, he was one of the greatest lawyers of England.

Thomas J. Semmes. Thomas J. Semmes, a brother of Admiral Raphael Semmes, is a name familiar to every Orleanian. He was Attorney-General of Louisiana, and a Confederate State Senator. After the close of the war he resumed practice in New Orleans, and soon became the undisputed head of the Louisiana bar, ranking among the greatest lawyers of his own or of any other time. He was the very incarnation of legal learning, and intellectually a giant before whom few could stand.

Ernest B. Kruttschnitt. Ernest Benjamin Kruttschnitt, a nephew of Judah P. Benjamin, was born in New Orleans, April 17, 1852, and

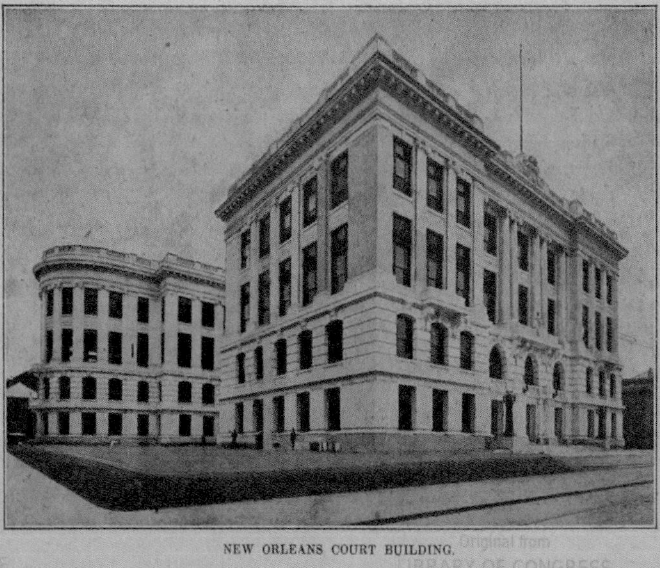

NEW ORLEANS COURT BUILDING.

died on his birthday, at fifty-four years of age. Mr. Kruttschnitt entered Washington and Lee College at fifteen years of age, and graduated with the highest honors in 1870. He accepted the chair of History and Literature at this university, and at the same time studied law. He returned to New Orleans in 1873 and began the practice of his profession. He was soon recognized as one of the leading lawyers. His brilliancy of mind and executive ability made him the leader of the Democratic party. His advice, legal and otherwise, was usually sought when matters of great moment were in question. His services for nineteen and a half years as a member and president of the School Board were most valuable. He was the moving spirit in placing the school work on a civil service basis and in establishing the Board as a business corporation. He was president of the Constitutional Convention of 1898, and guided that body through its strenuous sessions. His life is written in the laws of Louisiana and in its historic court records.

The Bench and Bar of To-Day. The New Orleans Bench and Bar of to-day ranks among the foremost in this great land, and many of its brilliant members have compiled editions of the Codes and Digests. The Louisiana Law Association, incorporated in 1847, was reorganized in 1899, and its name changed to the Louisiana Bar Association. In the thirty-seven years of its existence, the American Bar Association has three times honored Louisiana with the presidency of that eminent body. A Louisiana lawyer now holds, through merit, the exalted office of Chief Justice of the United States.

TOPICS: The Louisiana Laws; Early History; The Codes of 1808 and 1825; Distinguished Jurists and Lawyers; The Bench and Bar of To-Day.

REFERENCES: The New Orleans Book of 1851; Foote's Bench and Bar of the South and Southwest; The American (after 1875, Appleton's) Annual Encyclopedia, 1861-1902.

SECTION 2. HISTORY OF MEDICINE.

The demand for men possessing or claiming to possess the art of healing or alleviating the diseases and suffering of frail humanity must have been coëval with the appearance of man on the surface of the earth.

Indian Medicine Men. In America, long before its discovery and colonization by the Europeans, the Indians had their medicine men. The Natchez, so familiar to every student of Louisiana history, were superior to the tribes that dwelt around them. Their physicians claimed a knowledge of more than three hundred medicinal plants native to Louisiana soil, and taught the colonists the use of them. The curative powers of these plants so impressed De La Chaise that he sent a collection of them to France, with a memoir written by La Page du Pratz. The Natchez understood the art of blood-letting, and the water cure was familiar to them. It is to these Indians that the Louisianians owe their acquaintance with the medicinal qualities of sassafras, sarsaparilla, and maiden hair. They discovered the balsam of the copal-tree to be an excellent remedy for fever, and astonished the French by their rapid cures of the most dreadful wounds produced by fire-arms. Their physicians ranked very high and were looked upon as inspired. The Natchez believed that, for every disease, the Great Spirit had provided a remedy in the shape of a plant, and, if supplicated in the proper manner, would point it out to the physician. They paid most liberal fees to the physician in case of success, but frequently put him to death if the patient died, believing that it was the doctor's fault if he did not find the remedy.

Early History of Medicine. Very little has been written of the history of the practice of medicine in the early colonial days, as the documents of public interest were written in foreign tongues and have been entombed in the archives of distant lands. Many physicians who came to this colony had the sole object of acquiring a fortune and then returning to their European homes. The gradual development of medicine in New Orleans is of peculiar interest. The first physicians, who came with Iberville, were army surgeons. In 1722, when New Orleans became the capital, civilian physicians from various parts of France became residents of the colony and were the first to establish the contract system of annual payment. When Don O'Reilly took possession, his troops were provided with Spanish army surgeons. Shortly afterwards, Spanish physicians came to the colony, and, like the Frenchmen, entered into contract practice, which was continued long after the purchase of Louisiana. This contract system has, within the last fifty years, been almost superseded by the "Mutual Benevolent Society" practice, which exists to this very day in New Orleans. When their means permitted it, the first white residents of New Orleans sent their sons to Europe to acquire an education. A number of them studied medicine in the most celebrated schools and returned to practice in their native land. Later, some of the sons of Louisiana attended the schools of the East to acquire the English language, and while there obtained their medical education. After the purchase of Louisiana, many physicians from other states and from various European countries came to New Orleans, and entered permanently into the ranks of the profession, proving an honor to it.

The First Medical College. In 1834, a Medical College was founded by Doctors Luzenberg, Mackie, Barton, Hunt, Cenas, and Harrison, these talented men having for a clinic the great Charity Hospital. They soon rendered it unnecessary for medical students to visit other states and foreign lands to acquire the qualifications and title of Doctor of Medicine. A few years previous to the Civil War, the New Orleans School of Medicine entered into the field of education, but the war and financial troubles resulting therefrom caused the school to close after a short but brilliant career. During the war, many of the physicians proved their patriotism by abandoning their practice to follow the Confederate Army as surgeons. Their skill and the success of their operations will never be forgotten by the soldiers who wore the gray. The alumni of the schools of medicine of New Orleans have deservedly obtained such a reputation, both at home and abroad, that there is no longer need to seek outside their ranks for professors to fill any vacancy in the Medical Department of Tulane.

The Homeopathic School. The School of Hahnemann has been represented in New Orleans since 1841. The pioneer was Doctor Taxile of Toulon, France. Doctor Jules Matthieu was the first American member of this school. Doctor W. H. Holcombe was its most prominent representative in recent years.

Eminent Physicians. Physicians of the past and the present have contended with the gigantic forces of disease and devoted their scientific attainments to the preservation of the health of the community. Pages could be written of their noble lives. Doctor C. A. Luzenberg came to New Orleans in 1829 and revolutionized medical practice of that time in Louisiana. Doctor Warren Stone was the first physician in New Orleans to use chloroform for the alleviation of human suffering. Doctor T. G. Richardson was one of the most prominent physicians in New Orleans. He served as surgeon of General Bragg's staff during the Civil War. From 1865 to 1885, he was dean of the medical department of Tulane University. Doctor Quitman Kohnke was one of the pioneers of the modern doctrine of the transmission of yellow fever by the mosquito.

Medical Societies. The Orleans Parish Medical Society, which has a large membership, was organized in 1878, by a number of physicians who were desirous of affiliating with the State and National Associations. The Pan-American Medical Society was organized in March, 1914, to promote a high standard of professional efficiency and to develop a more thorough understanding among the laity of the study and knowledge of preventive medicine.

Medicine To-Day. To-day, New Orleans boasts of a great number of eminent surgeons and physicians, whose reputations are international. Many of them are recognized as authorities on medical topics, and the gold medal for the greatest achievement in scientific research in 1913 was awarded to a New Orleans physician, Dr. C. C. Bass.

TOPICS: Indian Medicine Men; Early History of Medicine; Development of Medicine; The Homeopathic School.

REFERENCES: Mumford's Narrative of Medicine in America; Parks's History of Medicine; Dr. Joseph Jones's Medical and Surgical Memoirs; J. C. Warren's History of Medical Education from the Most Remote to the Most Recent Times; American Medical Association Journals; Department of Archives.

SECTION 3. BANKING.

History of Banking. Louisiana owes its foundation to a bank, the Mississippi Company, which was the Royal Bank of France. The failure of John Law's scheme caused great financial distress among the colonists. Banking in Louisiana under the French domination proved a failure, but after the transfer to Spain, the system somewhat improved. When the United States took possession of Louisiana, Governor Claiborne, recognizing the poor financial conditions, established the Louisiana Bank in 1804. Julian Poydras was its president and John McDonogh a director. Two banks were established in 1811. One of these, the Louisiana Planters' Bank, was organized for the convenience and advancement of the agricultural interests of the Territory. The success of this plan of raising money for the development of the planting interests of Louisiana led to the formation of a number of improvement banks. Among these was the Gas Company Bank, formed for the purpose of introducing gas into New Orleans. The Canal Bank was chartered for the construction of a canal in the American portion of the city, and the Carrollton Bank for the building of the New Orleans and Carrollton Street Railway. The Commercial Bank was organized for the purpose of providing New Orleans with waterworks. The Mechanics and Traders' Bank was formed for the benefit of the manufacturing and mechanical interests.

When the panic of 1837 struck New Orleans, fourteen out of the fifteen banks suspended specie payment, thereby forfeiting their charters. In 1839, the Legislature, recognizing the fact that the suspension of the banks was due to the general derangement of the monetary system, reinstated them in their charter rights. Poor financial conditions continued until 1845. The banking history from 1845 until 1860 was devoid of incident. In 1860, Louisiana stood fourth in banking capital and second in specie holdings.

During the Civil War, deposits shrunk and the banks had to accept Conederate notes. General B. F. Butler insisted that the banks had violated their charter by suspending specie payment, and introducing Confederate notes as currency. During his and Banks' administration, there were frequent quarrels between the bank officials and the military authorities. A large number of claims resulted, and much litigation grew out of them. In 1877, in 1893, and in 1907, New Orleans suffered from the general depressed conditions of the money market.

The New Orleans Clearing House. The New Orleans Clearing House was organized in May, 1872. In all cases of financial trouble, the Clearing House has proved a great advantage to the banks and the business community, for its certificates are accepted everywhere, thereby relieving strained financial conditions.

The Present Banking System. There are now nine banks in New Orleans. The Whitney-Central leads with assets of $60,363,696.52. The Hibernia is second with $42,477,824.08. The oldest bank is the Canal Bank and Trust Company, established in 1831. It went into liquidation in 1843, but reorganized shortly afterwards. It is now the Canal-Commercial Trust & Savings Bank.

The contribution of the banking business to public wealth is measured by the facilities it offers for the transaction of business, and by the extension of credit in various forms. As a rule, the banks are required to keep a large reserve. In New Orleans, the conditions are liberal, the reserve being 25% of their assets, of which only 8% is in cash.

Insurance Companies. The largest life and fire insurance companies of the United States have branch offices in New Orleans. The home companies do a large business, not only for the city and the state, but for many neighboring states.

The Homestead Associations. The homestead associations have done a vast amount of good in facilitating the purchase and building of hundreds of houses for people of moderate means. They have encouraged the spirit of economy and have enabled many families to own their homes, who would not have been able to do so but for their help.

TOPICS: History of Banking; The Clearing House.

REFERENCES: Rightor's History.

SECTION 4. TRADES.

History. Very little has been written on this subject in New Orleans, because, before the Civil War, the crafts and trades received but scant attention in Louisiana. The wealth of the people was invested almost exclusively in agriculture, and New Orleans was a commercial center.

Slavery had a tendency to crowd mechanics out of New Orleans, and in ante-bellum days the general desire was to have mechanical work done by negro slaves, many of whom were skilled workmen. They often paid their owners for the privilege of hiring themselves to others, and by this means accumulated enough money to purchase their freedom.

The white laborers from 1860 to 1865 consisted of men over fifty, boys, women, and men of military age, exempted because of physical weakness or wounds. Industries calling for white skilled labor were but comparatively little developed in 1860. When the War ended in 1865, the labor system of the South was disorganized. One of the results of the War was to awaken the South to a full realization of her lack of knowledge concerning mechanical and other industrial pursuits. By 1880, with the help of the United States Government, mechanical and industrial colleges were established in the Southern States. The splendid work was begun which has resulted in the preparation of many men and women for industrial service in the country. These schools were ridiculed by thoughtless people and by some of the leading journals. Manual labor, among the white population, was considered more respectable, and as Northern and European capital began to flow into Louisiana, skilled labor found its way into the city.

Organization of Labor. The history of New Orleans' trade unionism begins in the first decade of the nineteenth century, when an association of printers was formed in 1810. From 1830 to 1836, local unions of printers were organized in New Orleans. The immediate cause of all organizations or wage labor has been and is the rise of prices in the cost of living. Following the natural trend, here, as elsewhere, combinations formed among the capitalists and workmen. The problems that have arisen from these combinations have steadily multiplied, and have become one of the chief features in our state and national government. Many of the problems have been solved through the efforts of trade unions. The adequate wage scale protects capital, to some degree, from profitless competition. The evils of child labor have been lessened by legislation.

There are more than 100 labor organizations in New Orleans all affiliated with the American Federation of Labor. The 30,000 organized workers are grouped under several Trades Council, viz., the Central Trades and Labor Council, Building Trade, Metal Trade, Allied Printing Trade and Dock and Cotton Councils. There is also the Central Labor Union, composed of colored organizations. Different unions in New Orleans, indicating trades followed here, are Boilermakers, Iron Ship Builders, Stereotypers and Engravers, Street Railway, Paper Hangers, Teamsters, Chauffeurs and Helpers, Moving Picture Operators; Coffee, Spice and Baking Powders, Bill Posters and Billers, Ship Yard Helpers and Laborers, Electrical Workers, Painters, Sheet Metal Workers, Railway Carmen, Iron Workers, Cigarmakers, Hoisting Engineers, Syrup Canners and Packers, Machinists, Mill Carpenters and Joiners, Carpenters, Federal Employers, Printing Pressmen, Plasterers, Broom and Whisk Makers, Locomotive Engineers, Plumbers and Steam Fitters, Drug Clerks, Ship Carpenters and Joiners, Marine Engineers, Boiler Makers, Railway Carmen, Sign and Pictorial Writers, Steam and Operating Engineers, Waiters, Bartenders, Railroad Trainmen, Railway Conductors, Locomotive Firemen and Enginemen, Railway Clerks, Freight Handlers, Station Employees, Sailors, Marine Cooks and Stewards, Draughtsmen, Blacksmiths and Helpers, Railway Clerks, Barbers, Marine Firemen, Oilers and Watertenders, Fire Fighters, Tobacco Workers, Bakery and Confectionery Workers, Retail Clerks, Theatrical and Stage Employees, Brewery Workmen, Book Binders, Newspaper Carriers, Building Trades consisting of Electricians, Painters and Decorators, Carpenters and Joiners, Structural Steel Workers, Building Laborers, Tile Setters, Marble and Stone Cutters, Pile Drivers, Hoisting Engineers, Plasterers, Bricklayers.

TOPICS: Trades; Past Conditions; Present Conditions.

REFERENCES: Archives of the Cabildo and City Hall.

CHAPTER XI.

Charitable Institutions.

SECTION 1. HOSPITALS.

A spirit of generosity has always been characteristic of the South and of New Orleans, in particular. The poor and the suffering, the aged and the infirm, the widowed and the orphaned have always found and, it may be hoped, always will find a tender chord of sympathy in the hearts of Orleanians. Looking back to the history of Bienville's time, we find the Ursuline nuns nursing the sick, caring for many Indian girls, and for French children orphaned by the Indian war.

Charity Hospital. The oldest charitable institution in the Mississippi Valley is the Charity Hospital, founded by an humble sailor, one Jean Louis, who, by trade and barter on his many voyages, had accumulated a fortune. This sum, $2,500, though small, judged according to present-day standards, was sufficient to purchase a building which was fitted up as the "Hospice des Pauvres." It stood upon the west side of Rampart Street, between St. Peter and Toulouse. The low, marshy ground rendered this a very unsuitable location for a hospital. The "Hospice des Pauvres," however, continued its humanitarian mission until destroyed by a hurricane in 1779. No concerted action was taken for rebuilding until 1784, when Don Almonaster y Roxas, the great benefactor of the colony, erected on the same site, a new building of brick and mortar. It was called the Hospital of St. Charles, in honor of the king of Spain. Although Don Almonaster had built the new hospital at his own cost and annually bestowed upon it a sufficient sum for its maintenance, he was bitterly opposed by members of the Cabildo. A communication from the king approved his action and declared him to be the "founder, patron, and endower" of the institution.

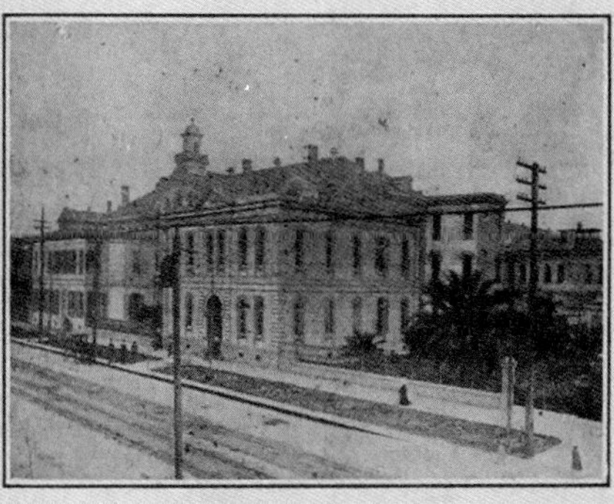

CHARITY HOSPITAL.

After the transfer of Louisiana to the United States, the affairs of the hospital passed from the hands of the Cabildo to the more practical management of American mayors and councilmen. A great fire totally destroyed the Hospital of St. Charles in 1809. All the patients were rescued and were quartered in a private residence, which continued to be used for this purpose until 1814. The square bounded by Canal, Common, Dryades, and Baronne was purchased as the site for a new building. Here, the institution entered upon the third stage of its career as the New Orleans Charity Hospital.

In 1830, it was removed to its present location in Tulane Avenue between Freret and Howard Streets, where, at the time, only the central building was erected. Built of solid masonry, this substantial structure has withstood the ravages of time. It has been so added to and extended that now the whole square and parts of those adjoining are covered with the buildings of the institution.

(See Chapter IV.).

SECTION 2. ASYLUMS.

Poydras Asylum. About the time that Louisiana was ceded to Spain, there arrived in New Orleans a young French refugee from San Domingo. His only assets seem to have been a handsome face and pleasing manner. What little capital he could command was invested in peddler's stock with which he ascended the coast to try his fortune. Enterprise and thrift were well rewarded, for soon we hear Julien Poydras, the one-time peddler, spoken of as the richest man in the Spanish settlement, a successful merchant, planter, and banker. In the midst of his wealth, he did not forget the poverty and struggle of earlier days; he gave unstintedly out of his abundance to help those in need. The city of his adoption received a large part of his munificent benefactions. Here, by the donation of a large lot and house in Poydras Street, he founded in 1816 the first orphan asylum in the state. The Legislature appropriated $4,000 for its benefit. It sheltered fourteen children the first year; but thereafter the number rapidly increased. The asylum was founded for girls, with the provision that any deserving girl, whether an orphan or not, should be received by the institution. The business section of the city gradually spread until it embraced Poydras Street, after which, the asylum was moved to its present location on Magazine Street and Peters Avenue. The administration is conducted by a board of directresses. The orphanage is supported by revenues from property left by Julien Poydras for that purpose.

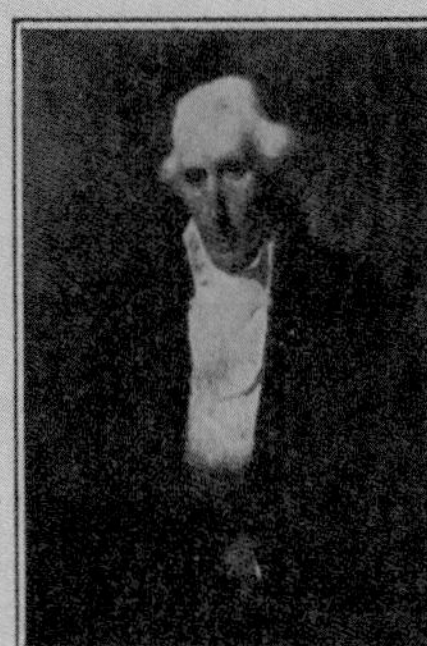

JULIAN POYDRAS.

St. Mary's Orphan Asylum. The history of this institution dates back to the year 1835. The Sisters of Charity have the care of the children, and the only condition of admission is that of orphanage. A board manages the business affairs of the institution, which is supported partly by private contributions and partly by revenues from property.

New Orleans Female Orphan Asylum. The Sisters of Charity withdrew from the Poydras Asylum to establish an institution of their own for the purpose of "receiving, harboring, nursing, raising, maintaining, and educating destitute female orphans under the age of fifteen." The girls were to be entirely under the control of the Sisters until they reached their majority, or were married. In front of the asylum is a triangle converted into a park graced by a monument erected to the virtues and benefactions of a woman. This is the statue of "Margaret," whose interesting history is intimately connected with that of the asylum she befriended.

Margaret Haughery, of Irish origin, came to New Orleans from Baltimore. Left alone by the deaths of her husband and child, she obtained employment in the Poydras Asylum. When the Sisters of Charity removed to their own establishment, Margaret went with them to manage the dairy. Soon after, she established and conducted a profitable bakery, so as to diminish the cost of bread used by the asylum. With little education, she mastered and directed the successful management of a large manufactory of flour, while personally aiding in the care of the largest female orphan asylum in the city. Her charities were numerous and bestowed without ostentation.

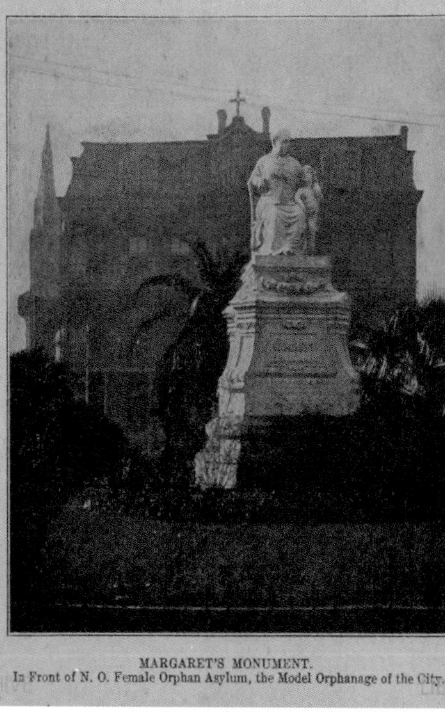

MARGARET'S MONUMENT.
In Front of N. O. Female Orphan Asylum, the Model Orphanage of the City.

St. Elizabeth's House of Industry. In connection with their Female Orphan Asylum, the Sisters of Charity opened in 1855 a branch in Napoleon Avenue to receive girls over twelve years of age. Here, they are given an industrial education, preparing them to make their way in the world. The institution, through the exquisite needlework, fine laundering, and other industries of the inmates, is largely self-supporting, although valuable property belongs to the asylum. Many a young lady is proud to say that her trousseau has been made at St. Elizabeth's.

St. Vincent's Infant Asylum. Another branch of the Female Asylum, conducted by the Sisters of Charity, is the St. Vincent's Infant Asylum, established in 1862. The kindergarten, nurseries, and dormitories are interesting sights and models of neatness. After the age of seven years, the children are no longer retained at this asylum; the girls are sent to the asylum in Camp Street, and the boys to some other institution.

Asylum for Destitute Orphan Boys. A society for the "Relief of Destitute Orphan Boys" was organized by members of the Presbyterian Church. When, in 1841, a fire destroyed the home, John McDonogh gave to the society $100,000 with which a house on St. Charles Avenue was built. This property has recently been sold and the asylum removed to more commodious quarters and advantageous location on the west side of the river, just below Algiers.

Seventh Street Protestant Orphans' Home. The terrible yellow fever epidemic of 1853 left so many orphaned children that the asylums of the city were taxed beyond their capacity. To relieve conditions, the Howard Association devoted a fund of $5,000 toward a new asylum; this was supplemented from other sources, and the outcome was the Seventh Street Protestant Orphans' Home. Both boys and girls are received by this institution.

Jewish Widows' and Orphans' Home. The Hebrews of the city maintain a well kept home for the widows and orphans of their faith. In 1888, the present spacious and substantial building on the corner of St. Charles and Peters Avenues was occupied by the "Home." The society that controls the institution dates back to 1855.

St. Anna's Asylum. St. Anna's Asylum was founded in 1850 by Dr. W. N. Mercer in memory of his daughter, Anna. Its object is the relief of impoverished gentlewomen, but small children whose mothers are inmates of the institution are also recipients of its beneficence.

Episcopal Home. The Sisters of the Protestant Episcopal Church conduct a well managed home for girls in Jackson Avenue.

The Soldiers' Home. The Soldiers' Home, sometimes called Camp Nicholls, as it was founded during the administration of Governor F. T. Nicholls, is situated on the banks of Bayou St. John. It is a retreat for maimed and disabled Confederate veterans. The board of directors for the Home consists of five members from the Association of the Army of Tennessee, five from the Association of the Army of Northern Virginia, and five appointed by the Governor of Louisiana.

The Touro-Shakespeare Almshouse. Those whose poverty and infirmities make them objects of public charity find shelter at the Touro-Shakespeare Almshouse.

Other Institutions. Several institutions for needy colored people are conducted in the city, one of the most notable being the Tomy Lafon Orphan Boys' Asylum on Gentilly Road.

There are many other institutions in the city, whose object is the alleviation of suffering.

TOPICS: Section 1, Hospitals; Section 2, Asylums.

REFERENCES: Standard History of New Orleans, Rightor; History and Present Conditions of New Orleans (1880), Waring and Cable; Cyclopedia of Louisiana, Fortier; Guide Book.

CHAPTER XII.

Education.

SECTION 1. COLONIAL EDUCATION.

Father Cecil's School for Boys. The early history of New Orleans was so filled with the struggle for existence that little time or energy was devoted to education. There were forests to be cleared, homes to be built, sickness and attacks of Indians to be guarded against, and an ever-increasing number of unworthy or worthless colonists to be provided for. Amidst such unsettled conditions, neither the governor nor individuals could turn their attention to schools. In 1724, Father Cecil, a Capuchin monk, opened a school for boys near the St. Louis Cathedral. He was the first teacher in Louisiana and was successful in imparting a fairly good elementary education to the youth of the day.

THE URSULINES.

Bienville Secures the Services of the Ursulines. Father Cecil was offering educational opportunities to the boys, but a generation of girls was growing up with only the limited training of the home circle. Bienville realized this and consulted the Jesuit priest, Father Beaubois, about securing teachers for the girls. The Ursuline nuns who were conducting flourishing and well patronized schools in France were recommended and their services secured in 1726. Although Bienville was no longer governor when the Ursulines arrived in Louisiana, he deserves the credit of having established the first girls' school in the colony.

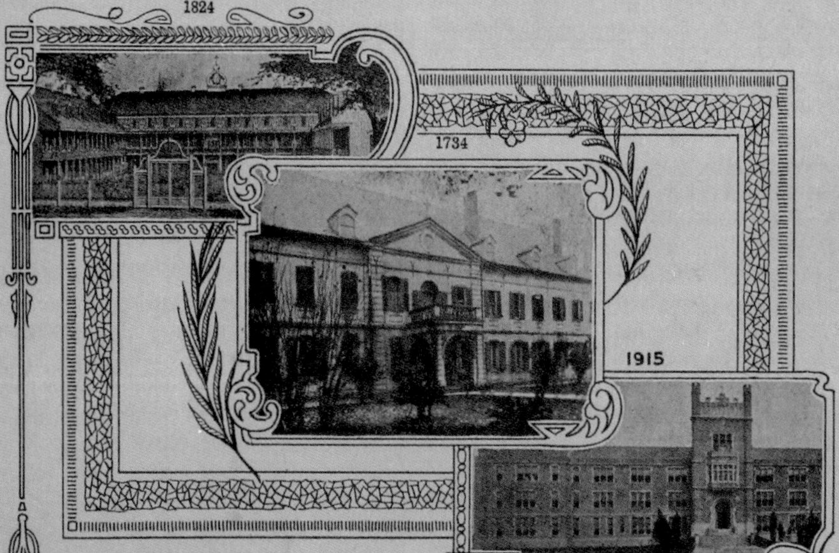

THREE HOMES OF THE URSULINES.

Establishment of the Ursulines. Eleven Sisters under the direction of Mother Tranchepain embarked at Lorient, France, on February 22, 1727. After a long and hazardous voyage they reached the land of their adoption on August 7th of the same year. Joyful crowds assembled on the river banks and along the streets to welcome them, and every courtesy was extended to them. Governor Perrier and his wife were most cordial to the Sisters and saw them installed in Bienville's house, which was the best in the colony. Here, they were to remain until their own convent could be erected.

Treaty With the Company of the Indies. A treaty was drawn up between the Company of the Indies, then in control of Louisiana, and the Ursulines before the latter left France. The provisions were that in return for the care of the hospital and the education of girls, the nuns were to receive from the company a convent and a plantation and 500 livres (livre 18½ cents) each, besides having the expense of the voyage paid. They were guaranteed 600 livres until they could realize something from their plantation, and this contract did not bind them to remain in the colony should they find it distasteful.

Removed to Their Convent. There is no record of any Sisters having returned to France. All were satisfied with their work in a strange land. Their convent on Chartres Street was completed in 1734 and they took possession of it with great ceremony. The beloved Superioress, Mother Tranchepain, had ended her days of usefulness, but Bienville, patron and benefactor of the Sisters, had returned to the colony as governor for the third time and took an active part in the ceremony. At the time of this change of residence, many day scholars, twenty boarders, three parlor boarders, and three orphans were under the care of the nuns.

System of Education. Religious classes were conducted for two hours every day for the benefit of Indian and negro women. The Sisters, through the influence of religion and education, sought to uplift the inferior races and lead them into the ways of civilization. The daughters of the colonists were taught languages, history, literature, some science, mathematics, and the art of letter-writing. Great emphasis was laid upon instruction in music and sewing, accomplishments required of every girl of the time. Nimble fingers that could lighten dull hours with gay music or fashion dainty garments made their owners more attractive helpmates. Wives were scarce, though, and so readily did the girls exchange the duties of the classroom for those of the household that Sister Madeleine writes, "Henceforth no girl was allowed to marry without being first instructed by the Nuns."

Influence in Colony. This instruction bore fruit throughout the entire colony. The girls carried from the convent to the home circle polish, charm and refinement, the result of education, and seldom found in the rough surroundings of pioneer life.

Lack of School for Boys. As a result of this training, the women far surpassed the men in culture, for the latter had no means of obtaining higher education without going to Europe. The fundamentals were taught in a few primary schools, but Bienville, realizing the lack of opportunity for young men in Louisiana, petitioned the government to establish a college for boys in New Orleans. According to his letter, the sons of wealthy parents were reared in luxury and idleness, utterly ruinous to character, or at great expense were sent to France to be educated, where they acquired a distaste for their colonial homes. He represented that many persons residing in Vera Cruz would be glad of the advantages offered by such a college and would help to maintain it. The government, however, considered Louisiana too remote and too insignificant to warrant any such establishment. So it was not until after the Americans assumed control of the colony that a college for boys was opened.

SPANISH SCHOOLS.

Interest Manifested by Spanish Governors. In 1768, Louisiana passed under the control of Spain. Unlike the French government, the Spanish authorities manifested some interest in education. Ulloa was a highly cultured man, but failed, through his unpopularity, to benefit the colony. O'Reilly and his successors fostered learning in the colony, but still no institution of higher education was founded. Many a débonair Spanish official married a convent-trained girl, thus forming a friendship for the Ursulines. The Nuns' school was well patronized under this régime and they received several Spanish ladies into their convent.

Spanish School Founded. An effort to make the use of the Spanish language more universal in the colony, and to train the youth according to Spanish ideals resulted in the government ordering a school to be established in New Orleans in 1772.

People's Distrust of Spanish Schools. The Louisianians, tossed from one king to another, felt intense resentment against the Spanish and clung with fierce pride to their own customs and languages. Although Spanish was used for all official proceedings, French was the language of the home, the church, and the school. Complaint was made to Spain that merchants refused to keep their books in any language but French. Even the influence of just and politic rulers like Unzaga, Galvez and Miro was not sufficient to stamp out this prejudice. The Spanish school was, therefore, not well attended, never having had more than thirty pupils, which number dwindled down to eight or ten after a fire had destroyed the original building.

French Schools. Those who could afford to do so sent their children to France to be educated; but there were eight French schools where several hundred profited by the instruction. Many refugees from San Domingo, who opened little schools to eke out a livelihood, received staunch support from the French families.

SECTION 2. EARLY YEARS OF AMERICAN RULE.

Private Schools. The influx of Americans, after the purchase in 1803, caused a greater demand for schools. As there was no system of free schools, this need was met by a number of teachers, who conducted private schools at moderate prices. According to the advertisements in the old newspaper files, learning flourished in the Faubourg Ste. Marie (the American quarter), where there were also evening schools and summer sessions.

Discipline. Frequently these pioneers of education in American New Orleans were men who exacted the most rigid discipline from their scholars by means of the dunce cap, the rod and in some extreme cases by enforced kneeling on brick dust and tacks.

Course of Study. The subjects accentuated then were almost as different from the present day curriculum as was the mode of discipline.

English, French, and other languages, writing, arithmetic, geography, history, mythology, chronology are mentioned in all advertisements, while "embroidery, print and crape work, French darning and every kind of fancy work, as well as plain sewing and marking" are specified for girls. No young lady's education was considered complete without music and dancing. These were frequently taught by special teachers who went from house to house and also gave lessons in "deportment," that is, the correct manner of entering a parlor, of standing, of sitting, of addressing persons."

COLLEGE OF ORLEANS.

Foundation. American legislators were more impressed with the necessity for public education than the French or Spanish had been, but they made the mistake of establishing too many academies and colleges instead of elementary schools. The most noteworthy of these was the College of Orleans, opened in 1805, where many prominent men received their education, among them being Gayarré, the historian.

Course of Study and Discipline. The course of study was comprehensive, including Greek, French, Latin, English, Spanish, arithmetic, algebra, geometry, mechanics, history and literature. Interest in composition was stimulated by literary exercises. Poetic as well as prose composition was encouraged, and occasionally, a paper published verses by some enterprising student. Lessons in music, dancing, and fencing were given those who paid extra. Life at the College of Orleans was not luxurious; the rising sun found the boys about their tasks; a half loaf of dry bread constituted breakfast.

Support of College. As there was no definite arrangement for the support of the college, its finances were very unsettled. To the small and irregular appropriations by the Legislature, were added funds from two lotteries established for this purpose. Even these sources of revenue proved insufficient to maintain a flourishing institution, and the proceeds from the licenses granted to gambling houses was utilized.

Decline. The College of Orleans flourished for about twenty years, but with the appointment as principal of Lakanal, one of the parties who caused the death of Louis XVI., the school began to decline. Parents refused to commit their children to the guidance of a regicide and the College of Orleans passed out of existence. Its failure was also the result of injudicious regulation of the terms of admission. Parents, who could afford to do so, were required to pay for their sons' tuition; but many sons of destitute parents were admitted without charge. These pupils were dissatisfied, because they received the sobriquet of charity students from the boys.

"Public Schools." In 1826 the college of Orleans was supplanted by one central and two primary schools. Though supposedly public schools, gratuitous instruction was limited to fifty pupils in each school. To the revenue obtained from the gambling houses was added about $3000 annually from theatre licenses.

SECTION 3. PUBLIC SCHOOL SYSTEM.

Louisiana was far behind the other states of the Union in organizing a system of public schools, because the idea of self-taxation for educational purposes was entirely new to its people. However, when Americans from other states began to form a large proportion of the population, the question of taxation for school support was agitated more fully.

Accordingly, the public school system of New Orleans was inaugurated by the Legislature of 1841, which decreed that "the councils of the different municipalities of New Orleans are authorized and required to establish within their respective limits one or more public schools for the free instruction of the children residing therein, to make such regulations as they judge proper for the organization, administration, and discipline of the said schools, and to levy a tax for the maintenance of the same. Every white child residing in a municipality shall be admitted to and receive instruction therein."

These schools did not spring immediately into popular favor; but within a few years their ultimate success was assured. The people soon became anxious to patronize schools supported by self-imposed taxes, and where the terms of admission were the same to all. The American quarter in 1844 had three schools, eleven teachers, and 615 pupils, but in the following year, to accommodate an enrollment of 1,029 pupils, the number of schools was increased to six and the number of teachers to thirty-six.

Public Schools in the State, 1845. Following the success of the new schools, the Legislature organized a similar system throughout the parishes, to be supported also by direct taxation. The eminent scholar, Alexander Dimitry, was appointed the first State Superintendent of Education and his influence was felt in New Orleans.

Normal School. The growth of the system created a need for a normal school where efficient teachers could be trained for work in the elementary schools. This need was met in 1858 by the establishment in New Orleans of the first normal school in the South.

From this as a beginning the New Orleans Normal School has grown to meet the needs of the present educational system, preparing teachers for instructing children of the elementary schools. These embryo teachers do their practice work in the city schools.

Civil War and Reconstruction. B. F. Butler, Commander of the Federal army of occupation in New Orleans during the Civil War, consolidated the four school districts under one board and one superintendent. There were to be a uniform system of grading and uniform text-books used throughout the city, which greatly facilitated the adjustment of pupils who moved from one district to another.

Education of Negroes. Troubles in educational circles came with the Emancipation Proclamation. The Freedman's Bureau, created by the United States Government to assist liberated slaves, furnished free transportation for teachers and supplies and expended large sums for negro schools in New Orleans. Little objection was raised to these schools, but the law passed by the "carpet-bag" Legislature of 1870, requiring the white schools to admit any negro children who would apply, caused great agitation and bitter feeling. Although there were but few actual admissions of colored children into the New Orleans schools, the furore did not subside until separate schools were provided for the two races.

School Buildings. As soon as the race question in the schools was somewhat settled, attention was directed to better buildings. Out of the funds left by John McDonogh for this purpose, six well-equipped schoolhouses were erected. This money has been utilized to meet the needs of increased enrollment until over thirty McDonogh schools have been built.

Overthrow of Reconstruction Government. The reconstruction government had spent vast sums of money for education, recklessly and injudiciously extending educational advantages to hundreds of non-taxpaying negroes to the exclusion of the whites, who bore the burden of taxation. One of the first acts of the General Assembly, after the overthrow of "carpet-bag" rule and the assumption of power by the better element, which elected Francis T. Nicholls governor, was to provide for education. Louisiana, mercilessly crushed by four years of war and left burdened with a monstrous debt yearly increased by the extravagant rule of unscrupulous politicians, had been given a setback from which she rallied bravely, but the effects of which are felt even to the present time.

R. M. Lusher—William O. Rogers—Warren Easton. Taking all of this into consideration and remembering the natural prejudice of Louisianians to a system of gratuitous education, the schools of New Orleans rank very favorably with the best of those of northern cities, where public schools are an inherited institution of the people, and where revenue from taxation has been uninterrupted. The services of Robert M. Lusher as Superintendent of Schools have left a marked impress on the schools of the city. William O. Rogers as Superintendent of the New Orleans schools rendered valuable service to this system for many years. From 1887 until his decease in 1910, the position was held by Warren Easton, whose success is attested by the devotion of teachers and pupils during his long incumbency and the universal reverence now accorded his memory.

Within the past few years the schools have made wonderful advancement in organization.

Management and Maintenance. Before the adoption of the new city charter, the schools were governed by a board of seventeen members, one elected from each ward in the city. Under that system each member of the board had the appointment of all teachers to schools in the ward which he represented.

Since 1912, the Orleans Parish School Board has been distinct from and independent of the State Board. Under the new city charter, it consists of five members who serve gratuitously and have complete control of the affairs of the Public Schools. (See Chapter XV. for Maintenance of Schools.)

Division of Schools. At present, the system includes elementary schools, secondary or high schools, a normal, and an industrial school for girls, which is soon to have its counterpart in a trade school for boys. The school year of about nine months is divided into terms, and promotions are made semi-annually, so that a retarded pupil has to repeat only one-half year's work.

Elementary Schools. The elementary schools comprise kindergarten, primary grades, covering four years work, and grammar grades, covering four years more. Previous attendance at kindergarten is not a requisite for admission into the primary grades. Any child six years of age or over, who complies with the rules of the schools, is eligible.

Departmental Teaching. The system of departmental teaching having been tested in several schools and found successful was introduced throughout the city in 1913 in the sixth, seventh, and eighth grades. Each teacher handling one principal subject and, according to conditions in the school, one or more minor subjects, is enabled to attain greater knowledge of her specialty and more efficiency in imparting it. Arithmetic, English, History, Geography, and Literature are given more time and attention in these grades than are other subjects. Some schools are supplied with a stereopticon or a moving picture machine, by which historical and geographical facts can be presented pictorially. Drawing and Music are taught in the schools as necessary elements of cultre.

High Schools. The city supports three splendid high schools. The Esplanade Avenue Girls' High School for the benefit of the girls below Canal Street, the Sophie B. Wright Girls' High School in Napoleon Avenue, and the Warren Easton Boys' High School in Canal Street. The high school courses are elective, and the pupils have a wide selection of subjects, as some are designed simply for a business course, others to prepare for normal school or college. For graduation, the pupil must attain a certain number of points, that is, successfully complete so many subjects. The standard of graduation is being raised, so the number of points required is changed from year to year.

Modern School Buildings. The three high schools are among the handsomest educational buildings in the city and their classroom arrangement and laboratory equipment equals that of most colleges. Many of the school houses have been erected through the generosity of philanthropic citizens. The new McDonogh 14 building is as fine as any in the country. The Beauregard School in Canal Street is especially attractive because of the beautiful grounds that form a setting for its artistic architecture. The oldest public school building now in use in the city is Jackson School, named after the hero of the Battle of New Orleans. One portion was built in 1845, and around that various additions have been made.

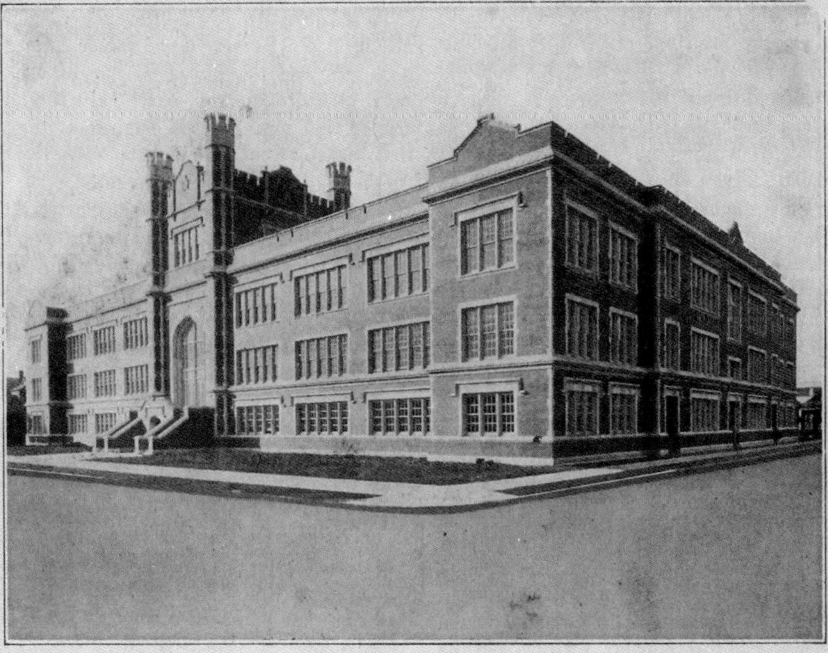

WARREN EASTON BOYS' HIGH SCHOOL.

Evening Schools. Three times a week, evening classes are given for the benefit of boys and girls over fourteen years of age, who have to work. There are also adult classes for those who did not receive an early education and for foreigners desirous of learning English.

Manual Training. The aim of the present-day education is to develop the powers and activities of the child as far as practicable. To this end, manual training has been introduced for the boys of the seventh and eighth grades. The boy in measuring, planing, sawing, fitting, and staining has the pleasure of seeing the work advance from a piece of rough lumber to the finished product—a rack, an ornamental box and sometimes a chair or table.

Domestic Science. A domestic science and a domestic art department train the girls for the more practical affairs of life. One period, each week, is given to the girls of the seventh and eighth grades. Under the supervision of a skilled teacher, the Eighth A and Eighth B girls in the domestic science department learn the chemical constituents of the materials they handle, the relative food values, and the most wholesome combinations. They are taught to plan a perfect meal, perfect not only from an epicurean, but from a healthful standpoint.

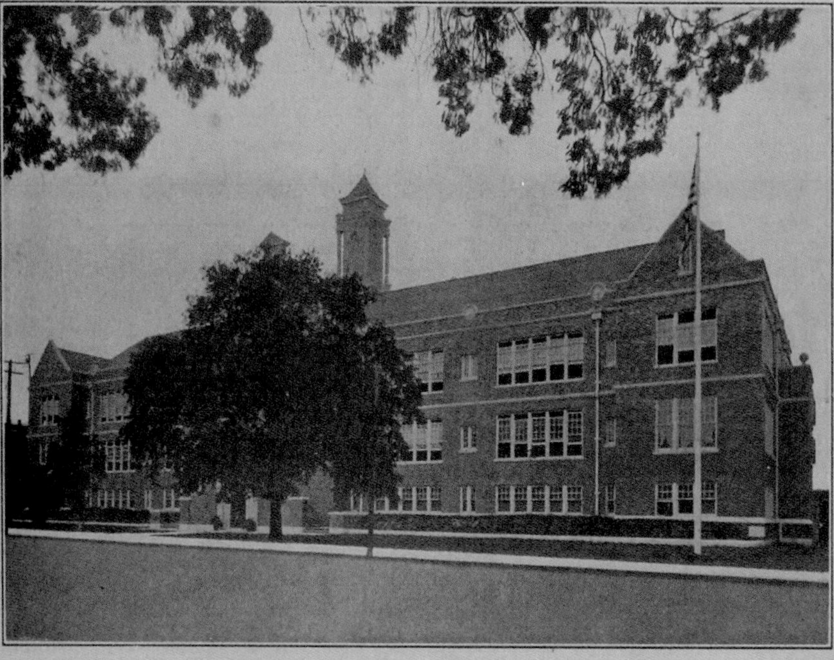

McDONOGH No. 14.

Domestic Art. The girls of the Seventh B and Seventh A are taught sewing. This department has been most successful. The girls of the Eighth A have made their dresses for the closing exercises of the grammar schools.

Department of Physical Training. As the happiness of an individual depends largely on his mental and physical well-being, proper training of mind and body are essential to complete education. Daily calisthenic drills and class athletics for boys and girls help to insure straight bodies, active limbs, and well-developed lungs. Competitive games between teams selected from the different schools assist in this physical development and create for many an interest in school affairs, which otherwise would be lacking. The boys' games are basket-ball, indoor-ball, and base-ball, according to the season of the year. The girls play basket-ball and indoor-ball. The victorious teams are awarded trophies, which the winning schools keep for one year. The "Spring Meet" in May is well attended and much enthusiasm prevails among the pupils, teachers and parents.

Department of Hygiene. To further insure the physical welfare of the community and the best possible hygienic conditions in the schools, the services of several competent physicians are secured. It is the duty of this department to instruct and supervise those in charge of the hygiene and sanitation of school buildings, to enforce the exclusion of contagious diseases from the schools, and to require from every child and teacher a certificate of vaccination.

Its activities cover a much broader field in the medical inspection of pupils. Through these examinations it has been found that many children, who were thought slow or even dull, were suffering from physical defects such as poor eyesight, poor hearing, or adenoids. A careful examination of the pupils' teeth proved a revelation to many parents, who were unaware of any defects. In most cases, they gave their immediate attention to the matter, and those who could not afford to pay a dentist were given gratuitous treatment.

Department of Attendance. There is a law in the State of Louisiana compelling children between the ages of eight and fourteen to attend school. In order to enforce this law, the School Board of New Orleans has appointed officers whose duty it is to see that this law is carried out and to investigate cases of truancy. If the conditions do not improve, the children are brought before the Juvenile Court.

Francis T. Nicholls Industrial School. A movement for industrial or vocational education has spread over the entire country and attracted attention in New Orleans. The aim is to offer to persons whose educational opportunities are limited one, two, or three years of training in some trade or industry. The trained worker always commands a higher salary than the raw recruit. Those, who have finished courses at a trade or industrial school, are fitted to earn a livelihood in one field or another. The Francis T. Nicholls Industrial School for Girls, occupying a handsome building similar to the new high schools, has been opened to girls over fourteen years of age, who have completed the sixth grade of the elementary course or its equivalent. Girls above the age of seventeen, who have not completed the sixth grade, may be admitted upon the approval of the Superintendent. The courses offered are dressmaking, home economics, garment making, millinery, fine laundering, art needle work, design making, Commercial Arithmetic, and English. The school has proved so popular that other courses will be added as soon as the need arises and provision can be made for them. Many girls, who either had no aptitude for or time to devote to higher intellectual culture, have been equipped with the means of making their way in the world, where year after year greater skill is exacted in every occupation.

Delgado Central Trade School for Boys. Isaac Delgado bequeathed to the Public Schools of New Orleans a fund of a million dollars for a trade school for boys, which as nearly as possible, must be centrally located. This school is now being erected, but a department of Educational Research has been established to furnish the School Board with accurate data concerning the industries, trades, and commercial activities of New Orleans, so that the school, when opened, may best meet the needs of the community.

SECTION 4. TULANE UNIVERSITY AND LOYOLA UNIVERSITY.

Medical College of Louisiana. The history of Tulane University dates back to the foundation of the Medical College of Louisiana in 1834. This College was chartered the following year, and in 1836 issued the first degree in medicine and science ever conferred in the southwest. Some of the most famous doctors in the country have added prestige to the institution by holding chairs in the different branches.

University of Louisiana, 1845. The Constitution of 1845 provided for the establishment of a university in New Orleans, embracing the Medical College, to which were to be added law and academic departments. The law department then, as now, gave instruction in common and in civil law, with more stress on the latter. As the civil law of Louisiana differs so widely from that of other states, few students are drawn from these sources. The academic department ceased all instruction in 1859 and was not reopened until after the restoration of civil government in Louisiana. During the years of 1863, 1864 and 1865 (war times), the University held no sessions. Through the strenuous efforts of a new board of administrators, the academic department was reopened in 1878 and sixty students matriculated. The following year the Legislature recognized the University of Louisiana in its three departments—medical, law, and academic, and pledged state aid to the amount of $10,000 annually. Such was the foundation on which Tulane University was built.

Paul Tulane. Louis Tulane, father of Paul Tulane, was a Frenchman who had emigrated to San Domingo with his brother-in-law, a wealthy planter and slaveholder. The brother-in-law's entire family was exterminated during the insurrection of the slaves, but Louis Tulane and his wife managed to escape in an open boat to the United States. They settled in Cherry Valley, near Princeton, New Jersey, and there Paul Tulane spent his boyhood. A cousin from France, touring the United States for his health, took the youth as "traveling companion." Much of the traveling, in those days, was done by steamboat, and the two descended the Mississippi to New Orleans, which so charmed Tulane that he returned a few years later to make it his place of residence. Establishing here a business for the sale of general supplies to planters and country merchants, he amassed a fortune. His charities were numerous, though so unostentatious as rarely to come to public notice. In 1873, he returned to New Jersey, where he died. Paul Tulane never forgot the city where most of his wealth had been accumulated; his generosity to it in the cause of education amply proved his devotion. In 1881, he donated all the property he then possessed in New Orleans to the education of the white youth of Louisiana. A board of administrators selected from the most prominent men of the city was chosen to execute the trust. In all, Tulane donated one million and fifty thousand dollars to the fund, which he intended to increase, but, as he died without a will, this intention was never carried out.

Tulane University, 1884. Tulane had not specified what should be done with the fund beyond that it should be devoted to the education of the white youth of Louisiana; so the administrators decided to establish an institution of higher learning. They entered into an agreement with the State by which the University of Louisiana, with all its property, would become a part of the new institution, thenceforth to be known as Tulane University of Louisiana. The $10,000 annually contributed by the state was to be withheld, but the property belonging to the University was to be free from taxation, in return for which the right of appointing to a scholarship was reserved to each senator and representative in the state. Colonel William Preston Johnston, a man of scholarly attainments and upright character, then president of the Louisiana State University at Baton Rouge, was selected as the first president of Tulane University.

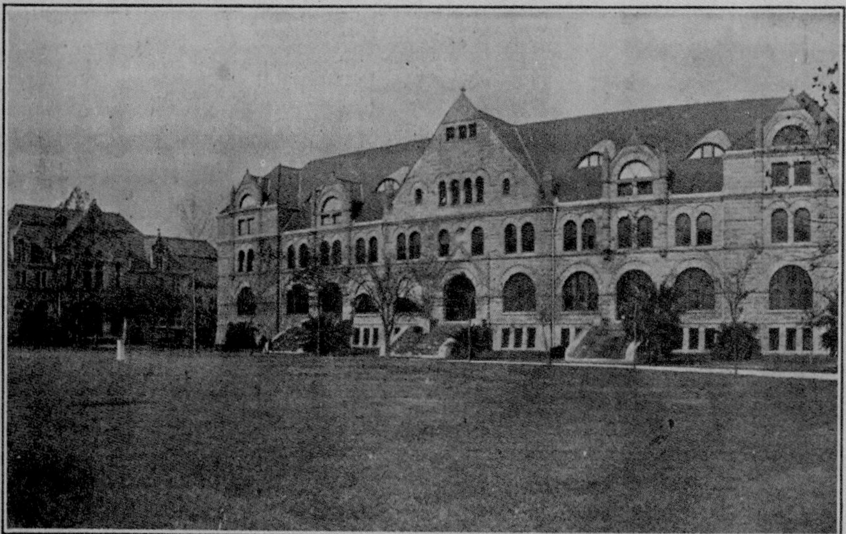

GIBSON HALL, TULANE CAMPUS.

Courses Offered. At present, the University comprises the College of Medicine, with the schools of medicine, of pharmacy, of dentistry, of hygiene and tropical medicine, of post-graduate medicine; the Department of Law, with the school of Louisiana Law and Common Law; the College of Arts and Sciences; the College of Technology, with schools of mechanical and electrical engineering, of civil and sanitary engineering, and chemical engineering, of architecture and architectural engineering. The College of Commerce offers a business course.

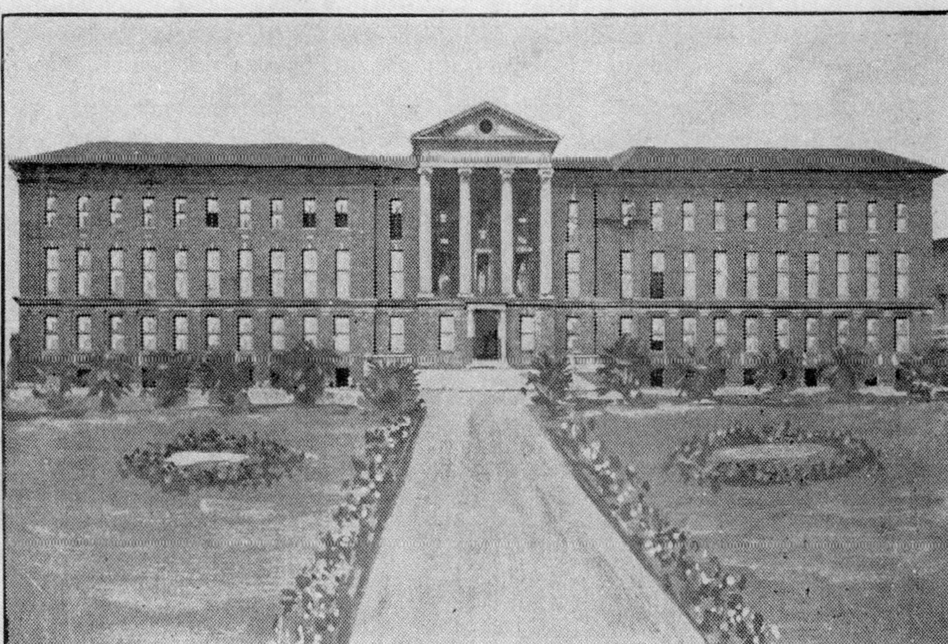

NEWCOMB COLLEGE.

Location. The University at first occupied the buildings of the University of Louisiana, which it had absorbed. Sufficient funds were given by Mrs. Ida Richardson to erect and equip a modern building as a memorial to her husband, who had long been connected with the medical department. The building was erected in 1904, facing Canal Street, in the square between Villeré and Robertson, and until 1908 was known as the Richardson Memorial Medical School. In that year, however, the building was sold to the Hutchinson Fund and the name "Richardson Memorial" was given to a building erected on the campus of Tulane University. Here, the first two years' instruction in medicine is given the students. The buildings of the former University of Louisiana became too crowded for the growing institution, which was removed to the present spacious grounds in St. Charles Avenue, facing the pleasant prospect of Audubon Park. The cornerstone of the main building, known as Gibson Hall, was laid in 1894. Since then, many handsome and well-equipped structures have been added and form an imposing group on the campus. Many of them are donations of generous patrons of education; such is the Tilton Memorial Library, the repository of the very valuable collection of books belonging to the University.

Government. The student body of Tulane University is self-governed. Each of the four classes (freshman, sophomore, junior and senior) of the academic department select a president, vice-president and secretary. These twelve students from the Academic Board of which the president of the senior class is ex-officio president. This court of honor is entrusted with nearly all matters of discipline, except neglect of work or absence. Its judgments are referred to the president of the University, who approves or sends them on to the faculty. That body seldom does more than ask the Board to reconsider a decision. This system, inculcating a certain amount of moral responsibility in each individual, has worked with admirable success.

Sophie Newcomb. Mrs. Josephine Louise Newcomb, wishing to perpetuate the memory of her daughter, Sophie, founded a college for young women. The original fund of $100,000 was entrusted to the administrators of the Tulane fund. The Sophie Newcomb Memorial College was opened in 1887 as a department of Tulane University. The courses offered are regular collegiate work, the high standard of which ranks Newcomb among the best colleges in the country. One of the most noteworthy features of the institution is the School of Art, which covers a four years course, supplemented by post-graduate work. Drawing, music, painting, modeling, art needle work, tapestry, jewelry, and pottery are some of the subjects comprised in this course. Newcomb pottery is far-famed for its beauty of outline and design. The exhibit of the Newcomb School of Art received the highest award at the Panama Exposition held in San Francisco in 1915.

Education Work of the Jesuits. Although the Jesuits had been in Louisiana since the earliest colonial days, they did not undertake educational work until after it became a state of the Union. The first college established within the present limits of the state by this illustrious teaching order was at Grand Coteau in 1835. Twelve years later, upon the invitation of Archbishop Blanc, they opened the College of the Immaculate Conception, now Jesuits High School, on the corner of Baronne and Common Streets in New Orleans. Adjoining the college building is one of the handsomest churches in the city.

Loyola University. In 1904, the Jesuit Fathers opened a select school in the uptown section of the city, in St. Charles Avenue opposite Audubon Park. To this was soon added a collegiate course. The ambition of the Society for a Catholic University in the State was realized in 1912, when the Legislature granted them full powers to confer "degrees in the arts and sciences and all the learned professions, such as are granted by other universities in the United States." Marquette Hall, a magnificent building in the Tudor Gothic style of architecture, has been erected and equipped with up-to-date apparatus for laboratory work.

The buildings are grouped in the form of an open quadrangle. Marquette Hall to the rear, Thomas Hall on the downtown side, and a church built on a magnificent plan occupies the thrid side of the quadrangle. The University now offers, besides an academic course, a pre-medical course, a law course, a course in pharmacy, and a course in dentistry.

Seismic Observatory. The most interesting instrument in the excellent scientific equipment of the University is the seismograph, one of the few in the country. The seismograph is an apparatus, which records vibrations of the earth. A cylinder, revolving by clockwork, moves a piece of carbonized paper on which two delicately poised needles trace parallel lines. These needles move from side to side with any vibration, causing the lines to be wavy. The instrument is so sensitive to the slightest vibration that it will be affected by an earthquake anywhere in the world. A special observatory, donated by W. B. Burke in memory of his son, houses this mechanical wonder. The seismograph is pro-

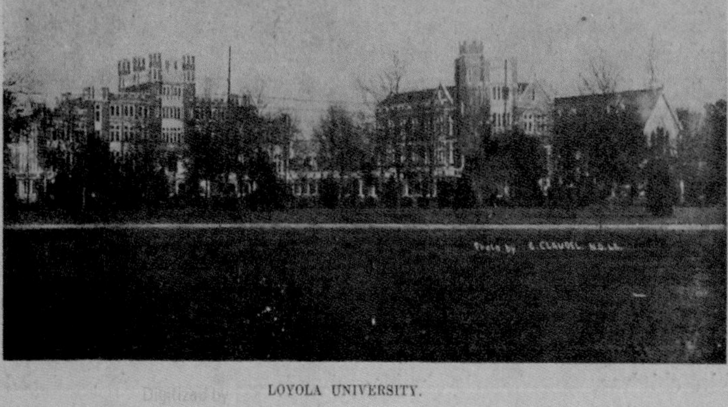

LOYOLA UNIVERSITY.

tected from atmospheric disturbances by the double walls of the observatory and by a special little room of glass within the larger room. The instrument does not rest upon or touch any part of the building, but is supported by an independent concrete column extending eight feet under ground. The Jesuits own the principal seismic observatories in the United States, and they have been asked to co-operate with the government in the compilation of seismic data. This university has also the equally wonderful and better known apparatus, the wireless telegraph.

SECTION 5. PRIVATE SCHOOLS AND COLLEGES.

Convents. Several Catholic religious orders conduct splendid schools for girls. The Ursulines, the Ladies of the Sacred Heart, and the Dominicans have been qualified by the Legislature to confer the degree of Bachelor of Arts.

The Ursulines, having been forced to abandon their historic buildings in the lower part of the city because the site was needed for a new levee, have erected a very imposing structure in State Street.

The Ladies of the Sacred Heart have an Academy in St. Charles Avenue, just above Napoleon Avenue. This order was founded in France in the beginning of the nineteenth century and, for over a hundred years, has successfully been devoted to the education of young ladies; their schools, established on all continents, have gained for them world-wide renown as cultural educators and moral instructors. The aim of their education has always been to mould the character and to infuse into their pupils that exquisite culture which is the mark of true refinement. Before the convent in St. Charles Avenue was established, there was one in Dumaine Street. This older institution has lately been abandoned owing to the shifting of population.

Parochial Schools. The Catholic Church conducts a well organized system of parochial schools. Each parish church has a school adjoining under the direction of the parish priest and, in most cases, taught by Nuns. Uniform text-books are used throughout the city and the classes are graded according to public school standards. The unity and efficiency of the system is further increased by a general supervision of all the Catholic Parochial Schools in New Orleans. Music, art, and, of course, religious instruction are given special attention. A graduate of Newcomb College, eminent for her art work, has been appointed supervisor of the art department. The teachers are thoroughly prepared for the work and the buildings are well equipped. The school adjoining the Sacred Heart Church is considered one of the most up-to-date in the city. Stereopticons and even moving picture machines are utilized to illustrate moral stories, history, and practical science lessons, importing vivid and realistic sense-impressions to the child, thereby stimulating interest.

Preparatory Schools. There are several well-known preparatory schools. The Christian Brothers' College, renowned for thoroughness, the Holy Cross College, and Rugby Academy are very successful in pre-collegiate work.

Soulé College.—Since 1856, this institution has been successfully carried on, excepting during the years of the Civil War, when the president, Colonel Soulé, entered the Confederate Army. It ranks very high as a business college and its graduates have little difficulty in securing positions. In 1884, it became co-educational to meet the demands of women for commercial education.

SECTION 6. INSTITUTIONS FOR THE COLORED.

Public Schools. The city conducts elementary public schools and a public high school for the children of the negro race similar to those provided for the white children.

Xavier College. This institution, richly endowed by Mother Drexel of Philadelphia, occupies the site of the old Southern University in Magazine Street. It is a well-equipped school, modern in all details and offers every advantage in way of educational opportunities.

Straight University. The American Missionary Association was instrumental in establishing this school in 1869, which was named for Seymour Straight, a produce merchant of New Orleans, and one of its earliest benefactors. At present, the University occupies large buildings with ample grounds in Canal Street.

New Orleans University. In 1869, the Freedman's Bureau established the Union Normal School, which in 1873 the Legislature chartered as the New Orleans University. The affairs of the institution are controlled by a board of trustees. Two-thirds of the members must belong to the Methodist Episcopal Church.

SECTION 7. LIBRARIES.

Library Societies. According to tradition, as early as 1801, the first public library of New Orleans was established; but there are no authentic records to attest its existence at so early a date. In 1805, the Legislature chartered the New Orleans Library Society, a joint stock company with an unlimited number of shares at $25 each and the privilege of conducting a lottery. The finances of the Society did not prosper and its ultimate fate is uncertain. A similar attempt was made in 1824, when the Touro Free Library Society of New Orleans was incorporated. Its term of usefulness was short, for it lasted only six years.

The State Library. There is no record of any public library for eight years after the dissolution of the Touro Free Library Society; but in 1838, the State Library was established by act of the Legislature, chiefly for the benefit of the legislators, but open to all citizens. From a beginning of 3,000 volumes, it increased to 50,028 in 1861. These had been removed to Baton Rouge with the change of capital, consequently many very valuable books and documents were destroyed when the State House was burned during the war. The volumes that were left were brought to New Orleans and are now deposited in the new Court House.

"Commercial Library." This owed its existence to private enterprise, but in 1842, through the generosity of B. F. French, it was turned over to the public.

The Lyceum or Public School Library. The Second Municipality was by far the most progressive in the educational line. In 1845, a library in connection with the schools of the district was established through the efforts of Mr. Shaw, superintendent of the public schools, Samuel J. Peters, and others. A monthly subscription of 25 cents for pupils and a yearly subscription of $5 for others, gave free access to the library, while a fee of $10 entitled the subscriber to life ownership. The Lyceum contained about 7,500 volumes and it is interesting to note that a few of them still bearing the mark of the Lyceum are to be found on the shelves of the present Public Library. The books were placed in the newly founded and unfinished municipal hall, the same whose classic Grecian architecture now adorns Lafayette Square.

The Fisk Library. About 1849, Mr. Alvarez Fisk bought the "Commercial Library" from Mr. French to carry out the designs of his deceased brother for the establishment of a public library in New Orleans. The collection then consisted of about 6,000 volumes, which, with a building in Customhouse Street, he offered to the city. It was used successively by the Mechanics' Institute, the Louisiana University, and Tulane until 1897; then it was that the Lyceum and the Fisk Library were consolidated to form the "Fisk Free and Public Library." The City Council has annually made an appropriation for its maintenance. This library continued to be the chief public library of the city and was frequently changed from one building to another until the city received a donation from Mr. Carnegie with which the present handsome structure was erected.

SECTION 8. THE NEW ORLEANS PUBLIC LIBRARY.

Buildings. The library building was erected in 1908 at a cost somewhat over $260,000. Mr. Carnegie's gift amounted to $375,000, but as the Fisk Library was to be embodied in the new, the city refused to accept the sum unless the condition of naming it "Carnegie" be removed. The structure and grounds occupy the length of the block on St. Charles Avenue, between Lee Circle and Calliope Street. The building is of gray stone and a portico supported by graceful Corinthian columns extends beyond the main entrance. A terrace, several feet in height, gives the building an imposing setting. The interior of the main building is like one great hall supported by massive marble pillars. A domed skylight and many large windows keep it well lighted. Almost one-half of this huge room is occupied by the Juvenile Department, secluded by a low partition running from side to side. Here, the long low tables with their rows of dark shaded electric reading lamps, the small chairs, the drinking fountains, row upon row of interesting books, the carefully arranged collection of pictures show that everything is planned for the comfort, entertainment, and instruction of the little folks. On the other side of the hall is the reference room, containing a large collection of valuable books which are not allowed to circulate, but which can be taken from the shelves and read at leisure. Just beyond the reference room is the magazine reading room, where one can peruse at will the latest copy of 339 different magazines—fashion books, literary periodicals, religious publications, and magazines of science, art, invention, agriculture, education, published in all parts of the English-speaking world and some in foreign languages. Behind the main building and connected to it by a wide vestibule is the annex where the books for circulation are kept. Three stories are stacked with well-filled shelves, having only narrow passageways between. The books are catalogued by means of the Library of Congress cards. Each book is listed at least twice—first on a card bearing the title of the book followed by the author's name, and this is filed alphabetically, according to the name of the book; secondly, on a card bearing first the author's name, then the title of the book, and this is filed according to the alphabetical order of the author's name. All the books are numbered and the cards in the catalog bear the numbers of the books.

Branch Libraries. In connection with the New Orleans Public Library there are five branch libraries, namely, the Royal Branch, Algiers Branch, Canal Branch, the Napoleon Avenue Branch, and the Dryades Street Branch for negroes.

System of Circulation. The use of these libraries is absolutely free to all, and any one holding a card may borrow books from the circulating department. All that is necessary to obtain a card is to have some one sign a guarantee that he would be liable for any fines incurred by the borrower. Fines are incurred if the book is kept longer than the time allowed, if the book is damaged, or if it is lost.

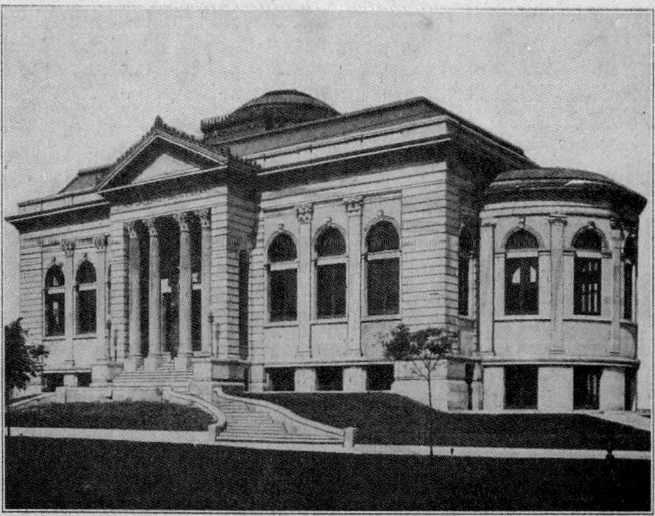

NEW ORLEANS PUBLIC LIBRARY.

Howard Memorial Library. Just on the other side of Lee Circle from the New Orleans Public Library is a much smaller, but handsome structure. This, too, is a library, a memorial to Charles T. Howard, erected by his daughter, Mrs. Parrot, in 1888. The plans were drawn by Richardson, and were the last from the hand of that famous architect. The original cost of the building was $115,000, and Mrs. Parrot's generosity led her to bestow an endowment of $200,000 upon the library. The interior consists of a fine hall containing stacks, and a circular, domed reading room. Among the valuable articles owned by the library are copies of the original editions of the works of Audubon and an unrivaled collection of Louisiana maps.

The Confederate Memorial Hall. Adjoining the Howard Library is the Confederate Memorial Hall built in 1891 by Frank T. Howard. The Hall with its invaluable collections is in charge of the Louisiana Historical Association. Many and varied are the relics gathered here—flags tattered and stained by time and battle, swords of gallant officers, the uniforms of some fallen hero, a lock of hair, the cord from a hat—sad but soul-stirring mementoes of those heroes, who went forth gladly to give their lives for their beloved South.

The Louisiana State Museum. The Louisiana State Museum, which now occupies the two historic buildings on either side of the St. Louis Cathedral, was created by act of the Legislature in 1906. The Cabildo contains valuable and interesting historical collections, including original documents and letters; maps, especially of New Orleans dating from the earliest days of the city; General Jackson's battle flag and other relics of the battle of New Orleans; slave-sale certificates, Confederate money, and mementoes of the Civil War; pictures of scenes connected with the history of the state, portraits of the governors of the state and many other historical personages; and collections of china, silverware, furniture, and trinkets, representing different periods in the history of the State and city. The old Presbytery is devoted to the natural history and commercial history of the State. The chief agricultural products—cotton, sugar cane, rice and corn, the lumber and mineral products, and a wonderful collection of native birds and animals are scientifically classified and attractively exhibited.

TOPICS: **Section 1,** Colonial Education; **Section 2,** Early Years of American Rule; **Section 3,** Public School System; **Section 4,** Tulane University and Loyola University; **Section 5,** Private Schools and Colleges; **Section 6,** Institutions for the Colored; **Section 7,** Libraries; **Section 8,** New Orleans Public Library.

REFERENCES: Louisiana Studies, Fortier; Standard History of New Orleans, Rightor; History of Education in Louisiana, Fay; Annual Report of the Superintendent of Public Schools; Annual Report of the New Orleans Public Library.

CHAPTER XIII.

Literature of New Orleans.

SECTION 1. INTRODUCTION.

Meaning. The word "literature" is derived from the Latin word "litera," which means a letter, written records, or writings. By literature is meant "the best expression of the best thought reduced to writing." As people's emotions and thoughts are influenced by their individual character, mode of life, and social conditions, so is literature, which is the written record of these emotions and thoughts; hence literature is an important factor in understanding a people. Literature requires settled conditions in order to flourish. The North American Indian had no literature because his life was one continuous struggle for food and life; he had no time to record his emotions, thoughts, and deeds. The earliest form of literature is the writing of the priests of the ancient tribes; their life was quiet; they led the people spiritually, in return for which, they were exempt from fighting; this condition of their life enabled them to give permanent expression to their religious beliefs and the prowess of the warriors. Literature is therefore the product of peaceful times, though struggles and turmoils of different kinds are often taken for the theme.

Two Kinds of Literature in Louisiana. For a full century, French was the principal language in Louisiana. The Spanish domination had no effect on the language of the colony. Even after the American occupation French held first place for about forty years. The sons of wealthy Creole families of antebellum days were sent to France for their higher education; thus the French language was retained in its purity. Even to-day, the French language is generally well spoken in New Orleans. From this has resulted a French as well as an English Literature.

SECTION 2. FRENCH LITERATURE.

First Literary Effort. Literature grows slowly in new countries. In the early days of the colony, the hard conditions of life repressed any literature aspirations. **"Le Moniteur,"** the first newspaper, was not founded until 1794. Copies of it are to be found in the archives of the city. The first literary work produced in New Orleans, in fact in Louisiana, was an epic, which appeared in 1779, during the time of the Spanish control; it was written in French by **Julien Poydras**, a native of Brittany, then living in New Orleans. The poem celebrated Galvez's capture of Baton Rouge and was entitled "La Prise du Morne du Baton Rouge par Monseigneur de Galvez." The work is devoid of literary merit, but is worthy of notice as the first attempt at a literary work in Louisiana. Julien Poydras's fame rests on his philanthropy and public-spirited citizenship. He came to New Orleans penniless; by peddling along the River, he gradually amassed enough money to become a merchant and planter, and thus acquired the fortune, which he spent so freely in assisting less fortunate in Louisiana. Poydras Street received its name from the fact that Julien Poydras's New Orleans home was located there.

Drama. The second literary work was a tragedy, "Poucha Houmma," by **Le Blanc de Villeneufve**, published in 1814. The subject is a Houmma Indian chief's sacrifice of his life so as to save that of his son. Cula-Bé, the son of Chief Poucha Houmma, had escaped from the Choctaw village after killing a Choctaw. At the feast of the "Young Wheat," the Choctaws sent to the Hoummas to demand the murderer. The old chief sent his son away and gave himself up instead to the Choctaws. Villeneufve endeavors through his work to prove to the world that the Indians were not destitute of human feeling. **L. Placide Canonge** in 1849 wrote a one-act comedy, "Qui Perd Gagne" (Who loses gains). **Dr. Alfred Mercier** and **Dr. C. Delery** also wrote some plays.

Poetry. A number of fine poems were written at different times during the last century. In 1846, **Mr. Felix de Courmont** published a poetical journal called "Le Taenarion." **Dr. Alfred Mercier,** besides his drama, wrote some poetry; "La Rose de Smyrne" and "Erato" are ranked among his best. **Dr. Chas. Testut** published in 1849 a volume of verse called "Les Echos." The works of the French poets do not enjoy the wide recognition they deserve.

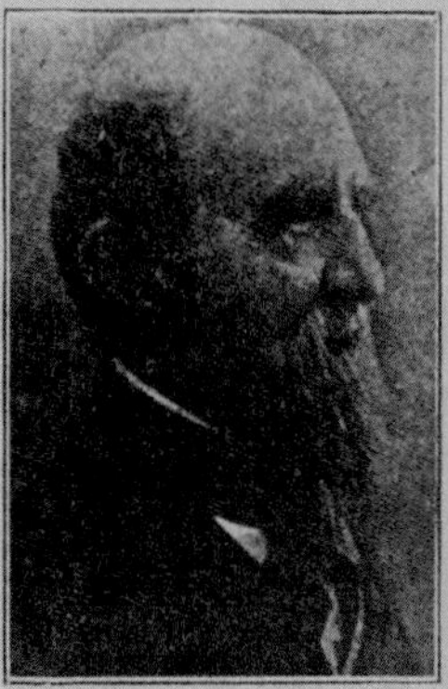

CHARLES GAYARRE.

Prose. Charles Gayarré's first work was in French, "Essai Historique sur la Louisiane" (Historical Essay in Louisiana). This work appeared in 1830. Charles Gayarré is one of the best known names in Louisiana, as a lawyer, legislator, and historian. He was born in New Orleans, January 9, 1805, of French and Spanish parentage; his mother was the youngest daughter of Etienne de Boré. He was graduated at the age of twenty from the College of Orleans and then went to Philadelphia, where he studied law with a well-known jurist, Mr. Rawle. He was elected in 1835 to the United States Senate, but his poor health prevented him taking his seat. He then spent eight years in France and returned with his health much improved. While abroad, he began the work on which his fame rests, his "Histoire de la Louisiane," the first two volumes of which appeared in 1846 and '47; in 1854, he completed the volume on the Spanish Domination, and during the Civil War that on the American Domination. After the Civil War, appeared a comedy, "Dr. Bluff," "Philip II. of Spain," "Fernando de Lemos or Truth and Fiction," and its sequel, "Aubert Dubayet or the Two Sister Republics." He contributed many articles to prominent magazines and reviews. He helped to reorganize the Louisiana Historical Society and became its president. Gayarré has given a valuable account of his life as a child on his grandfather's (Etienne de Boré) plantation in "A Louisiana Plantation Under the Old Régime." He held many political positions, such as member of the General Assembly and Secretary of State. The last years of the distinguished scholar's life were rendered painful by ill health and pecuniary embarrassments. Death claimed Charles Gayarré on February 11, 1895.

Besides his poems, **Dr. Testut** wrote two novels, "Le Vieux Salomon" and "Les Filles de Monte Cristo." **Dr. Alfred Mercier** wrote "Le Fou de Palerme," "La Fille du Prêtre," and "L'Habitation St. Ybars"; the latter is generally considered his best; it gives a vivid and accurate account of life on a large sugar plantation before the War.

French Literary Society. The "**Athénée Louisianais**" is a society for the preservation of the French language in Louisiana. It is affiliated with the **Alliance Française** of Paris and the United States. The society publishes a journal, "Les Compterendus d l'Athénée Louisianais," which contains many of the best literary efforts of its members.

SECTION 3. ENGLISH LITERATURE.

DeBow's Review. In January, 1846, appeared the first number of the "Commercial Review of New Orleans"; the Review was edited by **James D. B. DeBow,** who had removed in 1845 from Charleston, South Carolina, to New Orleans. Its original title is now scarcely known, it being familiarly spoken of as DeBow's Review. The Review became one of the foremost journals of the United States in the years before the War; it is a rich source of historical material about the Old South. De Bow, the editor, was a pioneer in the study of political economy, which he taught at the University of Louisiana, then located in New Orleans. Besides contributing to the Review and the Encyclopedia Britannica, DeBow published "Encyclopedia of Trade and Commerce of the United States" in two volumes, and various other works. The Review was published regularly until 1864, when it was discontinued; after the war, the office was removed to Nashville, Tennessee, where the journal was published for two years, 1866-'68, and then permanently stopped. The Review's influence on the development of the city commercially and educationally was great; its pages are rich with the best thought not only of New Orleans, but of the entire South.

Poetry. Many New Orleanians have written poetry, though few have attained distinction as poets. Before the War, the two best writers of verse were not native New Orleanians, but citizens by adoption. **Joseph Brennan,** born 1829, was an Irish patriot exiled from Ireland because of his connection with the revolutionary movements in 1848. He lived in New Orleans for the last ten years of his life, and for three years was connected with the "Delta." About his best poem is "The Exile To His Wife"; it is a pathetic account of his loneliness in a foreign land and his longing for his wife, for her presence, her love, and tenderness; it is rich in beauty of thought and musical rhythm. **Richard Henry Wilde** was also a native of Ireland; he was born in Dublin in 1789; he came to Maryland as a child and then lived in Augusta, Georgia, where, after studying law, he was sent to Congress. In 1843, Wilde removed to New Orleans, where he died four years later. His two best known poems are "Ode to Ease" and "The Lament of a Captive; or, My Life is Like the Summer Rose." Both poems sound a note of sad loneliness; the last is an exquisite lyric.

Colonel William Preston Johnston, a former president of Tulane University, published a volume of poems, "My Garden Walk," in 1895.

There have been three noted poetesses, **Mrs. Mollie E. Moore-Davis, Mrs. Mary Ashley Townsend,** and **Mrs. Eliza Poitevent Nicholson.**

Mrs. Davis was the wife of Major Thomas Edward Davis; she was born in Alabama in 1852, but, when a small child, her parents moved to Texas, where she lived until her marriage caused her to reside in New Orleans. Many of her early poems were gathered into a volume entitled "Minding the Gap and Other Poems." "Père Dagobert" and "Wanga" are among her principal later poems. There is an appealing note of truth and sympathy and sweetness in Mrs. Davis' writing; her thoughts are fresh and original. Mrs. Davis was also a novelist.

Mrs. Mary Ashley Townsend was born and spent her early life in New York. After her marriage in 1856, New Orleans became her home. Mrs. Townsend has published three volumes of verse and a collection of sonnets; she usually wrote under the name of "Xariffa." "Creed" contains beautiful thoughts beautifully expressed. "A Georgia Volunteer" is a sympathetic musing over the grave of an unknown Confederate soldier. "A Woman's Wish" and "The Captain's Story" are among other well-known poems.

Mrs. Eliza J. Poitevent Nicholson was born in Mississippi in 1849, but removed to New Orleans after her marriage. Mrs. Nicholson was the owner of the former "Picayune" newspaper. "Pearl Rivers" was the name under which she wrote. Mrs. Nicholson died in 1896. Besides many unpublished poems and poems published in newspapers, there is a volume of "Lyrics." The lovely poem, "Singing Heart," is in this volume. Mrs. Nicholson generally wrote of the things of nature; she had a deep understanding and love of nature's workings.

Drama. No great dramatic work has been produced. Judge Gayarré and W. W. Howe, and Mr. E. C. Wharton wrote a few plays, but achieved no distinction thereby.

History. **Judge Francis X. Martin** was the first historian of Louisiana. Judge Martin published his history in 1827; he recounts the history of Louisiana from the beginning of its settlement to the close of the year 1815. Judge Martin was also an eminent jurist. (See Chapter X., Professions—Trades.)

Judge Gayarré wrote a romantic History of Louisiana. Other historical writings of Judge Gayarré are: "A Historical Sketch of the Two Lafittes," "A Louisiana Sugar Plantation of the Old Régime," "The New Orleans Bench and Bar in 1823," "Literature in Louisiana," and "The Creoles of History and the Creoles of Romance"; the last was a refutation of George W. Cable's misrepresentation of the Louisiana Creoles.

Professor Alcée Fortier devoted his life to the study of Louisiana history, people, and their language. Professor Fortier was born in St. James Parish, June 5, 1856; he was the son of Florent Fortier and Edwige Aime, the daughter of Valcour Aime. He received his early education under private tutors, in the schools of New Orleans, and at the University of Virginia. He then studied law for two years, but his father's financial reverses compelled him to give it up and accept a clerkship in a bank. Shortly afterwards, he became a teacher in the city high school; later, he was made principal of the preparatory department of the University of Louisiana. In 1880, he was made Professor of French, at the University. The following year, he married Miss Marie Lanauze of New Orleans. From the professorship of French, he was changed some years later, to that of Romance languages. In 1913, he became Dean of the Graduate Department of the University. He died at his home in Audubon Street, February 14, 1914. Professor Fortier served for ten years on the State Board of Education; he was president of the Civil Service Commission and of the Board of Curators of the State Museum. It was largely through his exertions that the Louisiana Historical Society was kept from perishing; he served as its president for many years. The French government honored him by appointing him an officer of public instruction and presenting him with the cross of the Legion of Honor. Professor Fortier was president of the following organizations: Athénée Louisianais, Modern Language Association of America, American Folk Lore Society, and Federation Alliance Française of United States and Canada, and the Public School Alliance of New Orleans.

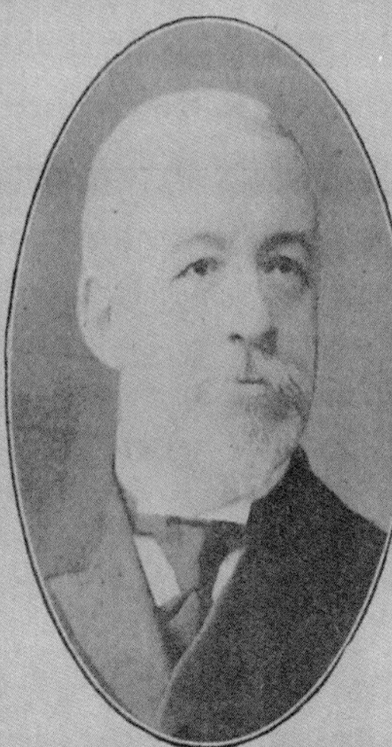

ALCEE FORTIER.

Besides his labors in the classroom, in clubs and societies, Professor Fortier did much writing, both in French and English. "Bits of Folk Lore" appeared in 1888, followed successively by "Sept Grands Auteurs du Dixneuvième Siècle" (Seven Great Authors of the Nineteenth Century), "Histoire de la Litérature Francaise" (History of French Literature), "Louisiana Studies," "Louisiana Folk Tales," "Voyage en Europe," "Précis de l'Histoire de France" (Abstract of History of France), "History of Louisiana," "History of Mexico"; editor of "Encyclopedia of Louisiana," and of many French texts. Professor Fortier contributed to many magazines in the United States and in France.

Judge Alexander Walker wrote in 1860 the "Life of Andrew Jackson and Battle of New Orleans"; his son, **Mr. Norman McF. Walker,** published in the Magazine of American History, September, 1883, an interesting paper entitled "The Geographical Nomenclature of Louisiana." **Colonel William Preston Johnston** wrote the life of his father, "Life of Albert Sidney Johnston." Another work dealing with the Civil War is **Colonel Alfred Roman's** "Military Operations of General Beauregard." **W. W. Howe** published the "Municipal History of New Orleans" in the Johns Hopkins University Studies in Historical and Political Science. There are many other books of a similar character.

The Novel. Charles Gayarré wrote two so-called novels, "Fernando de Lemos" and "Aubert Dubayet." **Charles Dimitry,** the son of the able educator, wrote, "The House on Balfour Street." **Dr. W. H. Holcombe** published "Mystery of New Orleans in 1890."

One of the most noted names in the literature of New Orleans is that of **Lafcadio Hearn.** Hearn was born in 1850 on the island of Santa Maura, one of the Ionian group; his mother was a Greek and his father an English army surgeon; he was educated partly in England, in Ireland, and in France. Hearn came to the United States after his father's death, making his residence in Cincinnati; here, he learned the printer's trade, then became a travelling correspondent of a Cincinnati paper; he spent a vacation in the South and, unable to cast off the spell of the Southland, removed to New Orleans. It was in New Orleans, most of his literary work was done; he wrote at times for the Times-Democrat. His first book was "Stray Leaves from Strange Literature." "Chinese Ghosts" relates legends of China. "Chita" is a local story based on the terrible storm that destroyed Last Island. Later Mr. Hearn removed to Japan, where his death occurred. Lafcadio Hearn's writing is characterized by its brilliance and vivid coloring.

George W. Cable may be claimed as a writer of New Orleans, even though he no longer resides in the city. George W. Cable was born in New Orleans in 1844. After serving in the Civil War, he became a civil engineer, but ill health forced him to give up his profession. Cable wrote for the Picayune and in 1869 became one of its editors. Scribner's Magazine published his "Old Creole Days"; the success of this book decided him to adopt literature as a profession. After a lecture tour with Clemens (Mark Twain) through the Northern States, he removed to New England. George W. Cable has also written "The Grandissimes," "Dr. Sevier," "The Creoles of Louisiana," and "The Silent South." His portrayal of the Creoles has sometimes been faulty. One of Mr. Cables ablest works is "History of New Orleans and Its Present Condition," written for the United States census of 1880; it is a rich source of information about New Orleans. His last work is "Lovers of Louisiana." Mr. Cable has much power as a descriptive writer, delighting his readers with exquisite word-paintings.

Besides her poems, **Mrs. Mary E. M. Davis** wrote several charming novels, "In War Times at La Rose Blanche," "An Elephant's Track," "The Queen's Garden," "The Price of Silence," "Keren-Happuch," clever accounts of life and scenes in New Orleans.

Mrs. Ruth McEnery Stuart was born in Avoyelles Parish, the daughter of James and Mary McEnery; she was educated in New Orleans. Mrs. Stuart is the widow of Alfred O. Stuart, a cotton planter, to whom she was married in 1879. Mrs. Stuart began writing in 1888; her first book was "The Golden Wedding," a portrayal of negro character; this was followed by "Christmas Gifts," a story of slave times; "Carlotta's Intended," which deals with Dago life; "In Simpkinsville," "The Gentleman of the Plush Rocker," "George Washington Jones," and "A Christmas Gift That Went A-Begging." Mrs. Stuart also did clever magazine writing.

Miss Grace King is among the foremost writers of New Orleans. Knowing intimately the Creole life of New Orleans, Miss King has generally devoted her books to the portrayal of the character and manners of the Creoles, in which the best critics agree that she has entirely succeeded. Miss Grace Elizabeth King was born in New Orleans, November 29, 1859; her father, William Woodsen King, was a prominent lawyer in ante-bellum days. Miss King passed her childhood in the midst of the Creole quarter of the city and on her father's plantation in St. Martin Parish. She received her education in the schools of the city and from private tutors. Miss King early spoke French and Spanish fluently and was thus enabled to easily study the history of the Creoles from original documents. Her first literary work was done for the New Princeton Review, which article she later developed into her first novel, "Monsier Motte" (1888). "Tales of Time and Place," and "Earthlings" followed. "New Orleans, the Place and the People," then followed; this is one of Miss King's most delightful books; it is written in an easy, charming manner, replete with vivid descriptions and interesting details, and reveals the Creole character at its best. Other works are "Jean Baptiste Lemoyne, Founder of New Orleans," "Balcony Stories," "De Soto and His Men in the Land of Florida," and "Pleasant Ways of St. Médard." Miss King wrote a school history of Louisiana, in collaboration with Mr. Ficklin. Miss King has received world-wide recognition of her work.

Mrs. Cecilia Viets Jamison is a writer of beautiful stories for children. Mrs. Jamison is a native of Canada, but New Orleans became her home after her marriage in 1878 to Samuel Jamison, a well-known lawyer of this city. Among Mrs. Jamison's most popular books are "Lady Jane," "Toinette's Philip," "Seraph," "Thistledown," and "The Penhallow Family." Mrs. Jamison writes for such magazines as Appleton, Harper, and St. Nicholas.

Mr. Thos. McCaleb has written a novel, "Anthony Melgrave," which met with a cordial reception on its appearance in 1892.

Miss Fannie Heaslip Lea (Mrs. Hamilton Pope Agee) is among the latest recruits to the literary ranks. Miss Lea has written principally for magazines. Two of her novels are "Quicksands" and "Chloe Malone." Miss Lea has just begun her literary career.

TOPICS: **Section 1**, Introduction: Meaning, Two Kinds of Literature in Louisiana; **Section 2**, French Literature: First Literary Effort, Drama, Poetry, Prose, French Literary Society; **Section 3**, English Literature; DeBow's Review, Poetry, Drama, History, Novel.

REFERENCES: Fortier, Louisiana Studies; Fortier, Encyclopedia of Louisiana; McCaleb, The Louisiana Book; J. E. Clarke, Songs of the South; Literary reviews of current magazines and newspapers.

CHAPTER XIV.

People—Customs.

SECTION 1. PEOPLE.

Composition of Population. The population of New Orleans, like that of other large American cities, is cosmopolitan, the result of its people's foreign parentage and of foreign immigration. It must be borne in mind that the people of the United States are not native to the country; their ancestors, following in the wake of Columbus, pushed their way across the seas and assumed control of the Americas as their forefathers had of Europe.

According to the United States census of 1910, the population of New Orleans was 339,075, consisting of Creoles, Americans, negroes, and foreigners; the foreign element was then slightly more than 7 per cent of the population, and included representatives of every nation of Europe and of several countries of Asia and of Central and South America. This percentage compares favorably with such cities as New York, in which the foreign element is 27 per cent of the entire population, Chicago 33 per cent and St. Louis 16 per cent. It is much smaller than that of Boston, where the foreign element is 38 per cent of the entire population.

Creoles. The Creoles are the descendants of the French and Spanish settlers of Louisiana. When Louisiana passed under the American flag, the Americans built up a quarter for themselves above the Terre Commune. This Terre Commune is now Canal Street and thus marks the division between the old city and the new, and between the Creoles and the Americans. Below Canal Street is the French or Creole quarter and above Canal Street the American district; the line is not as strictly drawn now as in former times; many Creole families now live in the American section and there are numerous American residents north of Canal (downtown). The Creoles have many characteristics of the French and Spanish people, tempered, however, by the different conditions of their life in America. They are quick-tempered, care-free, sociable, gay, possess the power of enjoying life, and are generally religious; they are kindly in their intercourse and possesses a pleasing charm of manner. The Creoles differ in appearance from the other inhabitants of the city; their physique is slight, but muscular and strong, and their movements light and graceful; they have olive complexions, dark eyes and hair. The Creoles, as a rule, speak French and English.

Americans "Americans" in New Orleans generally means the people who are not descendants of the French and Spanish settlers. The appellation, "American," was given by the Creoles to the English-speaking settlers, who, from the time of the Revolutionary War, came at intervals to Louisiana. This name has clung to them ever since. These people rapidly obtained control of the commerce of the city and made their quarter, the Faubourg Ste. Marie, (the First District), the business and political center of New Orleans. These Americans, unlike the Creoles, have no distinctive physical characteristics, except that generally, their build is larger. Their temperament is the same as that of the average American; having become acclimated, the long summers do not cause them to lose their energy as frequently happens to their brothers from northern States; they adjust their mode of living to suit the conditions of the place. Though the "Americans" are a happy people, yet they are not as fond of gaiety as the Creoles; they generally prefer home pleasures to social affairs.

Latin Americans. The Latin Americans come from the West Indies, Mexico, Central and South America; they are descended from the Spanish settlers of these countries and have the same character and appearance as the people of Spain. Though not very numerous heretofore, revolution in Mexico is occasioning the number of Mexican immigrants to increase rapidly.

Europeans. Every country of Europe is represented in New Orleans and in all classes, occupations, and sections of the city. Among the foreigners, the "Italians" are the most numerous; they are found in the different walks of life from the humble, loud-voiced vendor, driving his cart of fruit along the streets and calling out the different varieties in English impossible to understand, to the wealthy fruit merchant, who is helping to develop the city's ocean commerce. The French are perfectly at home in the Creole part of the city, where they hear their native language spoken with but a slightly different accent. French opera is sung exclusively at the Opera House; a troupe of singers is brought from France for the winter season. The Irish are almost as numerous as the French. Irish immigration began in the early forties of the past century and has continued almost uninterruptedly. Trade is the avocation in which they are most conspicuous. The English in New Orleans belong as a rule to a wealthier class than the other foreigners; they are largely engaged in foreign trade; like the Italians and Germans, they are scattered among the inhabitants of the city, not congregating more in one quarter than another. The Russians occupy sixth place on the list of foreigners in New Orleans; in the main, they are Russian Jews, who have fled from persecution in Russia; many are engaged in conducting little second-hand shops on Dryades Street, and in peddling. Besides these nationalities, there are a few Austrians, Greeks, Swiss, Spaniards, Belgians, Danes, Norwegians, Swedes, and Scotchmen.

Asiatics. Of Oriental nations, the Chinese, Japanese and Turks are more prominent in New Orleans, as is the case in other cities of the United States, where they have congregated in any numbers. The Chinese have established a quarter of their own in New Orleans; they are located on Tulane Avenue between South Rampart and the Criminal Court House. Here, they have small restaurants, junk and pawn shops, and laundries; they are experts in laundering, especially clothes requiring stiffening, and their little laundry places are found everywhere in the city. The Japanese, the most highly developed people of the Mongolian race, operate many shops for the sale of Japanese ware and curios of all kinds; some of the more interesting of these little stores are in Royal Street, and, through them, may be obtained most delightful glimpses of the life in far-away Nippon. The swarthy Turk earns his livelihood in the Crescent City by peddling linens, embroideries. laces, and various products of Western Asia.

Negroes. The negroes are the descendants of the slaves of ante-bellum days, who originally came from Africa. Schools and missions, maintained for their betterment, are well attended and have accomplished good results. A kindly feeling exists between the white and "colored" races.

SECTION 2. CUSTOMS.

Carnival. Carnival is the season between Twelfth Night and Lent. It is the gayest season of the year in New Orleans, the climax being reached by the costly festivities of Mardi Gras, "fat Tuesday," the eve of Ash Wednesday. The name "Carnival" is derived from two Latin words "carne," "flesh," and "vale," "farewell," hence "farewell to the flesh"; the pleasures of "carnival" are a gay good-by to the flesh which is to be mortified during the penitential season of Lent.

Carnival is of pagan origin. The Romans celebrated the feast of the Pastoral god, Lupercus, on February 15th; goats were sacrificed and two youths clothed in goat skins ran through the streets hitting with leather thongs the persons they met. The celebration in modified form was kept by the Christian Romans and has been continued to the present day. The custom spread from Rome to other places. New Orleans adopted the Carnival from Paris, but has improved upon it so greatly, that, today, her Carnival is the most noted in the world. The brilliant balls and gorgeous pageants of the last week of Carnival annually attract thousands of visitors to the hospitable metropolis of the Southland.

The custom of having pageants reproducing scenes from history, literature, or art, by means of gorgeously decorated floats was introduced into New Orleans from Mobile. In 1831, an organization of Mobile known as the "Cowbellions," held the first parade of the kind in America. The Mystic Krewe of Comus was the first to delight the populace of New Orleans by its appearance in the streets. In 1857, they presented scenes from Milton's "Paradise Lost" and then repaired to the old Varieties Theatre for the grand ball with which they entertained their more intimate friends. This merry god and his court annually parade in exquisitely artistic guise in the evening of Mardi Gras; their ball later at the French Opera House is the climax and close of the brilliant social season.

Rex first came to rule in 1872 for the benefit of the city's distinguished guest, the Grand Duke Alexis of Russia. Since then, the royal yacht, coming from over distant seas, bears the merry monarch and his court of dukes and peers of the realm, to the landing at the foot of Canal Street at noon of Monday, the eve of Mardi Gras. Rex's arrival is hailed by a prolonged salute of cannon and whistles from every craft in the harbor. A procession, composed of the dignitaries of the city, the soldiers from Jackson Barracks, the crews of the visiting warships, the state militia, and part of the city police force, then escorts Rex to the City Hall. Here, the Mayor of New Orleans presents him with the keys of the city and he begins his frolicsome rule of thirty-six hours, during which time the air resounds with the royal anthem, "If Ever I Cease to Love." At noon on Mardi Gras, Rex parades in fanciful array through the principal streets of the city, pausing in front of the Pickwick or Boston Club's balcony in Canal Street, to salute the Queen of the Carnival and the members of her court and present Her Majesty with a bouquet in the carnival colors, purple, green, and gold.

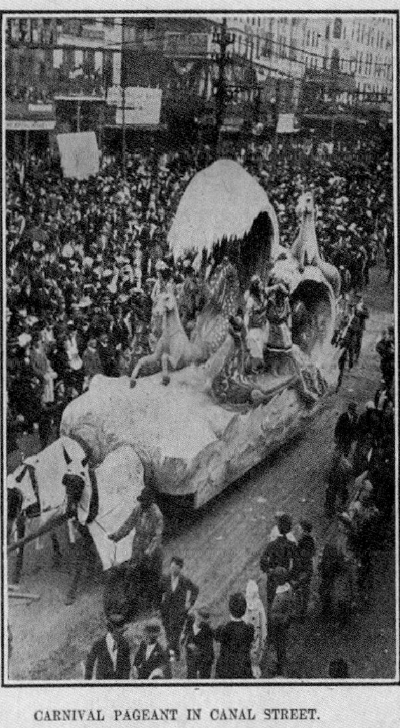

CARNIVAL PAGEANT IN CANAL STREET.

Mardi Gras night Rex entertains at a public ball at the carnival palace (the Athenaeum, corner of St. Charles Avenue and Clio Street); at midnight, Rex and his Queen, accompanied by the members of the court, visit Comus, at the French Opera House; the union of the two courts in the grand march following the arrival of the royal guests is one of the most gorgeous spectacles in the social life of the United States.

The Thursday night before Mardi Gras witnesses the appearance of the Knights of Momus. This parade inaugurates the Mardi Gras festivities. Momus's advent occurred in the same year as Rex, 1872, when he showed scenes from Sir Walter Scott's romance, "The Talisman." After the parade, Momus entertains at a ball at the French Opera House.

The Mystic Krewe of Proteus made its first appearance in 1882, on Mardi Gras eve, in a parade illustrative of "The Dream of Egypt." Proteus seems not to limit the cost, so beautiful are his annual pageant and ball both in thought and execution.

There are other organizations that entertain at brilliant balls; among these, the more prominent are the Twelfth Night Revellers, Nereus, and the Atlanteans. A queen and attendant maids are chosen at all these balls and the beauty and rich attire of the court contribute to the splendor of the entertainment, which generally occurs at the French Opera House.

One of the most important factors in arousing the Mardi Gras spirit is the secrecy and mystery enshrouding the great pageants; the public knows nothing about them until they see them appear in the streets. The expense of these parades is borne by members of the Mystic Krewes, and ranges from $20,000 to $30,000 and sometimes more for a single pageant. As soon as one Mardi Gras is over, preparations begin for the next. A Mystic Krewe numbers about 250 members, about 100 of whom are selected to participate in the display. A design committee is elected at the organization's first meeting; a "captain" is appointed to be the head of this committee, and is given absolute power. The committeemen propose subjects taken from history, literature, mythology, etc.; five or six of these suggestions are given to the artist, who presents a few weeks later crayon sketches of them to the committee. After the committee makes its final selection, the artist designs in detail and in water colors each float and costume. The characters are then assigned the members and the costume cards are sent to the manufacturer; the costumes are received by December and given to the court tailors for fitting and altering. The float Committee has charge of the construction of the floats. Carpenters, painters, papier-maché workers, and many others are kept busy building the floats in the "Float Den," which is located in an out-of-the-way place, such as the yard of an abandoned cotton-press. The ball at the Opera House is arranged by the "Ball Committee." When the appointed day for the parade arrives, preparations are begun in the afternoon, if the display is to be at night. The drivers, torch-bearers, and other attendants are well drilled. The maskers' costumes are in readiness in some building near the Float Den; the members repair to this building and don their costumes, placing their formal dress suits in the costume boxes; these boxes are later taken to the Opera House to be in readiness for the maskers at the close of the ball. About seven o'clock, the maskers line up and the roll is called. A police squad keeps the streets cleared for several squares about the den. The torch-bearers form in ranks and the floats, about twenty in number, are driven out. At the "Captain's" command, the maskers mount the floats, which parade through several of the principal thoroughfares of the city to the enjoyment of thousands of spectators. The floats are then taken away to their secret home.

These pageants are not only exquisite and entertaining, but instructive as well. The subjects are worked out in a highly artistic manner, beautifully illustrating bits of the world's treasure house of fact and fable, as for instance, Tasso's "Jerusalem Delivered," "The Adventures of Telemachus," "Chaucer's Tales," and many others.

McDonogh Day. One of the most prominent persons in the commercial and social world of New Orleans between the Transfer and 1850, was John McDonogh; first, social favorite, then melancholy recluse. John McDonogh was born in Baltimore in 1778, of Scotch parentage. A visit to New Orleans in 1800 revealed its commercial possibilities, and, in 1804, he took up his permanent residence here. His business flourished so well that, five years later, he opened a sumptuous house at the corner of Chartres and Toulouse Streets. At the Battle of New Orleans, he served as a member of Captain Beale's company of rifles. The story is that, about this time, McDonogh fell in love with a Miss Johnson, whose parents had removed to New Orleans from Baltimore in 1814. Because of differences in religion, the young lady's parents refused their consent to her marriage with John McDonogh; a few years later, Miss Johnson became an Ursuline Nun. Thereupon, McDonogh closed his house in the Vieux Carré and repaired to his plantation across the river, now McDonoghville. As there were no steam ferries prior to 1835, McDonogh crossed the river daily in a skiff, continuing to do so after the ferries were operating. Because of this habit, many persons accused him of stinginess. Unaffected by the sarcasm, ridicule, and condemnation of his former admirers, McDonogh spent the remainder of his days in solitude, dealing out justice and charity to his employees and slaves, freeing many of his slaves and providing for the future freedom of others, and all the time amassing a fortune. "And for what purpose?" every one asked. John McDonogh never said. It was not until his will was read after his death in 1850, that his secret purpose was revealed, namely, to benefit by education the youth of New Orleans and Baltimore. The passing years have removed from his name the stigma of miser, and, today, we know him to have been honorable, steadfast, kind and self-sacrificing, a patriotic citizen, and an upright Christian.

The opening of the will of John McDonogh revealed to the public that he had left the bulk of his fortune to the cities of Baltimore and New Orleans for the education of their youth. All that John McDonogh asked in return for his gift, was that, once a year, the children of the city would strew flowers on his grave. As his remains were removed to Baltimore, the monument erected in his memory by the public school-children of the city, has been substituted for his grave. On the first Friday of May, delegations from every public school in New Orleans, gather in Lafayette Square, and mass beautiful flowers about McDonogh's monument, while singing the pretty McDonogh song. Owing to other benefactors of the public schools being honored on this day, the name of the day has been changed to Founders' Day, but uppermost in the minds and hearts of all is the name of John McDonogh, the foremost of the public school benefactors.

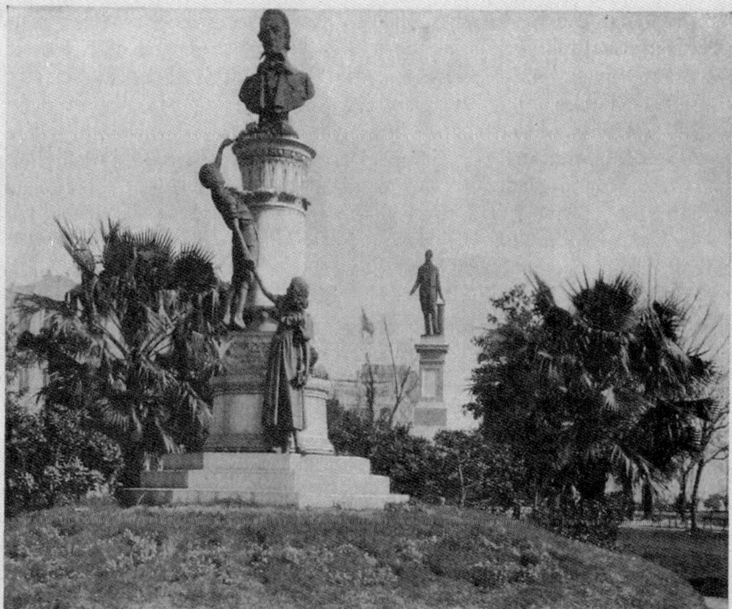

McDONOGH MONUMENT IN LAFAYETTE SQUARE.

All-Saints'. All-Saints' Day is celebrated on the first of November; it is of Catholic origin, being the day on which the memory of all the saints is honored by the Catholic Church. All-Saints is now a state holiday. The cemeteries are beautifully decked with quantities of gorgeous flowers; the large, handsome chrysanthemums being the most used. All day, the cities of the dead are thronged with the living, whose presence and the lavish floral display give a festive air to the otherwise sad scenes. The day is prepared for months ahead of time by thrifty florists. So popular has become the chrysanthemum for all Saints' decoration, that several hundred persons are engaged in their cultivation, principally for this festival.

Thanksgiving Offering. Thanksgiving Day is celebrated in New Orleans much in the same way that it is in the more northerly state in which the custom originated. In addition to this, the children of the public schools bring a Thanksgiving offering to school on the eve of the holiday. This offering consists of anything from an onion and an Irish potato to a delicate pastry or jelly. After all the offerings have been collected, they are sorted and sent to the needy homes, orphan asylums, and homes for the aged in the district of the school. Thus do the more prosperous share with their poorer neighbors, and Thanksgiving morning sees all united in thanking God for His public and personal benefactions.

St. Roch's. St. Roch's is one of the most interesting cemeteries in New Orleans; principally because of its unusual origin. An epidemic broke out in the city in the year 1866-'67. Father Thevis, then pastor of the Catholic German parish in the rear of the Third District, made a vow that if none of his parishioners should succumb to the epidemic, he would with his own hands erect a chapel in thanksgiving.

The whole parish united in prayer to St. Roch. As the epidemic did not cause the death of any of his congregation, the old pastor built the chapel and called the place "Campo Santo," "Holy Field." The chapel is of beautiful Gothic architecture and is similar to the mortuary chapels found in Austria and Hungary. Over the altar is a statue of St. Roch, which represents him with his favorite dog that fed him when he lay suffering from the plague, in the forest near Bingen, Germany. St. Roch's became famed as a miracle-working shrine, attested to by the hundreds of votive tablets expressive of the gratitude of the donors; these are placed on all sides of the altar, and many candles are kept continually burning before this altar. A little cemetery has grown up about the chapel; within the little edifice, the side tiers of vaults are reserved for the members of the societies of St. Anne and St. Joseph; the holy founder lies buried in the crypt under the sanctuary. There are many legends connected with St. Roch's, such as, that if a young woman prayed in the chapel regularly every evening she would have a husband before the year would be out; another is that if a maid look into the well at St. Roch's, she would see reflected on its smooth surface the face of her future husband; of course, she must not look into the well when alone.

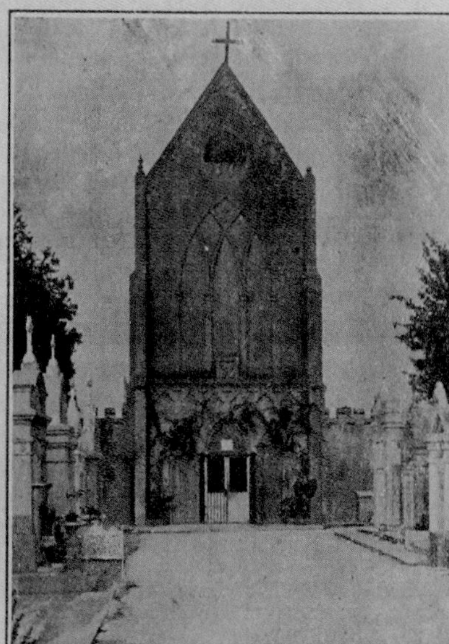

ST. ROCH'S CHAPEL.

Charivari. The charivari was among the distinctly odd customs of New Orleans. In mediaeval times in France, persons entering into a second marriage were given a "mocking serenade, produced by the beating of pans and kettles mingled with groans and hisses"; this peculiar serenade was called a "charivari." There have been numberless "charivaris," but perhaps none have attained the celebrity of the one accorded the fair, young widow of Don Andres Almonaster y Roxas. Miss King relates in "New Orleans: The Place and the People," that for three days and three nights the crowd followed the fleeing couple, "up and down the city, to and fro across the river," until finally they made their escape from the city.

July Fourteenth. Frenchmen's Day is celebrated annually on July fourteenth. It was July 14, 1789, that the Paris mob, in whom oppression had aroused the spirit of revolution, attacked the Bastille, the state prison, for five hours. The huge stronghold withstood the attack, but the guard within forced De Launey, the captain, to surrender; he did so, however, on the condition that no harm should be done. Seven prisoners, well deserving their fate, were the only ones found in the prison. Five officers and three men were killed by the populace. De Launey was murdered in the street and his head stuck on a pike. This began the Revolution in France, known as the "Reign of Terror," which overthrew the rule of the Bourbon kings, and was itself crushed only by the despotism of Napoleon Bonaparte. The republican form of government, different however, from that in the United States, finally obtained control in France. The French of to-day, thus celebrate July Fourteenth as their Independence Day.

SECTION 3. WAR ACTIVITIES.

War Savings. The Louisiana State Committee on War Savings carried on a ceaseless, intensive and patriotic campaign to induce people to save and to serve the Government by the purchase of War Savings and Thrift Stamps. Up to December 1, 1918, the sales in the city of New Orleans exceeded in value $4,500,000, or more than $6.50 per capita.

Liberty Loans. The success of the Liberty Loans is a credit to the city of New Orleans and to its people. In every instance "Over the Top" was realized by the determined spirit of a people who "never say die." The Fourth Liberty Loan called forth the genius of the Crescent City and the advertising campaign was the most thorough and systematic ever conducted in this section of the country; the longest street sign ever put up in the world was raised on Canal Street.

Resumé of New Orleans' War Finance Activities.

First Liberty Loan	$ 9,226,350
Second Liberty Loan	15,248,900
Third Liberty Loan	15,667,500
Fourth Liberty Loan	30,800,000
Fifth Victory Liberty Loan	22,000,000
War Savings Stamps	8,000,000
War Camp Recreation Fund	33,000
First Red Cross War Fund	672,250
Second Red Cross War Fund	1,265,789
Christmas Membership Drive Red Cross	85,000
Young Women's Christian Association	165,000
Y. M. C. A. Fund	116,000
Total	$103,279,789

Foot-note: United War Workers Fund not yet compiled.

Food Conservation. Food control and conservation played an important part in winning the war. The Food Administrator for Louisiana, John M. Parker, helped the State to make a splendid record. It began with almost a hundred per cent. conservation pledge, and ended by reducing sugar consumption to 3.3 pounds per capita, for all uses, one of the lowest marks set anywhere in this country.

Sugar, rice, and cottonseed industries were organized and stabilized, grades and prices fixed, and the government aided in popularizing and disposing of Louisiana crops. The Louisiana food work was divided into a dozen departments with deputy administrators in districts, parishes, and communities. Poster pictures, oratorical demonstration and other campaigns were conducted, and churches, schools, fraternities and clubs, and men and women contributed splendid services.

Red Cross. The American Red Cross is the largest and most efficient organization for relief of suffering that the world has ever seen. Chapters of this organization were established in practically every city in the United States; the New Orleans Chapter, with branches, was formally organized December 1, 1916, and performed a splendid service in the great humanitarian cause; it is arranging to continue its efficient work through departments for the study of Elementary Hygiene; through a Sanitary Department; and a First Aid Department.

The Junior Red Cross, composed of pupils of all public, private and parochial schools, was as equally efficient in the duties entrusted to it. The children participated in the great war work of the American Red Cross to an extent that won distinction for New Orleans in its wonderful record of 100 per cent. in war work. The Junior Red Cross is permanent and will continue all activities as outlined by the parent body.

TOPICS: Section 1, People; Section 2, Customs; Section 3, War Activities.

REFERENCES: Guide to New Orleans, 1884; Picayune Guide Book; Eliza Ripley, Social Life in Old New Orleans; Grace King, New Orleans—The Place and The People; Alcée Fortier, Louisiana Studies.

CHAPTER XV.

City Government.

SECTION 1. INTRODUCTION.

The Well-Governed Home. "Ah! what a splendid home!" said the visitor, smiling approvingly. The house of which he spoke was very modest; but let us approach it as did the appreciative visitor. The banquette was clean and in repair; the simple iron fence was well painted; within was a small garden, where lovely flowers blossomed unhampered by any rank growth of weeds. The home sat in the midst of the garden and lawn and, like its surroundings, was in good condition, not in the least in need of repair; its cleanliness fairly sparkled. A peep into the interior of the home revealed every comfort and a few luxuries. Children's merry voices resounded about the premises. At the sound of the dinner bell, there was a flurry of movement and then the family gathered about the inviting board. At one end of the table, the smiling mother saw to the needs of each of the rosy-cheeked youngsters, amid a happy chatter about the doings of each one, discussions of which were referred to the proud father at the other end of the table. Each had his report to make about that day's activities.

What was it that made that home "splendid," as the visitor said? GOVERNMENT. The father and mother were the head of the family. They saw that each member had his or her special task to accomplish, and that each one did his share and took up responsibility for the whole, inasmuch as each one would **not** do anything to cause disorder. No one would throw paper, fruit peelings, etc., about the premises, nor ruthlessly tear up the grass and flowers, nor jab holes in the pavement, nor scribble on the paint.

What was the result? A fair home, the joy of the inmates and the admiration of the visitors.

Need of Government in the City. If government is so necessary in the home for the maintenance of order, securing of coöperation, and making progress, how much more necessary is it in a home of hundreds of thousands of people, a big city! And as the needs of the city are the vastly magnified needs of the family, so the tokens by which the visitor judges the family, are those, vastly magnified, by which he judges the city, namely, the appearance of the city, the spirit of the citizens (the members of the city family), and the work accomplished by the citizens.

As the father and mother governed the family, so the persons chosen by the people of the city, govern the city; and when, like the two parents of whom we have been speaking, they do their work well, the citizens are busy and contented, and make annually (everything is on such a bigger scale) reports about their wonderful work.

Civic Interest—A Duty. Do you think the home we have been considering would be so splendid if all the members of the family were not interested in making and keeping it in such condition? Surely not. Suppose four-year-old Tommy decided to use a flower-bed as a garbage can, and threw all the banana peelings into it. Six-year-old Mary might happen by and carefully remove it to its proper receptacle; but, while Mary would be so engaged, the task, that had been assigned to her, of gathering the violets for the dinner table, would be neglected. Some one else, trying to accomplish Mary's work, would leave his own undone. So, because of poor Tommy's disorderly act the entire household arrangement would be somewhat upset.

Now let us make the application to our huge family—our city. A couple of thousand Tommies unthinkingly throw peelings, paper wrappings, bits of old clothes, food, etc., in the streets, even in the beautiful squares and parks. A large number of workmen are kept employed cleaning up after these careless citizens; another set of men have to mount guard to protect the public grounds and prevent these thoughtless citizens from committing such disorderly acts. And all this labor and money spent on cleaning up and preventing disorderly deeds could be used in improving the city,—if there were no disorderly Tommies.

It is then the duty of each one to refrain from committing disorderly acts, and to labor, each one according to his ability and position, to improve the city; to discover the needs of the city, and how to meet these needs; to take an interest in the government of the city, since it is all the voters of the city who choose the government and select the persons to do the governing of the city; to see that the work of governing is assigned to responsible persons; to recognize and appreciate good governing, as well as condemn and punish bad governing.

Charter of New Orleans. New Orleans became a chartered city in 1805, that is, she was then granted a charter by the Legislature of the Orleans Territory. The charter gave her the right to govern herself in a special manner described therein. Every time the people of New Orleans have desired a change in the government, they have had to apply to the State Legislature for such permission; when it was to be a complete change, a new charter would be granted.

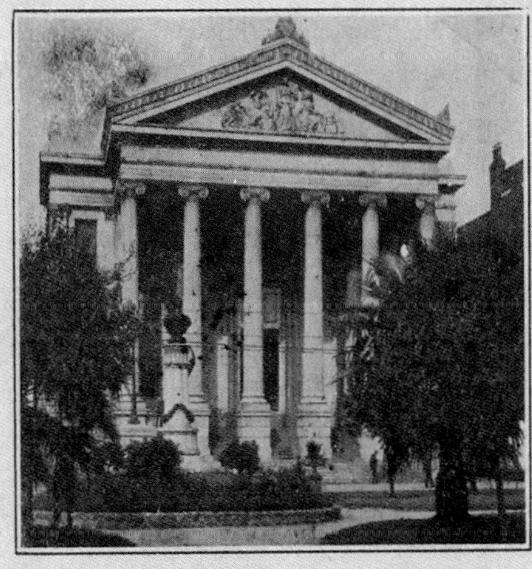

THE CITY HALL.

Government of New Orleans, 1805-1912. Between 1805 and 1912, the government was generally "aldermanic." The city was governed by a mayor and aldermen; the number of aldermen varied under different charters. The mayor and aldermen formed the city council and made and enforced the laws and took charge of the city's finances.

The last form of government in the city before 1912 was the "aldermanic." This form of government with the large number of councilmen, was considered to be unsatisfactory, principally because it prevented the holding of any one in particular responsible for the government's acts. A change was then agreed upon.

Commission Plan of City Government. A form of government known as the Commission plan had become popular among medium-sized cities in the Mississippi Valley. It was started by Galveston, Texas, after the great storm of 1900 and has since been adopted by more than four hundred cities.

This plan provides for conducting the business of governing a city in the same manner as operating a large corporation. The advantage of this plan is that with so small a number it is easy to fix responsibility. A few men, usually five, are elected by the people to make the laws and see to their execution, also.

Commission Plan of Government in New Orleans, 1912. It was decided in 1912 to try this plan of government in New Orleans. There was much opposition. Many persons held that such a form of government was satisfactory in small cities, but would prove a failure in a city of the size of New Orleans. However, a bill providing for a new charter giving New Orleans the commission form of government, was introduced in the legislature in May, 1912, and was passed after amendment. The general opinion at present seems to be that the commission form has proved better than its predecessors. A new era of civic activity has certainly come to life since 1912.

Political Divisions of New Orleans. New Orleans is divided into seven municipal districts, corresponding to the growth of the city by the annexation of adjoining towns. Besides the municipal districts, there is the division of the city into wards; each of the seventeen wards is entitled to one representative in the General Assembly of Louisiana. The wards are subdivided into precincts—police precincts and polling precincts. A police precinct is the district under the supervision of one police station. A polling precinct is a certain district within which there is a polling booth, where the voters residing in that precinct must cast their votes.

Community Civics. In the proper study of city government, the citizen not only learns how the government works but acquires an interest in helping to improve it.

It is an ideal of every good citizen to leave the world a little better than he found it.

Citizens have duties and responsibilities as well as rights and privileges. There are many problems facing those in authority, who live in a large community. A great deal of our comfort and well-being depends upon the government, which is deeply concerned in the inspection of milk, in screening the markets, in reducing fire risks, etc.

Therefore, we should take an interest in knowing what is done to secure pure food, in which effort the United States government, the state, and the city co-operate. We should find out what the city and state do in the matter of inspection of factories where clothing is made in order to see that they are healthful and safe.

New Orleans has a woman factory inspector to see that the laws in regard to women and children are properly observed. In order to protect the health of the citizens, the city makes laws regulating the way in which tenements shall be built with a view to securing proper air-space and ventilation.

In addition to government agencies for the well-being of the people, kind and public-spirited citizens have formed organizations that help those who are sick or are unfortunate.

SECTION 2. COMMISSION COUNCIL.

Members of the Commission Council. The Commission Council is composed of five members; namely, the Mayor and four Commissioners. Their duty is to make laws for the city and to see to their being carried out. The members of the Council must be qualified electors of the City of New Orleans; they are elected at large, that is, all are voted for by all the electors of the city without any regard to districts; they serve for a term of four years. The Mayor receives an annual salary of $10,000, and each of the Commissioners, $6,000.

Vacancies. When a vacancy occurs in the Commission Council, the Council must appoint a qualified person to serve for the unexpired portion of the term; during the vacancy, a quorum (a majority) of the whole Council exercises the powers of such officer.

Meetings. The Commission Council meets on the first Tuesday evening of each month, and as often as is thought necessary. If the returns of an election are to be opened, the meeting must be held in daylight. Meetings of the Commission Council are open to the public. The Mayor, or in his absence, the acting Mayor, presides at the meetings; the Mayor cannot veto a measure, but either he or two Commission Councilmen must sign every resolution or ordinance passed by the Council, after which it must be recorded before going into effect.

Publication. The Mayor must have all ordinances and resolutions of the Council published and the clerk of the Council must have all proceedings of the Council published for the information of the public. These publications must be in a daily newspaper of New Orleans, which shall have been in existence at least a year previous to the contract; a contract for publication must be given out at least every two years at public auction to the lowest bidder. The newspaper so contracting has to give security for the faithful performance of the work.

Council Elections. Many important city officials, such as the City Attorney, City Notary, Clerk of the Commission Council, Auditor of Public Accounts, City Engineer, City Chemist, Chief Engineer of the Fire Department, and others, are elected by a majority vote of the Commission Council, either at the first meeting of the Council or as soon thereafter as possible.

Powers of the Commission Council. The entire powers and duties of government of the city are vested in the Commission Council. The Council has not only the power, but it is their duty, to preserve peace and good order in the city, and to that end may make and see to the execution of the laws, and provide for city improvements. The Council must see that cleanliness and health are maintained in the city; that thoroughfares are kept open to traffic; that there are efficient police and fire departments, and a good system of public lighting; that the education of the city's youth is properly provided for by means of schools and libraries; that public works are maintained.

SECTION 3. DEPARTMENTS.

Distribution of Powers. The Mayor, because of his office, is Commissioner of the Department of Public Affairs. At the first regular meeting after the election, the Commission Council by a majority vote assigns one Commission Councilman to each of the other four departments (public finances, safety, utilities, and property) to be Commissioner of that department. The Commissioner of the Department of Public Finances, because of his office, is City Treasurer and serves as acting Mayor in the absence of the Mayor.

Department of Public Affairs. The Mayor is the head of the city government and has supervision of all parts of the city government. He sees to the execution of the laws of the city and state. He must sign all contracts entered into by the city and sign all bonds issued by the city. He is by virtue of his office a member of all city boards and commissions. He has charge of the seal of the city, which he affixes to all official acts. He has the power to administer oaths. He represents the city in all legal matters.

Department of Public Finances. This department has charge of the city's moneys. Accounts must be kept of the receipts and expenditures of all public moneys. The Commissioner of this department is, in the absence of the Mayor, the acting Mayor.

Department of Public Safety. The Public Safety Department is charged, as its name tells, with the maintenance of public safety. For this purpose, there are maintained the police and fire departments, board of health and public charities. The fire department has charge of the inspection of premises, with a view to their being to a certain extent fire-proof, and maintains an efficient force of firemen and engines to combat fires. The police department has a body of policemen whose duty it is to see that the laws are obeyed and that violators of the laws are brought to trial in court. The board of health has to see that sanitary conditions are maintained in the city. (See Chapter IV. Health Conditions.)

Department of Public Utilities. This department has charge of public utilities, such as street cars, telephones, gas, etc. The Commissioner of Public Utilities awards at public auction franchises, contracts, and grants to the highest or lowest bidder, according as the case may require. A franchise is a privilege granted by the city to an individual or corporation to operate a public utility under certain conditions for a specified time.

Department of Public Property. Streets and alleys, parks and playgrounds, public buildings, public baths, and other public property, except the Public Belt Railroad, are controlled by this department. The Commissioner of Public Property, with his assistants, has charge of the draining, paving, lighting, cleaning, and beautifying of the streets, parks, playgrounds, and other public places; much of the work is given out in contracts; there are park commissions that have charge of the parks and different public squares and places. This department, however, sees directly to the cleaning and watering of the streets, removal of garbage, and street paving. (See Chapter XVI., The City Beautiful.)

SECTION 4. CITY BOARDS.

Commissioners of Civil Service. In order to have better service in departments, where it is necessary that the employees have a certain educational training, the employees in such departments have been placed under civil service. By being placed under civil service is meant that they are examined as to their qualifications necessary to hold the position, and after being permanently appointed cannot be removed from office without grave cause, until the term of the appointing officer shall have expired. Positions under civil service thus have a certain permanence.

The civil service is controlled by the Board of Commissioners of Civil Service. This board is composed of the Mayor and two Commissioners selected by the Commission Council. Applicants in order to become eligible to appointment must make an average of at least seventy per cent; this eligibility expires on January thirty-first of each year. The first six months after an applicant is appointed is a period of probation; if he is not discharged during that time, he is entitled to hold the position until the expiration of the term of office of the appointing officer.

All Confederate veterans with good records are excused from any examination.

Board of Directors of the Public Schools. The Board of Directors of the Public Schools of the Parish of Orleans consists of five members, who must be electors. In 1916, five members were elected; the three receiving the highest number of votes shall serve for four years and the two receiving the lowest number of votes shall serve for two years. After that each group shall serve for four years. By this regulation, the entire membership of the board will not be changed at the same time. The election of the members of the Board of Public School Directors must be non-partisan, that is, without regard to political parties. There must be a separate column on the ballot with the heading "Board of School Directors;" the names of the candidates are placed in alphabetical order in this column. All the public schools of the Parish of Orleans and the management, property thereof, course of study and grading thereof, including text books to be used therein, are under the control of this Board of Directors.

The Board of Directors must elect a competent and experienced educator to be superintendent of the schools; this election must take place on July thirteenth of every fourth year after July thirteenth of the year 1913. The Board must also elect as many assistant superintendents as may be necessary; there must be an attendance officer and such other officers, clerks, and assistants as may be necessary to properly conduct the public schools of the parish.

The schools are supported by funds derived from the following sources:

1. Receipts from levying of school tax on assessable property of the city.
2. State appropriation, which is in proportion to the number of educable children.
3. City poll taxes.
4. Interest on daily balance in bank.
5. Smith-Hughes Fund.

Board of Commissioners of the Orleans Levee District. This board is composed of nine members possessing all the requisites of an elector; seven members are appointed by the Governor of the State from the seven municipal districts of the city; the other two members are the Mayor and the Commissioner of Public Works, who are ex-officio members. The board has charge of the construction and repair, and is vested with the control and maintenance of all levees in the Orleans District.

Board of Directors of Public Libraries. The public libraries are managed by a board of ten members. This board was originally appointed by the Mayor and City Council; vacancies, since occurring, are filled by the board itself. The members serve for life or until resignation. The Mayor is ex-officio a member and, on going out of office of the mayoralty, becomes a permanent member. The libraries are maintained by means of donations and special city appropriation; the city is under contract with Mr. Andrew Carnegie to appropriate annually for the support of the libraries, an amount equal to at least ten per cent of Mr. Carnegie's gift, which was $375,000.

SECTION 5. ELECTIONS.

Elections. An election is a choice of officials or acceptance or rejection of laws by popular vote. The parish and municipal elections in New Orleans are held on the Tuesday following the first Monday of November, 1916, and every fourth year thereafter.

Electors. Electors are those persons whom the state permits to vote in elections. In Louisiana, electors are males over twenty-one years of age and having certain qualifications; namely, residential, educational or property, and poll tax qualifications.

(1) **Residential**—An elector must be a resident of the state for two years, of the parish one year, and of the precinct six months preceding an election. Removal from a precinct, however, does not operate against an elector until six months thereafter.

(2) **Educational**—An elector must be able to write his application for registration in English or in his own tongue, or, if prevented from so doing by a physical disability, the registration officer or deputy may write it at his dictation, under his oath attesting his disability.

(3) **Property** The possession of property assessed at $300 and on which all taxes are paid, serves in place of the educational qualification.

(4) **Poll Tax**—Electors between the ages of twenty-one and sixty years must pay a poll tax of a dollar a year, which tax is used to help support the public schools of the parish. In order for an elector to vote at an election, he must have paid his poll tax for the two years preceding the year in which he offers to vote. This tax must be paid on or before December 31st of each year.

Registration. No elector may vote in an election without first registering. There is a special registration office in the City Hall, where electors register; this office is closed to registering for thirty days before an election. An elector registers by going to the registration office and filling in or having filled, as the case may be, the registration blank; this blank, when filled out, is a statement of the elector's residential and educational or property qualifications. When the elector has filled in the registration blank, the registration officer gives him a certificate of registration; this certificate is similar to a check; it bears the elector's registration number and is attached to a stub, which remains in the book when the certificate is given to the elector. The registration officer compiles books for each polling precinct, containing the name, address, registration number, and qualifications of each elector in that precinct. These books are kept at the polling booths on election day for verification of the certificates presented by the electors.

Ballot. The ballot is the official form for voting. The names of the candidates for office are arranged in parallel columns according to parties, each party has a column at the head of which is the party name and emblem. There is a space left by the parties and candidates' name for checking by the electors.

In the case of a primary election, the names are arranged on the ballot according to offices, as the ballot is a party ballot.

Voting. The polling precincts are open from six o'clock in the morning until seven in the evening. During this time, an elector must cast his vote. He must present to the election commissioners his certificate of registration and his poll tax receipts; should he have lost his poll tax receipts, he is still allowed to vote if his name is on the official list of poll tax payers, issued by the City Treasurer, copies of which list are kept at every polling booth. He is then given a ballot by the election commissioners. The elector casts the ballot in secret; he votes by checking the space after a party name, thus voting for all that party's nominees for office, or else he checks the space after each preferred candidate's name, checking not more than one name for each office; he then folds the ballot, the names inward, and drops it in the ballot box.

Counting the Votes. The polling booth is closed at seven o'clock in the evening. The commissioners of election then compile lists of the number of votes awarded each candidate for office. These statements are sworn to, placed in sealed packages, and delivered to the Mayor or acting Mayor. The Mayor or acting Mayor opens in public on the Monday following the election these sealed packages and declares the result of the election.

SECTION 6. TAXATION.

Purpose. The people are taxed for the support of the government, public education, and libraries, the operation of the sewerage and water plant, the maintenance of levees, and the payment of the city debt.

Assessment. There is a board called the

Board of Assessors, whose duty it is to assess all property, real and personal, within the limits of the city. To assess property is to place a certain value upon it. Property may not be assessed above its actual value.

At present the assessment is fixed at 75% of its actual value.

Rate of Tax. The city has fixed a rate of 18½ mills upon a 75% valuation of real and personal property, which is distributed as follows: 6½ mills for city expense tax, 10 mills for the interest and redemption of the city bonds, and 2 mills for the payment of sewerage and drainage bonds.

In addition, the School Board of the city of New Orleans, which coincides with the Parish of Orleans, levies a tax of 2¾ mills for the support of the public schools. This rate will be applied to a 100% valuation of property.

The city taxes are collected in July. Besides the city taxes, there are the state taxes for the support of the State and maintenance of the levees in the parish of Orleans; four mills on the actual cash valuation will be collected beginning with the year 1919 for defraying the expenses of the State; the levee tax for 1919 has been fixed by the Orleans Levee Board at two mills on 100% valuation. This is a variable tax from year to year.

SECTION 7. COURTS.

Necessity For Courts. In order to try persons accused of violating the city laws, such as speeding an automobile, being disorderly on the street and other offenses, three police courts have been formed for the City of New Orleans which are known as Recorders' Courts. There is also a Night Court which tries persons arrested at night in order to prevent their having to spend the night in jail if they are not guilty.

Officers. Each such court has one judge called the Recorder, appointed by the Commission Council at a salary not exceeding $2,500. He must be at least thirty-five years old and a resident of the city for five years prior to his election to office. The Council also appoints a clerk and the necessary assistant clerks. The Board of Police Commissioners details four policemen to each Recorder's Court to keep order and execute the orders and decrees of the Recorders.

Control. These courts are under the control of the Commission Council.

Appeals. Appeals may be made from these courts to the Criminal District Court.

Powers of the Recorders' Courts. All fines, penalties or forfeitures imposed by the Recorders, must be collected by them and by them paid daily to the City Treasurer; they must give to the person paying the fine or penalty, a receipt stating the amount of the fine or penalty, the date, from whom collected, name of the person fined, and for what offense. The punishment imposed by the Recorders shall not exceed a fine of twenty-five dollars ($25.00) or thirty days imprisonment.

City Criminal Courts. For offenses of a more serious nature there have been constituted the First and Second City Criminal Courts, which have authority or jurisdiction for trial without jury and the punishment of all offenses against the State where the penalty does not exceed six months' imprisonment or a fine of three hundred dollars.

Above such cases the Criminal District Court has jurisdiction.

First and Second City Courts. Two civil courts have been constituted in New Orleans to have authority over cases when the amount in dispute does not exceed one hundred dollars. One of these courts has three judges and is situated on the east bank of the Mississippi River; the other has authority over the Fifth District, which is Algiers, and has one judge only.

Above such cases the Civil District Court has jurisdiction.

SECTION 8. DISTINCTIVE FEATURES OF THE COMMISSION FORM OF GOVERNMENT.

Initiative, Referendum, and Recall. The commission form of city government has three distinct features, namely, the "initiative," "referendum," and "recall."

By the "initiative," the voters may originate legislation; this is done by 30 per cent of qualified voters demanding of the Council the passage of a measure; should the Council not pass it, they must submit it to the vote of the electors, a majority of whom can pass it over the opposition of the Council.

Ordinances, except for the immediate preservation of the public peace, health, or safety, do not go into effect before ten days following their final passage; by the "referendum," the qualified electors may within those ten days demand of the Council to repeal the ordinance or submit it to the vote of the qualified voters. Ordinances that are passed by the majority of the electors, may be repealed only by a majority vote of the electors. Special elections for passing or repealing ordinances may not be held oftener than once in a period of six months, nor within ninety days of a general municipal election.

The charter provides that "the Mayor and Commission Councilmen may be removed from office or recalled therefrom in the manner now or hereafter provided by the Constitution." The Constitution as originally written did not provide for the recall of officers, but an amendment establishing the recall was passed by the vote of the people November 3, 1914.

TOPICS: **Section 1**, **Introduction**; **Section 2**, **Commission** Council; **Section 3**, Departments; **Section 4**, **City** Boards; **Section 5**, Elections; **Section 6**, **Taxation**; **Section 7**, Courts; **Section 8**, **Distinctive Features of** the Commission Form of Government.

REFERENCES: Charter of the City of New Orleans, 1912; Constitution of the State of Louisiana.

CHAPTER XVI.

The City Beautiful.

SECTION 1. CITY BUILDING.

Conditions Governing the Location of Cities. In the early history of nations, cities were located where the best natural means of defense were offered. As the strength of their armies increased, natural means of defense were considered of secondary importance in the selection of a site. Commerce and industries were developed during eras of peace. Consequently, cities grew and flourished where easy access by water and good harbors favored trade, where swift streams afforded power to run their mills, or where mineral deposits awaited the hand of man to convert them into wealth. The perfection of the railroad has largely removed dependence upon water communication: inland towns, far from navigable lakes or rivers, have sprung up as the distributing points for great agricultural districts. One or more of these conditions has led to the establishment of American cities. The natural fortifications around Quebec made that city an early center of western civilization; New York, on the other hand, possessed peculiar commercial advantages; the New England cities were the outgrowth of manufacturers and most of the cities of the Rocky Mountain States owe their rise to the untold mineral wealth of the section and the construction of great railroads.

City Building in Ancient Times. A woman, Queen Semiramis, had decided to construct upon the banks of the Euphrates River the greatest city in the world, and thus, for the first time known to history, a city, Babylon, was built in accordance with a definite plan.

The Greeks, laboring for the attainment of knowledge and beauty, enjoyed the highest civilization of ancient times. The city of Athens, a city of exquisite beauty and long the western world's center of art and letters, was the noblest expression of their cultured civilization.

Rome becoming by her military prowess the supreme power in the western world, drew to herself the best talent of the conquered peoples. Thus she was able to erect the magnificent temples and palaces that adorned her seven hills, and to construct the military roads, solid masonry bridges, and remarkable aqueducts that displayed engineering skill of the highest order.

Value of Permanency. The works of the Greeks and Romans in great part have defied the ravages of time and the elements; this is the result of the work of builders to whom permanency was as much an ideal as beauty. These people, to have left such wonderful monuments attesting their existence as proud and powerful nations, must have been actuated by a tremendous civic spirit.

Paris. The right building of modern cities, combining healthfulness, utility, and beauty, was first undertaken in France. In the early fifties, when Napoleon III. was emperor of France, Baron Haussmann and M. Alphand, the city engineer, drew up a wonderful plan for renovating and embellishing Paris. Crooked, narrow streets were straightened and widened into magnificent boulevards; broad avenues, connecting open space with open space were laid out through densely populated districts; places, parks, and avenues were beautified with trees and masterpieces of art. Hence it has been said of Napoleon III. in regard to Paris that "he found it brick and left it marble."

Garden Cities of England. The city planning movement in England has developed garden cities. The most noted of these are Letchworth and Hempstead, whose sites were purchased by companies. Neat, attractive cottages or apartments, surrounded by gardens, are provided the working classes at nominal rent. The result in beauty, convenience, health, happiness, and efficiency have fully justified the experiment.

City Planning in America. Few American cities have been built along any definite plan;

they have grown up haphazard, according to the press of conditions or the whims of individuals. Washington, which ranks as one of the most beautiful cities in the world, is a notable exception. When a site on the Potomac was selected for the national capital, President Washington, recognizing systematic planning to be necessary for growth, prosperity, and artistic development, employed Charles L'Enfant, a young French engineer, to lay out the city. The growth of Washington continued in accordance with L'Enfant's plan. The formal plan of rectangular blocks crossed by broad, diagonal thoroughfares, terminating at circles, civic centers, or open squares, is well adapted to a city so pre-eminently official and social.

The architectural features of Washington's imposing buildings are enhanced by the radial avenues, affording numerous leafy vistas, as the parks and streets of the city on the Potomac are the greenest and shadiest in the world.

Many American cities have drawn their inspiration in city planning from the beauty of the national capital. The Columbian Exposition, held in Chicago in 1893, demonstrated the advantages of spacious approaches and proper grouping of well-designed buildings, and exerted a marked influence. Chicago began to form a definite idea of the "City Beautiful" and to evolve a comprehensive plan for civic embellishment.

Cleveland, with characteristic enthusiasm, called upon the best talent to create for her a plan of utility and compelling beauty. The dominant feature in the renovation of Cleveland is the civic center. Along a broad thoroughfare are grouped the principal public buildings representative of the great functions of a city.

Boston, like New Orleans, is a city with traditions. These she cherishes and embodies in her churches, her inns, her architecture. No towering skyscrapers loom up beside dark, tunnel-like alleys, or shut out the blessed sunlight and fresh air from more lowly neighbors. Boston further shows her belief in the salutary effect of nature's restoratives by her admirable system of public parks, and her regard for the value of beauty and recreation by developing and embellishing the water front along the Charles River.

Experts are now at work on a plan that will render New York City pre-eminent in civic beauty as she is now in size and wealth.

Many other American cities are awakening to a sense of their responsibility toward the citizen. There is a growing realization of the need not only of hygienic conditions and business facilities in cities, but, also, of beauty; for people need, not only good health and means of earning a livelihood, but, also, sources of right enjoyment and inspiration, if they are to accomplish great works. This beauty is attained by spacious and tastefully adorned streets and parks and by an architecture characteristic and suitable to the people and place.

SECTION 2. BUILDING OF NEW ORLEANS.

Original Plan of New Orleans. Bienville, having convinced the authorities of the advantages of a town on the Mississippi River, sent de la Tour to plan the new city. Only a few huts built by voyageurs who had come down the River occupied the site Bienville had chosen. The engineer cleared a strip along the River and with the help of some piquers, located the streets, dividing the town into rectangular squares. De la Tour's plan embraced the rectangle now bounded by Bienville, North Rampart, Barracks, and the River; it provided for an open square or Place d'Armes around which were to be grouped the parish church, school, and government building, and it divided each square into plots or building sites to be given to settlers on condition that they should enclose the property with palisades and open along the street a ditch to serve as a drain for river water in times of inundation; Bienville selected a site on the outskirts for his residence, which, when occupied by the Ursulines in 1727, was still "in the depth of the forest."

Changes in the Shape of New Orleans. The city did not adhere in its growth to this rectangular plan. Owing to the greater height of land being along the river front and the boat landings all being there, the stream of settlement took that course also, and the rectangle was expanded on either side into a crescent, hence the name, "Crescent City." Growth in population has caused further advance up and down the curving River, so that now the harbor resembles an elongated "S"; the city is now also expanding towards Lake Pontchartrain, in fact reaches the Lake, between West End and Spanish Fort.

Influence of Climate and Available Building Material. Before long, the squares near the Place d'Armes were covered with rude habitations built of logs plastered with clay and thatched with palmettoes from the nearby swamp. Glass window panes were an unknown luxury in those days; even Bienville's house is described as having "the sashes covered with fine, thin linen which let in as much light as glass and more air." The primitive structures were gradually replaced by larger and better buildings of brick made from the abundant clay. Time hardened and strengthened this brick, and, as the framework and floors were of cypress, a wood unaffected by dampness, these buildings were remarkably durable. The first Ursuline convent, constructed of brick and cypress in the time of Bienville, is the oldest building in the Mississippi Valley and is still in splendid condition. Brick houses became more prevalent, not only because of their durability, but also because they were much cooler than frame houses. Climatic conditions favored the adaptation of broad central halls, long galleries shielding from intense glare, and thick walls through which little heat could penetrate.

Early French and Spanish Influence. New Orleans has an individuality, both charming and unique. The Vieux Carré, with its narrow streets and close rows of solid, somber houses with dormer windows and batten shutters, looks less a part of an American city than of some Old World town transplanted to this continent. One reason for the compactness of Old New Orleans was the need for defense against the Indians; and besides the early inhabitants brought with them ideas of French and Spanish cities, where the streets were made narrow to avoid the direct rays of the sun. Spanish architectural features predominate because most of the original French buildings were destroyed by the devastating fires of 1788 and 1794. After that the tiled roofs, still a picturesque feature of the French quarter, came into use. The solid walls of adobe or brick, paved courtyards, ponderous doors, iron-barred windows, massive arched doorways, and wrought-iron balconies over-hanging the banquettes bespeak Spanish influence. On three sides of Jackson Square are the most imposing relics of that influence, namely, the old St. Louis Cathedral, Cabildo, and Presbytere facing the River, and the red brick Pontalba buildings to the sides of the Square.

The courtyard, affording a cool secluded place for family rest or recreation, is one of the most attractive features of the section below Canal Street. Walled in by the great houses, these paved courts broaden out behind narrow entrances through which the passer-by may catch delightful glimpses of palms and ferns, old-fashioned parterres, and, occasionally, a graceful Spanish water jar or iron fountain. But the individuality of New Orleans is more strikingly emphasized by the second-story galleries extending over the banquettes from residences, shops, cafés, or old office buildings, offering generous shelter from sun and rain. There in the heart of the city, where every foot of ground bears its burden of masonry or timber, these galleries form hanging gardens, gay with feathery ferns and potted shrubs—bright color against the dingy faces of old weatherworn piles. The houses built after the American occupation are modifications of French and Spanish styles. Brick and timber, easily obtained from the surrounding country, were the chief materials used in their construction.

Building Ornamentation. Peculiarly characteristic of New Orleans architecture are the balustrades and fences of wrought-iron in elaborate and intricate patterns. Some show conventional designs, some flowers or trailing vines, but one very beautiful craftsmanship represents growing corn laden with ripened ears over which the flowering tassel waves with singular grace. Occasionally, as on the Pontalba buildings, there is a distinctive pattern formed by twining initials in the delicate traceries. The balustrades, so varied in design and beauty, are the work of mastercraftsmen, and are treasured as exquisite examples of a now almost lost art. The ingenuity and patient labor of these wondrous workers is strikingly proven by the fact that among the thousands of balustrades to be found in New Orleans, a duplicate is seldom seen.

American Influence. After the cession of 1803, the influx of Americans spread the city beyond its original limits and gradually transformed its architectural types. Some old American residences still standing in St. Charles Street and lower Carondelet, resemble those of the Vieux Carré, but with an open lawn or well kept garden instead of the closed courtyard. In the Garden District, still one of the most beautiful residential sections, fine homes with broad verandas supported by classic columns bespeak the influence of the Colonial style of the Georgian period. Large grounds enclosed by high iron fences, hedges, or walls complete the dignity and exclusiveness of these homes.

Modern Homes. To a city so accessible by rail and water, lack of material is no longer a stumbling block to diversity in building. Vermont granite, Tennessee marble, steel from Pennsylvania, cypress, oak, walnut, gum, and many other useful or ornamental woods from Louisiana's forests, have contributed to the construction of the New Orleans of today. Brick, artistically finished and as durable as stone, no longer needs a coat of plaster, and is used effectively; it is especially pleasing as a background for the white pillars of the English colonial residences. The cosmopolitan population, as well as variety of material, caused a defection from the early types of architecture. Indeed, except for public buildings, the architecture of the city at the present day, can hardly be said to possess a type. In architecture the practical need comes first, but parallel with this is the aesthetic need. Unfortunately, both are frequently overlooked in the construction of modern dwellings, which too often, are mere shelters for human beings or are modelled after plans totally unsuited to the climate. New Orleans, so rich in traditions, so indelibly marked by a distinctive type in her earlier architecture, a type, which, in itself, gives her individuality, and charm, should, like other cities with older associations, seek to perpetuate and vivify this individuality, and increase this charm. Imitation of other cities is a mistake. She has her own ideals. Why should they be forgotten in her progress?

One of the best examples of the Spanish colonial type is the old Newcomb pottery building. It is neither large nor pretentious, but with its small-paned windows and iron-railed balconies adheres closely to the style it represents, amply proving that an evolution of the native architecture is best suited to the natural environments.

Buildings of Note. As building is the outward expression of the life of a community, some of the most important structures in New Orleans have been described in relation to some phase of human activity. For example, the Post Office, the Custom House, the New Court building, are representative structures, and find their places in other chapters. Many churches are fine examples of the different architectural schools.

The City Hall was built in 1850 by Gallier after the plan of the temple of Minerva on the Athenian Acropolis. A broad flight of granite steps ascend to the entrance, high above the street. Massive Grecian columns support a lofty portico, the frieze of which is adorned by a bas-relief of Justice and figures emblematic of the commerce of the Mississippi Valley.

In the business section of New Orleans are several skyscrapers—the Grunewald Hotel, Maison Blanche, Hibernia Bank Building, and the Whitney-Central building—none however, rival the skyscrapers of New York. High buildings are unsuited to New Orleans, first, it is difficult to secure sufficiently firm foundations to bear their weight, and, second, the concentration of business within a small area congests traffic in streets which are scarcely wide enough to accommodate the usual procession of vehicles.

Streets. With the exception of the section laid out by de la Tour, New Orleans has never been officially planned. The streets have followed the line of least resistance or have been opened up by speculators who exploit the attractiveness of a particular section for immediate gain rather than for the permanent benefit to the community. The result has been great irregularity and lack of uniformity. In general, the streets running north and south conform in broad, sweeping curves to the direction of the River, and are crossed by other streets which converge or radiate, sometimes meeting to form triangles, sometimes ending abruptly at intersections. These curves become less evident in streets at a distance from the River, and the blocks of the newly developed section toward the Lake are, for the most part, rectangular. Some New Orleans streets have attained more than local fame. The narrow streets of the Vieux Carré are noted for the picturesqueness and Old World charm characteristic of that section. Canal Street, the broad thoroughfare 170 feet wide, which divides the city into two sections—north and south—is the great center of the city's retail trade, the heart of its business life. St. Charles Avenue, a shady boulevard from Lee Circle to Carrollton Avenue, curves with the winding of the River and its width of 128 feet affords splendid views on either side of the residences in the midst of their lovely gardens. The neutral ground is beautified with a green sward and crêpe myrtles, oleanders, palms, and oaks. The imposing buildings of Tulane and Loyola Universities facing Audubon Park, enhance the avenue's natural attractiveness. Besides good architectural features, many structures are enhanced by their exceptionally advantageous locations, as, for instance, the New Orleans Public Library. It was indeed a fortunate occurrence that caused the library to be erected where St. Charles Avenue terminates at Lee Circle, thus giving it several splendid prospects.

Present Movement in Behalf of Conservation and Improvement. The cry to abolish by city ordinance the galleries and balconies which shelter the sidewalks in the business section is raised in the name of progress by those who would rob New Orleans of a distinctive charm and reconstruct her according to the stereotyped pattern of some cities in the Middle West. Artists, architects, and travellers have praised these galleries. Edward Hungerford wrote of them: "The galleries of New Orleans! They are perhaps the most typical of the outward expressions of a town whose personality is as distinct as that of Boston, Charleston, or San Francisco.... She (New Orleans) well knows the commercial value of her personality. There are newer cities and showier within the radius of a single night's ride upon a fast train. But where one man comes to one of these, a dozen alight at the old French town by the bend of the yellow river." Concurrent with the movement for the retention of galleries is the still more recent agitation for conserving fine old trees, which having taken generations to attain maturity, cannot be repalced in a single day.

The Association of Commerce under the guidance of a zealous and energetic president, and the women's clubs are actively furthering the cause of the "City Beautiful." The campaign, earnestly waged in behalf of more harmonious architecture and more pleasing streets, strenuously opposes towering skyscrapers, and urges the abolition of violently assertive and glaring advertisements, unsightly shops in residential districts, and prosaic forests of poles with their burden of overhead wires. Street improvement has resulted in more spacious thoroughfares with ample provision for neutral grounds and banquettes, allowing free circulation of air; better pavement and drainage; and more lavish use of greenery, performing both a utilitarian and an aesthetic mission by absorbing carbonic gases and by giving out oxygen, by relieving monotony, and by speaking to the hearts of men the uplifting language of nature. The city government has manifested interest and a desire to co-operate in the movement. It supports a nursery to supply trees for civic adornment and it is gradually introducing a system of ornamental street lighting.

Monuments. The most imposing monument in New Orleans is that in memory of General Robert E. Lee. It surmounts a large grassy mound and is a shaft 107 feet high. At the top is a fine bronze statue of the great Confederate leader.

At the entrance to the City Park is a very handsome bronze equestrian statue of General Beauregard.

Surrounded by the wonderful live oaks and flowering shrubs, there is a beautiful monument to the great bird lover and scientist, John Audubon, who is claimed by Louisiana as a native son. The unique statute to a woman, the philanthropist, called Margaret, is mentioned in Chapter XI. on page 107.

Jackson Square has a very fine equestrian statue of General Andrew Jackson, the hero of the battle of New Orleans. Lafayette Square has a statue of John McDonogh, mentioned on pages 133-134, also a fine statue of Henry Clay.

Liberty Monument, at the foot of Canal Street, is a silent witness to the overthrow of reconstruction government. See page 38.

On the Jefferson Davis Parkway, there is a striking monument to the President of the Southern Confederacy.

SECTION 3. PUBLIC PLEASURE GROUNDS.

Need of Open Spaces in Cities. Public parks and squares have been called the lungs of great cities; they are as necessary to the health of a community as the organs of breathing are to an individual. Disease is fostered, human life shortened by the dusty, foul, ill-smelling atmosphere of congested districts. Since present economic conditions force people to live in such surroundings, it is the duty of the municipality to provide some means of alleviation. As many workers have neither time nor money to go long distances in search of fresh air, small parks distributed through every section of the city, supply this need. The trees and shrubs help to purify the atmosphere and afford a pleasant relief from the monotony of workshops or offices.

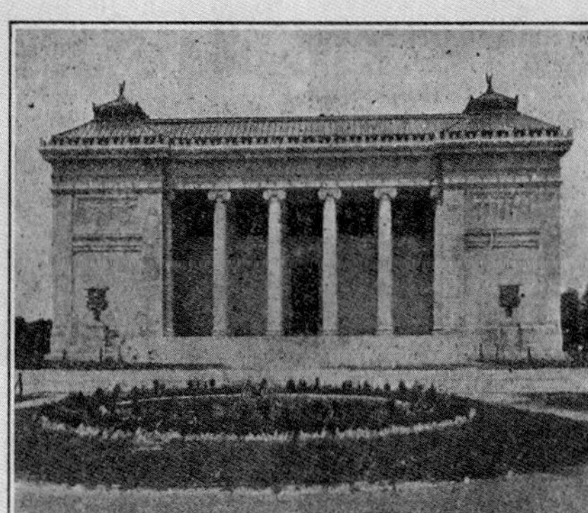

DELGADO ART MUSEUM.

The French Place. The French, particularly, make generous use of the small parks or places usually a center around which important buildings are grouped, or as parts of a system connected by splendid boulevards or driveways. When de la Tour planned New Orleans, he provided for an open square, the Place d'Armes, now Jackson Square, to serve the double purpose of a place of recreation for the public and, as the old name implies, a parade ground for the soldiers.

The Park: Function. The small parks and squares serve a purpose, but every city needs a large park, a place where people can seek rest and seclusion away from the noises and oppressive atmosphere of the heart of the city. The park supplies a physical need for sunshine, fresh air, and quiet, by offering a means of wholesome relaxation and change; it stimulates mental activity; and through the beauties of nature ordered and arranged by the art of man, it fosters a love of the beautiful.

New Orleans Parks: City Park and Audubon Park. A large portion of the area of City Park was the property of Louis Allard, which, being sold for mortgages, became the property of John McDonogh. The former owner, then in the decline of life, was allowed to pass his remaining years at his old home, and was laid to rest beneath the stately oaks he had loved so well. McDonogh willed the plantation with the rest of his estate to the cities of Baltimore and New Orleans. Baltimore abandoned her claim in payment of taxes; New Orleans then set aside the tract as a public park. It remained unimproved for many years, until placed in the hands of a commission. The commissioners had to solve the problem of converting a swamp through which sluggish bayous wound their tortuous course, into a beautiful spot for rest and recreation. The swamps were drained, the underbrush cleared, and the muddy, stagnant bayous transformed into winding lagoons arched by artistic bridges. City Park now charms all nature-lovers. The wonderful trees of City Park, in particular the mighty live oaks, are noted; nearly every tree found in Louisiana is represented; the principal ones beside the live oaks, being the magnolia, pine, cedar, cypress, and camphor. In the spring, the huge wistaria vines laden with their gorgeous lavender blossoms, give an oriental touch to the landscape. The open-air rose garden is an object of attention and admiration, the year round. The Delgado Art Museum is in the center of the park, by the side of the little lake. As its name implies, it was the gift of Isaac Delgado. Very fittingly, the edifice was fashioned after a Greek temple and is itself a work of art. The exhibit, though still small, contains many pieces of value. Mr. Delgado made a donation to the exhibit; Mr. Morgan Whitney bequeathed to it his collection of jades, and Mrs. Chapman Hyams, her beautiful art collection valued at $250,000. Mr. Cline has lent a very valuable collection of antiquities and Dr. Joseph Holt a beautiful collection of Japanese porcelain. A lovely prospect may be obtained of the museum, from the bridge that crosses Bayou St. John at the foot of Esplanade, through the long avenue of trees and palms that leads up to the museum.

Audubon Park was formerly the Foucher plantation. Pierre Foucher obtained the upper part in 1793, and the lower part in 1825. This lower section is of peculiar historic interest. It was part of Etienne de Boré's plantation where sugar was first granulated in 1794, and where Charles Gayarré, Louisiana's eminent historian, passed his youth. The Foucher plantation was purchased by the city in 1871, and was known as Upper City Park; in 1887, it was renamed "Audubon Park," in honor of the great naturalist. A statue in the central portion of the park, now also serves to honor his memory. The park was unimproved up to the Cotton Centennial Exposition; but the Exposition directed attention to the park as an important and easily improved asset to the city. Its natural advantages have been well utilized. Extending from St. Charles Avenue to the River, it has an unusual expanse. The broad green swards, clusters and avenues of palms and trees, and the far-famed grove of magnificent, old live oaks have an unfailing æsthetic appeal. A large artificial lake has been constructed and adds the final touch to the beautiful landscape of Audubon Park.

Two Park Commissions administer the affairs of the parks and see to the improvements.

Squares and Playgrounds. New Orleans is singularly fortunate in the number of small parks, or open squares and playgrounds distributed throughout the city. There is Jackson Square, the old Place d'Armes, famous in history and romance; Lafayette Square, between the City Hall and the new Post Office; Coliseum Place, a favorite resort for children; Annunciation Square, Washington Square, and many others serve as breathing spots for residents of crowded districts. The playgrounds, equipped with swings, see-saws, merry-go-rounds, and other apparatus that delight the hearts of children, are kept up in many parts of the city. Boys and girls not only reap the benefit of sunshine, fresh air, and exercise so necessary to build up the bone and tissue of growing limbs, but they are taught organization, self-control, and responsibility by means of supervised games. New Orleans has more fresh-air space per-capita than any other city in the world, for no city with equal population, and but one or two with greater population, include such a large area.

Flora of New Orleans. So varied is the vegetation of this semi-tropical climate that an attempt to list its trees, shrubs, and flowers would be a heavy task. Here, the

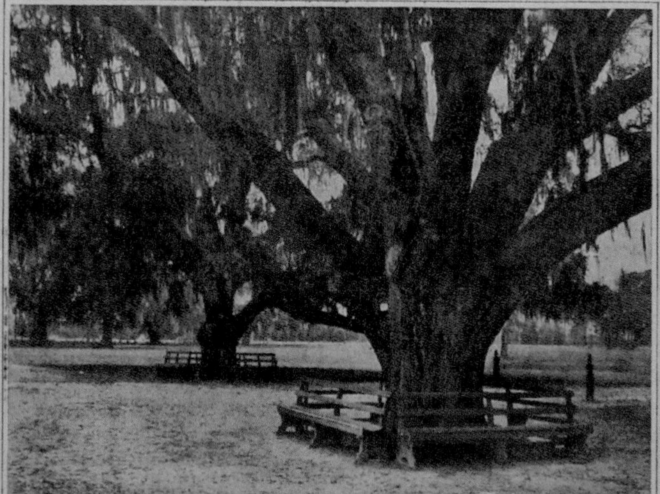

OAKS IN AUDUBON PARK.

hardy plants of colder climes thrive side by side with the delicate products of warmer regions. Many more varieties of trees are found in Louisiana than in the State of California; the most conspicuous are the varieties of oaks, the cypress, poplar, willow, pecan, beautiful white-flowering magnolia and linden. Among the shrubs that adorn the parks and gardens, are the crêpe myrtle and oleander of several different colors, the sweet olive, the camellia, white, pink, and red, and an endless variety of jasmines. Roses of every description and color thrive; the hibiscus, hydrangea, and beautiful crimson poinsettia adorn the gardens. "Parterres" are flled with a profusion of annuals, sweet alysum, marigold, petunia, phlox, pansies, portulaca, balsams. The wistaria, which in spring is massed with delicate and exquisite clusters of lavender blossoms, and the trailing rosa montana, whose delicate deep coral sprays burst into bloom in late summer, grace many a gallery, fence, and arbor. An eminent botanist has said, "Though perhaps the flora of Louisiana lacks the tropical beauty of Florida, or the stupendous grandeur of the forests of California, yet in the diversity and variety of its plant life, it is second probably to no State in the Union."

Birds. Altogether, about one hundred and fifty species of birds have been noted from time to time within the settled area of the city. About ten of these are common residents to be seen regularly at any season, and include the vultures, grackle, or crow blackbird, cardinal, mockingbird, and Carolina Wren. Added to this number in summer and nesting more or less freely in the parks and elsewhere in the residential sections, are the cuckoo, chimney swift, orchard oriole, purple martin, red-eyed vireo and gnatcatcher.

The bare trees of winter reveal the waxwing and myrtle and orange-crowned warblers, while the live oak often shelters the diminutive kinglet, all of which come to the latitude of New Orleans in fall from the north, returning there in the spring.

The largest class of birds found in this vicinity, however, consists of migratory species that appear for only limited periods in spring and fall as they pass between northern nesting grounds and winter homes in the tropics. Various warblers, several species of thrushes, vireos and fly-catchers, cat birds, indigo buntings, Baltimore orioles, scarlet tanagers, rose-breasted grosbeaks, and swallows in great numbers often make their appearance in favorable weather in spring and fall while the water bird-life at New Orleans in winter is justly celebrated because it includes the ducks, the aquatic species found there in summer are more showy than those of winter. The herons, gallinules, least bittern, and white ibis are attractive forms inhabiting the swamp and marsh in greater or less abundance.

Many favorable localities for the study of birds are found immediately about New Orleans, and in a comparatively small area, such diversified forms of bird-life as the anhinga, or water turkey, pileated woodpecker, crested fly catcher, painted bunting, white-eyed vireo, Carolina chickadee, prothonotary warbler and wood thrush may be found in summer, or some of these with the kildeer, sparrow hawk, phoebe, swamp sparrow, palm warbler and pipit in winter.

SECTION 4. PAVING.

Necessity for Paving. The question of pavements is one of great importance to a municipality. With the growth of a city and the consequent increase in traffic, paving becomes a necessity, for the continual hauling of heavy vehicles produces stifling dust in dry weather and impassable bogs during rains. And again, an unpaved street is both a hindrance to traffic, and a menace to health. It cannot be so easily or thoroughly cleaned as smooth pavement; even after sprinkling, the germ-laden dust soon rises with the passing of every vehicle; the drainage is less perfect than on a paved street; and, too often, it is an unsightly dumping ground for trash. Hence the needs of traffic, sanitary conditions, and the appearance of the city make paving necessary.

Early Paving. The conditions of New Orleans streets drained by open wooden gutters and bordered by wooden sidewalks was far from being sanitary. In 1817, in the face of much skepticism on account of the nature of the soil, the block on Gravier Street between Tchoupitoulas and Magazine, was paved with cobblestones. This was the first paving laid in New Orleans, and proving successful was gradually increased. In 1820, brick sidewalks replaced those of wood on the main thoroughfares, but it was not until 1821 that any systematic attempt was made to pave the streets. As there is no stone near the city, material for paving had to be brought from a great distance. In order to obtain stone, the city offered a premium for rock ballast. This plan was quite effectual. The heavy Belgian block was laid in a pretty diagonal pattern on many streets. Although some of the Belgian block still remains, the heavy traffic and the insecure foundation have caused the patterns long since to disappear. St. Charles Street was paved in 1822 and work begun on several commercial streets in the old and new town; but the impulse toward municipal improvements soon subsided. Up to 1835, only two streets had been paved for any considerable length; elsewhere, vehicles sank up to the hub in mire after heavy rains. The first paving with square granite blocks was done in 1850.

Paving at Present Time. New Orleans covers such an extensive area that, although there are several hundred miles of paved streets, there are many times that amount still unpaved. The kinds of pavement now being used in New Orleans are asphalt (pitch), rock asphalt, bithulithic, mineral rubber, granitoid, wood block, and granite block.

Asphalt. Asphalt is either obtained from natural lakes in Trinidad and Venezuela or is manufactured here from crude oil. The asphalt is not laid upon the soil. The model pavement of any kind must first have a six-inch concrete base next to the soil to give solidity and strength. The heat of the sun somewhat softens the asphalt, and heavy wagons passing over it in this condition indent it; in these depressions, the water collects and rots the pavement. To prevent the asphalt from slipping, a two-inch binder course of tar and crushed stone is laid over the concrete before the asphalt is applied. The tar sticks firmly to the concrete and the rough edges of the stone hold the asphalt in place. For the final layer, about 75 per cent. of river and lake sand is mixed with 12 per cent asphalt, the remaining portion consisting of mineral dust, or powdered granite used as a "filler." These are thoroughly mixed and heated to 250°, so that the total amount of expansion may take place in the mass. It is laid hot upon the surface of the street, and, in cooling, contracts, holding firmly to the rough surface of the binder. Immediately after the mixture is spread upon the street, it is rolled with a five-ton roller to compress particles of sand together in a solid mass. Asphalt pavement can be laid about as cheaply in New Orleans as elsewhere, because sand is easily procured and the asphalt is either made here or transported by water.

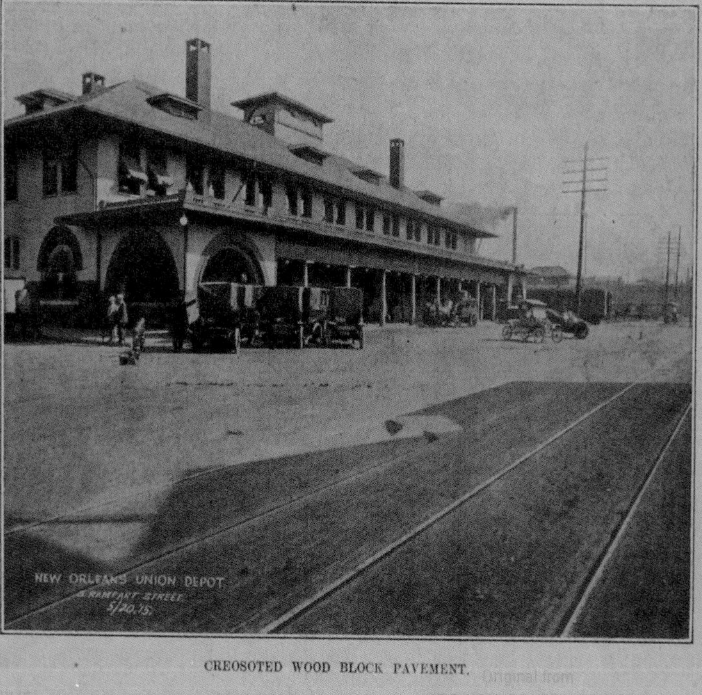

CREOSOTED WOOD BLOCK PAVEMENT.

Creosoted Wood Block. The best kind of pavement for heavy traffic is the creosoted wood block. It may be considered a home product, for the blocks are made from the native long leaf yellow pine. In the manufacture of the creosoted wood blocks, the pine is cut into blocks of uniform size. They are subjected to the vacuum process, which evaporates all sap and water, leaving the blocks porous. Creosote under heavy pressure is forced into the cylinder containing the blocks, which thus become permeated with the creosote. This pavement costs about 30 per cent. more than asphalt, as most of the creosote is imported, but the expense, ultimately, is not greater, for it lasts longer and does not require as frequent repair. The creosoted wood block is noiseless, compared with pavements of less elastic material; it is sanitary, as creosote is a germicide, and it endures without injury enormous weight and great shocks, as the falling of heavy machinery. Therefore the floors of foundries and other manufacturing places, and the docks are being paved with creosoted wood blocks. The government machine shops in Balboa, Canal Zone, are paved with this material.

Expenditure for Paving. The City pays one-fourth the cost of paving single streets and one-third the cost of double streets; the property holders pay the balance according to the frontage of their property along the street to be paved. On streets where car lines run, the railway company paves between the tracks and eighteen inches on either side, or the entire street, according to their franchise for each section.

SECTION 5. STREET LIGHTING.

Necessity of Street Lighting. Efficient street lighting serves a threefold purpose: it beautifies a city, prevents accidents, and lessens crime. Proper arrangement of lights supported by ornamental brackets or poles, adds to the artistic appearance of streets by day as well as by night. Robbers make use of dark streets where they can hide unobserved while waiting to attack unsuspecting persons; carriages, not having the powerful lights of the automobiles may come to grief, or pedestrians, groping their way in darkness may meet with some accident.

Street Lighting in the Past. Governor Carondelet, responsible for much municipal improvement, first established a system of street lighting in New Orleans (See Page 20). The use of oil lamps, suspended from wooden posts at the street intersections, continued well into the period of American rule. The light from these penetrated but a short distance, thus blocks where trees overhung the street, were shrouded in darkness. The sidewalks were inferior and those persons called forth for business or pleasure after nightfall, carried lanterns. Through the dim-lit streets, many a gay party made its way preceded by servants bearing swinging lights that daintily slippered feet might avoid foot-falls and mud-puddles. Gas street lamps were introduced about 1833 and continued in use for over half a century. Some of the old-time residents may still remember the lamp-lighter, who at dusk made his round; as the use of electricity gradually superseded gas, he became a less familiar figure and now is seen no more.

Present City Lighting. The cost of arc lights with underground connection, is greater than those with overhead wires; but the former are preferable because of the unsightliness of the overhead wires. Many cities require telephone, telegraph, trolley, and lighting wires to be placed underground. In some parts of the city, the arc lights at street intersections, are being replaced by incandescent lights along the block. The effect is much more beautiful, and the light more evenly distributed, especially where large trees overhang the street.

SECTION 6. CIVIC VIRTUES.

Kindness and Cheerfulness. By nature a social being, man should not ignore his relation to society. These very relations give rise to certain obligations; one of the greatest of these is to consider the happiness of others. The cultivation of a kindly cheerful disposition ready with little deeds of good will, sympathy, and hospitality to disseminate sunshine through the world is a duty both to self and to one's fellow-men. The value of a kind and cheerful disposition cannot be over-estimated.

Order and Cleanliness. Barbarous men do not know the use of water; the savages of Africa anoint their bodies with oil; the nomads of the desert rub their skin with sand; civilized people recognize the agreeable and salutary effects of the unstinted use of soap and water. Clean thoughts and clean language are even more obligatory than bodily cleanliness, because vulgarity of speech, profane or obscene language, not only offend sensitive natures, but poison minds and hearts. Personal cleanliness should be accompanied by good order in one's surroundings: the condition of a home indicates the character of its inmates. People who take pride in the attractive appearance of their property, who allow no breeding place for rats and roaches, who are too orderly to throw trash in public places, are a desirable element in any community.

Honesty and Courage. Honesty in public and private life has many phases; it implies freedom from pretense, truthfulness of speech, being worthy of confidence, fidelity to trust reliability in the performance of duty, sincerity, uprightness, integrity, and a high sense of justice in all human relations. Without such qualities in men and women, the whole fabric of law and order would be destroyed. The steadfast adherence to the dictates of honor, requires more moral courage than physical bravery. When boys and girls resist the inclination to cheat or tell untruths, they are laying a foundation of character, which will develop into right citizenship. This moral courage gives also the power to bear responsibility, which, as long as men live together, will fall to the lot of all.

Self-Control. Will power is needed for the governance of man's lower inclinations. Intemperance in any form, is a lack of self-control. Those who wish to preserve vigor of body and mind, to be useful to the community in which they live, and to render patriotic service to their country, must be temperate in the use of alcholic beverages, and narcotic stimulants and drugs which, especially during the period of youth, retard physical and mental growth. Self-control implies moderation in the pursuit of pleasure, the lack of which leads to wastefulness, poverty, and dissipation. Quiet conduct in public places and repression during performances, are necessary for the convenience and pleasure of others.

Industry. Thrift and industry go hand in hand. Idleness is far-reaching in its results; it is largely responsible for ignorance, poverty, and vice; it helps to fill prisons, reformatories, and insane asylums, throwing a heavy burden upon the municipality or the state. On the other hand industry brings self-respect, contentment, comfort, and increase in skill. All are not called upon to work in the same way; some are more proficient in lines of mental activity, while others succeed better at manual labor. But as every one has the power to work in some manner, every one must labor. The history of the world teaches the reward of labor and the punishment of idleness. For a city to be truly great, it is necessary that the citizens be industrious.

Respect for Authority. Authority is lawfully constituted power of control and direction. Respect for authority is the recognition of that power and rendering it obedience. In Chapter XV., it was seen how it was necessary in a city to have persons in authority, to have a government. Since that authority is necessary, it follows that it must be recognized and obeyed, else why have the authority? Lack of respect for authority, is a chief fault of the youth of the United States, resulting, perhaps, from a misunderstanding of freedom. The independence of a people cannot be maintained without authority, for, in its absence, unruly persons would disregard the rights of others in the attempt to satisfy their own desires. Respect for authority implies respect for all persons in whom authority is vested, whether it be parents or guardians, teachers, or officials of the city, state or nation.

Courtesy. Courtesy is an elegance of manner resulting from consideration of the needs of others. It is "the virtue of civilization." Its exercise is an indication of good breeding and intelligence, and requires compliance with the accepted rules of social intercourse. Reverence for old age without regard to station, dress, or other circumstances, and honor and respect for women, have become the essentials of the Southern ideal of courtesy, an ideal made world-famous by the past generations of Southern men. In the Southland men and boys do not speak to women without raising their hats; upon a woman entering an elevator, they remove their hats; in the street cars, the men stand that the women may have the seats; people say "please" when asking for something, and "thank you" on receiving it; the aged are assisted across thoroughfares, up and down stairs. A worthy example of this thoughtfulness is the kindly assistance the conductors on the cars extend to passengers entering or leaving the cars, especially in the case of the aged, whom they assist to ascend and alight from the cars. Such courtesy is possible only by the continual performance of courteous acts, resulting in the formation of a habit that gains the good-will of others for the possessor and adds grace and charm to his personality.

Civic Interest. Something has been said of what other cities with great civic spirit have accomplished. Every good citizen takes an interest in the affairs of his municipality, votes, pays his taxes, and lends his support to all movements for progress and improvements. Children can manifest civic interest by caring for public property, in particular, by not mutilating the interior or exterior of public buildings, trees, or flowers, by caring for library books, by being active workers in the cause of order and cleanliness. (Chapter XV.)

The Beauty of Right Living. In this chapter, many kinds of material beauty have been considered. Now, we come to view beauty which is far more than any of those; it is not a thing of matter like the beautiful flowers, nor is it generally short-lived, for it becomes in time the heritage of the generations; it is the beauty of right living. The beauty of right living is the root of happiness; if a person possessed every kind of material beauty in the world, and, yet, did not live rightly, that person would not be happy. And what is right living? Ordering one's life so as to do all the good possible, and to refrain from all the evil possible. For a child to live rightly, he must be like the most useful English verbs, active and passive; active in the commission of good deeds, but passive when it comes to the commission of bad ones. Right living gains for a person the admiration and affection of family and friends, and the appreciation of a worthy community. To live rightly, a boy or girl must act well not only at home and in school, but in the public thoroughfares and places, amusements resorts, etc. It implies an adherence to those civic virtues we have considered, and to other virtues, that may be known to us to be necessary, and requires continued effort for its attainment. The beauty of right living is the fruit of worthy deeds and is possible of attainment by all persons, for it is independent of wealth, great intelligence, and physical beauty, depending solely on the good will of the individual.

TOPICS: **Section 1,** City Building; **Section 2,** Building of New Orleans; **Section 3,** Public Pleasure Grounds; **Section 4,** Paving; **Section 5,** Street Lighting; **Section 6,** Civic Virtues.

REFERENCES: European Cities at Work, F. C. Howe; Personality of American Cities, E. Hungerford; History and Conditions of New Orleans, Waring and Cable; Commissioner of Public Property, City Hall.

SUPPLEMENT

DEFINITION OF A CONSTITUTION.

The State government is regulated by the State Constitution, which is a document made by the people through a convention held for that purpose. It prescribes the form of government, and is the basic law of the State. The Constitution is frequently changed by the majority vote of the people at election. The United States Constitution is above the State Constitution, just as the State is above the City.

The State Constitution begins with The Bill of Rights.

OUTLINE OF STATE GOVERNMENT.

Bill of Rights.

By the "Bill of Rights," the citizen has what are known as his civil rights secured to him, such as life, liberty, and property.

The "Bill of Rights" maintains that government originates with the people, rests on their will, and is established for the good of all. "To secure justice, preserve peace, and promote the interests and happiness of the people" is the only lawful end of government.

The people of the State are secure in the enjoyment of life, liberty, property, freedom of religion and of speech. The courts are thrown open to all for the enjoyment of impartially dispensed justice. Arms are allowed to be carried when not concealed. In trials, the accused is granted an impartial jury, the assistance of counsel, and the forced attendance of witnesses for his defense, and is confronted with his accusers and is informed of the nature and cause of the accusation brought against him. No person may be compelled to give evidence of a criminal nature against himself. There may be no excessive bail nor fines, nor cruel and unusual punishments. "The privilege of the writ of habeas corpus" can only be suspended in time of invasion or rebellion, or whenever else the public safety may demand it. The military is subordinate to the civil power. The listing of these rights does not deny or impair any other rights of the people not mentioned in the "Bill of Rights," as contained in the Constitution of Louisiana.

DEPARTMENTS OF GOVERNMENT.

Division. The powers of government are divided into three distinct departments, as follows: legislative, executive, and judicial. The members of one department may not hold office in another except in a few instances, which may be expressly provided for by law.

A. Legislative Department.

General Assembly. The legislative power is vested in a General Assembly, composed of a Senate and a House of Representatives. The General Assembly meets at noon in the capital city, Baton Rouge, on the second Monday in

May of the even years, for a session of not more than sixty days. Members of the General Assembly are privileged from arrest during their attendance at the sessions and in going to and from the same, except in cases of treason, felony, or breach of the peace. They are paid five dollars per day during attendance, and are allowed five cents per mile going to and returning from the capital. Each house has to keep a journal of its proceedings, which is preserved in the office of the Secretary of State. A quorum consists of not less than a majority of each house. Neither house may adjourn for more than three days nor to any place, without the consent of the other. No member may during his term of office nor for one year thereafter, be appointed or elected to any civil office of profit under the State, which may have been created or the income from which may have been increased, during the time he was a member of the General Assembly. The House of Representatives has the sole power of impeachment and the Senate of trying cases of impeachment. No person may be convicted without a two-thirds vote of the Senators present. When the Governor of the State is on trial, the Chief Justice or the senior Associate Justice of the Supreme Court presides over the Senate.

How a Bill Becomes a Law. A law may embrace but one subject, which must be expressed in the title. In order for a bill to become a law, it must be read on three different occasions in each house and reported by a committee and, in its final passage, receive the affirmative vote of a majority of the members elected to the house. When a bill has been passed by both houses and returned to the house in which it originated, it is sent to the Governor to be signed. Should the Governor refuse to sign it, he must return it with his objections, to the house in which it originated. It may then be passed over the Governor's veto by a two-thirds vote of all the members of each house. Should the Governor keep a bill longer than five days without signing it, it would become a law just as though he had signed it, unless the General Assembly adjourned sine die during the interval. An act does not become a law until it is promulgated, that is, until ten days after publication in the State Journal, unless it be a general appropriation act, or act appropriating money for the expenses of the General Assembly. A bill may not be again proposed in the house in which it was rejected without the consent of the majority of that house.

House of Representatives. Representation is based on population, but each parish, and each ward of the city of New Orleans must have at least one representative; representation is directed to be reapportioned after each United States census. The number of representatives may not exceed 120. The necessary qualifications of a representative are: (1) he must be an elector; (2) a resident of the State for five years; (3) for two years preceding his election, an actual resident of the parish or ward from which he is elected. A member's seat becomes vacant on his changing his residence from the parish or ward from which he was elected. The term of office is four years. The House of Representatives judges of the qualifications, elections, and returns of its own members, chooses its own officers, determines the rules of the proceedings, and may punish its members for disorderly conduct or contempt and, with the concurrence of two-thirds of all its members elected, expel a member. It may punish also any other person guilty of disrespect, or disorderly, or contemptuous behavior during the session; such imprisonment may not exceed ten days for each offense. All bills for raising revenue or appropriating money must originate in the House of Representatives, but the Senate may propose or concur in amendments, as in other bills.

Senate. Whenever the representation in the House of Representatives be apportioned, the State is divided into Senatorial districts; no parish, except that of Orleans, may be divided in the formation of such districts; when a new parish is made, it is attached to the senatorial district from which most of its territory was taken. There may not be more than forty-one senators nor less than thirty-six, and they are apportioned among the different districts according to the total population contained in the several districts. A senator must be at least twenty-five years of age and have the other qualifications required of a representative. The Senate, like the House of Representatives, judges of the qualifications, elections, and returns of its members, chooses its own officers, except the President of the Senate, determines the rules of its proceedings, and punishes its members for disorderly conduct and contempt, and, with the concurrence of two-thirds of all the members elected, may expel a member. It may punish any other person guilty of disrespect, disorderly or contemptuous behavior during the session; such imprisonment may not exceed ten days for each offense.

Limitations of Legislative Power. No money may be drawn from the treasury except as appropriated by law, nor may any such appropriation be for longer than two years. The General Assembly has no power to authorize the contraction of any debts, except for the purpose of repelling invasion or suppressing insurrection. There are numerous restrictions on the passing of local or special laws; for instance, no law may be passed for the opening and conducting of elections, or fixing, or changing the place of voting, etc. The price of manual labor may not be fixed by law. No member may vote on a bill in which he has any personal or private interest. No appropriations may be made for any church, or minister, or private charitable institution.

B. Executive Department.

Members. The members of the executive department are the Governor, Lieutenant-Governor, Secretary of State, Treasurer, and Auditor.

Election and Term. The officers of this department are elected at the general State election of representatives, for a term of four years. In case of the absence, resignation, death, or removal from office of the Governor, the succession devolves first upon the Lieutenant-Governor, then upon the President pro tempore of the Senate. In case of the absence, resignation, death, or removal from office of any of the other offices of the department, the Governor fills the vacancy with the advice and consent of the Senate. The Secretary of State has the right to appoint an Assistant Secretary of State.

Eligibility. Any qualified elector is eligible for these offices, except those of Governor and Lieutenant-Governor; for these positions he must be at least thirty years of age, ten years a citizen of the United States, and a resident of the State for ten years preceding his election to office. No person holding office under the United States government at the time of or within six months immediately preceding the election, may be elected to these offices. The Governor and Treasurer may not succeed themselves in office, but become eligible again at the expiration of one or more terms after they have served.

Salaries. The Governor's salary since 1916, has been $7,500 per year. The Lieutenant-Governor receives $1,500 per year. The Secretary of State and the Auditor receive $5,000 and the Treasurer $4,000 per year.

Duties and Powers of the Governor. The Governor enters into office on the third Monday in May. The Governor has the power to grant reprieves for offenses against the State, except in cases of impeachment or treason; he may, on the recommendation of the Board of Pardons, grant pardons, commute sentences, and remit fines and forfeitures. The Governor, with the advice and consent of the Senate, appoints all officers whose election is not provided for by the Constitution or by special act of the General Assembly. He is commander-in-chief of the militia of the State, except when they are in actual service of the United States. He must keep the General Assembly informed as to the affairs of the State and make such recommendations for its consideration as he may deem expedient. It is his duty to see that the laws are faithfully enforced and he may, on extraordinary occasions, convene the General Assembly, provided it be for a session of not more than thirty days. Before an act may become a law, it must be signed by the Governor; should he veto it, he must return it with his objections to the house in which it originated; it may then, by a two-thirds vote of all the members of both houses, be passed over his veto. Should the Governor keep a bill longer than five days before signing it, it becomes a law just as though he had signed it, unless the General Assembly had adjourned sine die during the interval. The Governor may veto any distinct item of a bill making appropriations for money and the part vetoed may become a law only by an affirmative vote of two-thirds of all the members of both houses.

Duties and Powers of Lieutenant-Governor. The Lieutenant-Governor enters into office with the Governor. He is ex-officio president of the Senate. When discharging the duties of the Governor, he receives the same compensation as that to which the Governor would have been entitled had he remained in office. He is a member of the Board of Pardons.

Commissions. All commissions to officials, whether elected or appointed, are in the name and by the authority of the State of Louisiana. They must be sealed with the seal of the State,[1] signed by the Governor, and countersigned by the Secretary of State.

C. Judicial Department.

Courts. The judicial power of the State is vested in a Supreme Court, Courts of Appeal, District Courts, City Courts, Juvenile Courts, Justices of the Peace, and other inferior courts.

1. Supreme Court.

Jurisdiction. The Supreme Court has appellate and original jurisdiction. It has control and general supervision of all inferior courts. Its appellate jurisdiction in civil cases extends to those involving an amount to exceed two thousand dollars ($2000), and in criminal cases where the punishment exceeds six months' imprisonment, or where a fine of over three hundred dollars ($300) has been imposed.

Members. This court is composed of one Chief Justice and four Associate Justices, a majority of whom constitutes a quorum. They are elected for a term of twelve years.

Sessions. The Supreme Court holds an annual session in the city of New Orleans, beginning not later than the first Monday in November and ending not sooner than June 30th in each year. All processes are conducted in the name of the State of "Louisiana."

Courts of Appeal.

Jurisdiction. The Courts of Appeal were constituted to relieve the Supreme Court of some of its work. Their jurisdiction, which is only appellate, extends to civil cases when the amount in dispute or the sum to be distributed does not exceed two thousand dollars ($2,000).

No criminal cases may be appealed to these courts.

Circuits. The State is divided into two circuits exclusive of the parishes whose appeals are returnable to the Court of Appeal for the Parish of Orleans. Each circuit is divided into three districts.

3. District Courts.

Jurisdiction. The District Courts except in the Parish of Orleans have original jurisdiction in all civil matters where the amount in dispute exceeds one hundred dollars and in cases where the title to real estate is involved, or to office or other public positions, or civil or political rights. They have unlimited and exclusive jurisdiction in all criminal cases with a few exceptions, in all probate and succession matters, and in cases where the State, a parish, municipality, or other political corporation is a party defendant.

Number. The State may be divided into not less than twenty, nor more than thirty-two judicial districts; there are at present thirty-districts exclusive of the Parish of Orleans, which has two District Courts, the Civil District Court and Criminal District Court.

Judges. There is usually one judge in each judicial district. In the case of large districts, however, there are two, as for instance, in the First District, composed of the Parish of Caddo.

In the Parish of Orleans there are five judges of the Civil District Court and two of the Criminal District Court. These judges are elected by the qualified voters of the district. Their term of office is four years, except in the Parish of Orleans, in which it is twelve years; their salary is $3,000 per year, except in the Parish of Orleans, in which it is $5,000. The district judge has power to issue the writ of habeas corpus at the instance of any person in actual custody in his district. The writ of habeas corpus releases from illegal detention or unjust imprisonment.

[1] The seal of the State of Louisiana, as it has existed up to April 30, 1902, had no absolute authority of record for its existence.

The first seal was chosen, supposedly, by Governor Claiborne, and was supposed to represent a pelican with a nest full of young. There was no change in this seal and no enactment providing for any seal until 1864. When Henry W. Allen became Governor of the Confederate portion of the State, and Michael Hahn of the Federal portion, each had his seal; both seals were a pelican—one with the head on the left and the other with the head on the right; one with a nest full of young and the other with four young. Up to that time, the inscription on the seal was "Justice, Union and Confidence"; subsequently, without any apparent authority, the inscription upon the seal was changed to "Union, Justice and Confidence."

In order to establish uniformity in the State seal and in its use among various departments of the government, on April 30, 1902, Governor Heard, acting under authority of Section 3471 of the Revised Statutes, directed the Secretary of State to use a seal, the description of which is given below, and this is the first directing order that has come from the chief magistrate and that stands of record legitimizing the seal for the State:

"A pelican, with its head turned to the left, in a nest with three young; the pelican, following tradition, in the act of tearing its breast to feed its young; around the edge of the seal to be inscribed 'State of Louisiana.' Over the head of the pelican to be inscribed 'Union, Justice and'; under the nest of the pelican to be inscribed 'Confidence.'" (W. O. Hart.)

Jury. Cases in which the punishment may not be at hard labor, are tried by the judges without a jury; cases in which the punishment may be at hard labor, must be tried by a jury of five, all of whom must concur to render a verdict; cases in which the punishment may be capital, must be tried by a jury of twelve, all of whom must concur to render a verdict. There are juries for trying civil and criminal cases. The Grand Jury, composed of twelve members, is impanelled in each parish twice a year; nine must agree to find an indictment or accusation.

Sessions. Continuous sessions are held during ten months of the year. In districts composed of more than one parish, the judge sits alternately in each parish as the public business may require. Judgments must be signed after three days from their being given and are to be enforced ten days after the signing.

4. Juvenile Courts.

Courts. In the parishes, the district courts serve when necessary as Juvenile Courts, but in New Orleans there is a special Juvenile Court.

Purpose. Juvenile Courts are established for the trial of all children seventeen years of age and under, charged as "neglected" or "delinquent," and all persons guilty of the violation of laws for the protection of the physical, moral, or mental well-being of children, not punishable by death or hard labor. Cases of desertion or non-support of children, by either parent, also belong to this court.

Terms "Neglected" and "Delinquent." By "neglected" child is meant any child seventeen years of age or under, found destitute, or without proper guardianship, or whose home because of neglect, cruelty, wickedness or poverty of parents or guardians, is an unfit place for a child; or having one parent undergoing punishment for crime, or found wandering about the streets at night without being on any lawful business. By "delinquent" child is meant any child seventeen years of age or under, found begging or receiving alms, singing or playing a musical instrument in any street or public place, for alms; or found living in places of bad repute, visiting any saloon, poolroom, etc., attempting to jump on moving trains or street cars for the purpose of stealing a ride; or found to be incorrigible or habitually using vile, obscene, or indecent language, or guilty of immoral conduct in public places or around schoolhouses, or growing up in idleness or crime, or running away from home or the State institution where he may be kept, or violating any law of the State, or ordinance of any village, town, city, or parish of the State.

Officers. There are the judge of the court and probationary officers. These probationary officers, discreet persons of either sex, are appointed by the court. The probation officers must attend court when cases assigned them are being heard; they have to investigate such cases and take charge of the child before or after the trial, according to the court's order; they have the power and authority of sheriffs to make arrests and perform other duties of their office.

5. Sheriffs and Coroners.

Sheriffs. At the general election, each parish, except that of Orleans, must elect a sheriff for four years. He must within thirty days of his election furnish bond. The sheriff has to see to the keeping of prisoners, conveying convicts, insane persons, juveniles, lepers, and other persons committed to any institution of the State; and must see to the service of process from another parish, and service of process or the performance of any duty within the limits of his own parish." For this, he is paid $500 a year for each representative the parish may have in the House of Representatives. He is also tax collector and receives five per cent of all sums collected. In Orleans Parish, there is a Criminal and a Civil Sheriff.

Coroners. A coroner is elected in each parish at the general election, for four years. It is the duty of the coroner to inquire into the causes of violent deaths occurring in his parish. The coroner takes the place of the sheriff when the office becomes vacant until it shall be filled, and when the sheriff is a party interested; he may not, however, perform the duties of tax collector. Coroners must be regularly licensed physicians.

6. Attorney-General.

Term. There is an attorney for the State, elected by the qualified voters of the State for a term of four years.

Qualifications. The attorney-general must be learned in the law and must have actually resided and practiced law as a licensed attorney in the State for five years preceding his election.

Salary. The attorney-general is paid $5,000 a year.

Powers and Duties. The attorney-general appoints two assistant attorneys-general at salaries, respectively, of $4,000 and $3,500 per year. It is the duty of the attorney-general to attend to all such legal matters as the State may have an interest in or be a party to, and to prosecute and defend all suits wherein the State may be a party or have an interest. He is the legal adviser of the Governor.

7. District Attorneys.

Each judicial district must elect a district attorney at each presidential election for a four-year term. He receives $1,000 a year and fees. He must be a resident of the district and a licensed attorney. He prosecutes or tries to prove guilty a person accused of violating a State law.

In the Parish of Orleans the District Attorney is now paid a salary of ten thousand dollars ($10,000) per year with no fees.

8. Justices of the Peace and Constables.

Justices of the Peace. Each parish must elect justices of the peace for a term of four years. Justices of the peace have exclusive original jurisdiction in all civil matters, when the disputed amount is not more than $50, and original jurisdiction with the District Court when the amount does not exceed $100. They also have jurisdiction in minor criminal cases. They are paid a salary fixed by the police jury of the parish.

Constables. Each court of the justice of the peace has a constable elected for four years. He is paid a salary by the police jury of the parish. The duties of the constable are similar to those of the sheriff; he must enforce the decisions of the court.

SOME GENERAL PROVISIONS.

Treason. Levying war against the State, or adhering to its enemies, giving them aid and comfort, constitute treason against the State.

Lotteries. The State of Louisiana prohibits lotteries and the sale of lottery tickets.

Gambling. The Constitution declares gambling to be a vice and that the General Assembly must pass laws to suppress it.

Convicts. The State may employ convicts on public works such as roads, farms, etc., but they must be under the supervision of State officers. They may not be hired out to individuals or corporations.

THE PARISH AS A UNIT OF GOVERNMENT.

The Parish, a Public Corporate Body. The State of Louisiana is divided into parishes, as other States are divided into counties, for the purpose of local government. The French called these divisions of the territory "Paroisses," hence their being called parishes instead of counties. The parish is a public corporate body that may own and sell property, sue and be sued, exercise power of taxation for purposes of local government, local improvement, paying off debts, and supporting schools. But the parish is made subordinate to the State by the Constitution, by which it was made.

Changing Parish Line. Parish lines may be changed only on the affirmative vote of two-thirds of the qualified electors of the parishes affected by the law. For instance, when in 1912 the Parish of Calcasieu was divided into the four parishes of Calcasieu, Allen, Jefferson Davis, and Beauregard, it was necessary for two-thirds of the qualified electors of Calcasieu to vote in favor of the division, otherwise it could not have been made. When such a division takes place, the property and assets, debts and liabilities of the former parish, are proportioned among its divisions. Similarly, for merging two or more parishes, it is necessary to have the consent of a majority of the qualified voters.

Parish Subdivisions. Parishes are subdivided into wards. When a parish is formed, the General Assembly decides the number of wards into which it may be divided, and the Police Jury arranges the limits of each ward.

Issuance of Bonds. Parishes may issue bonds for purposes of public improvement when authorized by the vote of a majority of the taxpayers; such bonds may not run for more than forty years nor bear more than five per cent interest, nor be sold for less than par. The total bond issue of a parish may not exceed ten per cent of the assessed valuation of the property within its limits. Taxes for the payment of interest and principal of such debts may not be higher than "five mills on the dollar of assessed valuation of the property" in such parish.

Police Jury. The electors in each ward of a parish elect a member of the Police Jury of the Parish. The Police Jury conducts the affairs of the parish; this jury may be said to be to the parish what the city council is to the city.

Other Parochial Officers. The Sheriff, coroner, clerk of court, assessors, justice of the peace, constable, board of health, board of school directors, and superintendent of schools, are the other officials who assist in managing the affairs of the parish.

Seat of Parish Government. In every parish there is what is known as the parish seat, in other States the county seat, where is located the courthouse and jail; where the Police Jury meets and the other officials, such as the sheriff, clerk of court, assessors, and superintendent of schools, have their offices. This forms a nucleus for a settlement, and in most cases, prosperous towns have thus been developed.

Commission Government. In 1914, the Legislature passed a bill allowing the parishes to change their government from that by the police jury to the commission form. According to this plan, three commissioners are elected at large; these commissioners replace the police jury, board of health, and assessors; they have charge of public buildings, sanitation, care of paupers, construction of roads, bridges, fences; the finances and assessment of the parish are under their control, as are all parish employees. The three characteristics of commission government, recall, initiative, and referendum, are provided for; by the recall, the electors may remove a commissioner from office and replace him; by the initiative, the electors may have ordinances and regulations passed; and by the referendum, the electors may compel the commissioners to submit a measure to the vote of the electors before putting it in force. This plan of government abolishes the division of a parish into wards.

THE TOWN AS A UNIT OF GOVERNMENT.

Municipal Corporations. When a hamlet or unincorporated village has a population of at least 250, on two-thirds of the electors petitioning the Governor to declare it an incorporated village, and he having verified the facts given in the petition, he must declare it incorporated as the village of ———, and appoint the first officials, but, thereafter, they are elected. The Governor must declare a village to be a town whenever the local authorities inform him that its population is or exceeds 1,000, or a city when the population is or exceeds 5,000.

Officials. In municipalities having a population of less than 200,000, the government is formed by the State and is of an aldermanic character; the governing body is composed of a mayor, aldermen, marshal, tax collector, and street commissioner. The number of aldermen varies according to whether the municipality is a village, in which case there are three; a town, five; or a city, not less than five nor more than nine. The voters elect the mayor, aldermen, and marshal; the aldermen appoint the other officials.

Powers and Duties of Municipal Officials. The management of the municipality devolves upon the mayor and aldermen, who enact ordinances for its governance, and improvement, levy and collect taxes. In towns, their power exceeds that in villages; in towns, they may open and maintain hospitals, have a system of street lighting, fire department, etc. With an increase in size, additional powers are obtained. The mayor is chief executive and, in municipalities of a population less than 5,000, judge in a court for cases of violations of the town ordinances. The marshal is the constable and chief of police. The tax collector collects the taxes. The street commissioner has to see that all alleys, streets, and roads are kept in good condition.

TAXATION.

Purpose. Taxes are levied for the support of the State Government and its institutions, the education of the children, preservation of public health, payment of interest and principal of the public debt, suppression of insurrection, repelling invasion, or defense of the State in time of war, providing pensions for indigent Confederate soldiers and sailors and their widows, establishing markers or monuments commemorative of the services of Louisiana soldiers on such fields, maintenance of a memorial hall in New Orleans for the collection and preservation of relics and memorials of the late Civil War, and for levee purposes.

Kinds of Taxes. (1) The poll tax is an annual tax of one dollar per year payable by all male inhabitants between the age of twenty-one and sixty years; this tax must be paid in order to vote, and property holders may be forced to pay it; the funds collected by this measure are given to the support of the public schools in the parish within which the collection is made. (2) The property tax to be levied on the 1919 assessment will not exceed 4 mills. This includes the 1½ mills tax for the public schools of the State, the Confederate Veteran tax, and the Good Roads tax. The remainder of the millage will be for the other expenses of the State government. Several fiscal amendments were adopted in 1918 with a view to having a 100% assessment on property for State purposes of taxation, but a much smaller rate of taxation than heretofore. This shows Louisiana to be a rich state with a low tax rate. (3) The license tax is a tax on trades, professions, vocations, and callings. (4) The inheritance tax is a tax on inheritances, legacies and donations; no inheritance or donation of less than $10,000 to ancestors or descendants may be taxed, and when over that amount may not be taxed for more than three per cent; collateral inheritance or donation to strangers may not be taxed for more than ten per cent; if the donation be to an educational, charitable, or religious institution, it is exempt from this tax. (5) The levee tax is levied by the Levee Board in each levee district. This tax varies from year to year.

Exemptions. Clerks, laborers, clergymen, school teachers, persons engaged in mechanical, agricultural, and horticultural pursuits, and manufacturers, except those of distilled alcoholic or malt liquors, tobacco, cigars, and cotton seed oil, are exempt from paying a license tax. No public property, nor property used for religious, educational, or charitable purposes, is taxed; neither is household furniture valued at $500, or less. The Constitution grants exemption from taxation to many corporations, bonds, etc., under certain conditions. See Constitution of 1913, Article 230.

Sheriff's Sales. If taxes are not paid before the expiration of the year in which they fall due, the collector shall, after giving due notice to the delinquent, advertise for sale the property on which the taxes are due, and on the day of sale shall sell such part of the property as the debtor shall point out, for the amount of the taxes, interest, and costs; if the tax debtor fails to point out sufficient property, the tax collector shall sell the least quantity of the property which any one will purchase for the taxes, interest, and costs. The owner may redeem the property within the space of one year by paying the price given, including costs and twenty per cent thereon.

State Board of Affairs. An amendment to the State Constitution was adopted in 1916 providing for a State Board of Affairs to take the place of the State Board of Appraisers and the State Board of Equalization.

The new Board is composed of three members appointed by the Governor. They began Jan. 1, 1917, the first three appointed to serve for two, four and six years, respectively. Their successors are to serve six years.

Their duty is to assess uniformly all the taxable property throughout the State not to exceed its cash value.

The Constitution by this act provides that the percentage of the actual cash valuation of the property assessed in any parish, for other than State purposes, shall not fall below twenty-five per cent of the actual cash valuation as fixed by the Board for State purposes.

VARIOUS STATE BOARDS.

Boards in General. The State has created several boards or commissions for the management of some special affairs of the State, and these boards form an important part of the machinery of the State government.

Board of Public Education. This Board is composed of the Governor, Attorney-General, State Superintendent of Education, and one member from each Congressional District, appointed by the Governor. The Board of Education has to appoint the chairman of the State committee for examining teachers; elects a State Institute Conductor, who has general charge of summer schools and institutes; prescribes standards for approved high schools, and makes appropriation to each high school of from $400 to $500 a year; makes recommendations to the parish board, gives special aid to departments of agriculture and home economics of the public schools, and provides courses of study for the different public schools.

Louisiana State Board of Agriculture and Immigration. This Board consists of a member from each Congressional District, appointed by the Governor with the advice and consent of the Senate, from men engaged in the leading agricultural interests of the State; these members hold office for six years, or until their successors are appointed. The Governor, Commissioner of Agriculture and Immigration, President of the Louisiana State University and Agricultural and Mechanical College, the Vice-President of the Board of Supervisors of the same institution, and the Director of the State experimental stations, are ex-officio members of this Board. The members of this Board receive no compensation, only their expenses when attending meetings. This Board has control and direction of all State agricultural organizations and State Farmers' Institutes, and adopts measures to secure proper immigration. It encourages State, district, and parish fairs and local agricultural organizations; maintains effective control of the manufacture and sale in this State of fertilizers and Paris Green, and suppresses adulteration and fraud therein. It has to perform other duties when assigned by the General Assembly.

Board of Charities and Corrections. Six members, appointed by the Governor for six years, form this board, of which the Governor is ex-officio chairman. They receive no compensation, but the secretary, whom they appoint, receives a salary fixed by the General Assembly. The board does not possess any administrative or executive powers, merely visitorial. It is their duty to visit all charitable, correctional, or reformatory institutions, whether public or private, and make an annual report on their condition to the Governor and General Assembly.

Board of Liquidation of the State Debt. The State's bonded debt was $11,108,300 on January 1, 1914. The State has created a special board to assume control of this debt, pay off the interest and principal.

Board of Commissioners of the Port of New Orleans. The Governor appoints the members of this board, five in number, has the power to remove them and fill all vacancies. The Commissioners have control of the bond issue for improving the water front, constructing wharves, sheds, roadways, etc. They must furnish the Governor with an annual detailed account of the receipt and expenditures, and this report must be published once in the official journal of the city of New Orleans.

The Board of State Engineers. The Board of State Engineers was created by Act 33, approved February 10, 1879. The duties of the Board, as defined by this Act, are to make surveys of water courses, public works and levees of the State; to "report to the Governor of the State the improvements necessary and levees to be constructed, which are of prime importance to the State at large"; to furnish estimates and specifications for the work so required; to examine and measure the work recommended by the Board, and done under contracts made by the State, and to specify the amount of payments due for the work thus executed.

Board of Health. The State Board of Health is composed of representative physicians from different parts of the State. It is the duty of this board to protect the people from the sale of injurious, or adulterated drugs, foods, and drinks, and against any and all adulterations of the general necessaries of life. See Chapter V.

A Department of Conservation has been established for the purpose of preserving the natural resources of the State. There is now one commissioner at the head of it. It is his duty to inspect and have improved all State reservation lands and waters; he must see that the State's natural wealth is properly used and not ruthlessly destroyed; he must find out what are the natural resources of the State and how they may be best developed. The reforesting of lands whose timber has been used, is one of the works undertaken by the department. The care and enlargement of the State's great oyster beds, falls within the province of the department.

Boards of Commissioners of the Levee Districts. The regularly incorporated Levee Districts in the State number, at this date, seventeen. All these Districts possess corporate powers, exercised under the administration of Boards of Commissioners, varying in number from three to nine; and all, except the Orleans Levee District, are empowered to levy ad valorem taxes for levee purposes, not exceeding the constitutional limit of five mills on the dollar. Up to the year 1913, the Orleans Levee District was restricted to an ad valorem tax of one mill on the dollar. However, by Act No. 251 of the General Assembly of the State, Session of 1912, the power to levy and collect an additional ad valorem tax of two mills on the dollar, or three mills in all, was authorized and provided for, commencing on January 1, 1913, and to maintain for a period of eight years.

EDUCATIONAL AND CHARITABLE INSTITUTIONS SUPPORTED BY THE STATE.

The State supports five large educational institutions, namely: the State University at Baton Rouge, the State Normal at Natchitoches, the two industrial schools at Ruston and Lafayette, Southern University for the education of persons of color, and several charitable institutions, the two Insane Asylums, at, respectively Pineville and Jackson, the schools for the deaf and blind, Charity Hospital, and other public charity institutions conducted under State authority.

SUFFRAGE AND ELECTIONS.

Electors. In Louisiana, electors are males over twenty-one years of age, who possess the following qualifications:

Residential. He must have been a resident of the State for two years, of the parish one year, and of the precinct six months preceding the election; removal from a precinct, however, does not operate against a person until six months thereafter.

Educational. He must be able to write his

application for registration in English or in his own tongue or, if prevented from so doing by a physical disability, the registration officer or deputy may write it at his dictation, under his oath attesting his disability.

Property Qualification. The possession of property assessed at $300 on which all taxes are paid, serves in place of the educational qualification.

Poll Tax Qualification. Men between the ages of twenty-one and sixty years must pay a poll tax of a dollar a year, which tax is used to help support the public schools. No man may vote at any election who has not paid his poll tax for the two years preceding the year in which he offers to vote; this tax must be paid on or before December 31st of each year. "Any person who shall pay the poll tax of another or advance him the money for that purpose in order to influence his vote, is guilty of bribery and punishable accordingly."

Voting of Taxpayers in Political Subdivisions. In order to vote as taxpayers, the only qualifications are those of age and residence; women of age who are taxpayers, have the right to vote in such elections either in person or by an agent authorized in writing. No other person may vote at such elections unless they be registered voters.

Debarment from Voting. "Persons convicted of any crime punishable by imprisonment in the penitentiary and who have not had the right of suffrage restored to them, inmates of any charitable institution except the Soldiers' Home, those confined in a public prison, interdicted persons, and persons notoriously insane or idiotic, whether interdicted or not," are not allowed to vote, hold any office or appointment of honor; trust, or profit in Louisiana.

Manner and Time of Voting. Voting is by ballot except "in elections by persons in a representative capacity," when the vote is viva-voce. The general State election is held once every four years on the Tuesday following the third Monday in April. The next State election will be held in 1920 and every four years thereafter.

Gain and Loss of Residence. Persons in the employ of the State or United States, whether civil or military, or "engaged in the navigation of the waters of the State, or United States, or of the high seas, or while a student at an institution of learning," are not considered to have gained a residence because of their presence, nor lost it because of their absence.

The Ballot. Ballots are furnished by the State for the general State elections. Ballots are so printed that an elector may vote a straight party ticket or vote individually. The ballots are cast in secret.

Voting. No registration may take place within thirty days preceding an election. A man desiring to vote, must register as an elector and present his registration papers and two poll tax receipts for the two years previous to the year of the election in which he offers to vote.

TOPICS: Bill of Rights; Legislative Department; Executive Department; Judicial Department; Various Officials; Some General Provisions of the Constitution; The Parish as a Unit of Government; The Town as a Unit of Government; The Town as a Unit of Government; Taxation; Various Boards; Support Given to Educational and Charitable Public Institutions; Suffrage and Elections.

REFERENCES: Constitutions of 1913 and 1898 and amendments adopted in 1916 and 1919; J. R. Ficklen, History and Government of Louisiana.

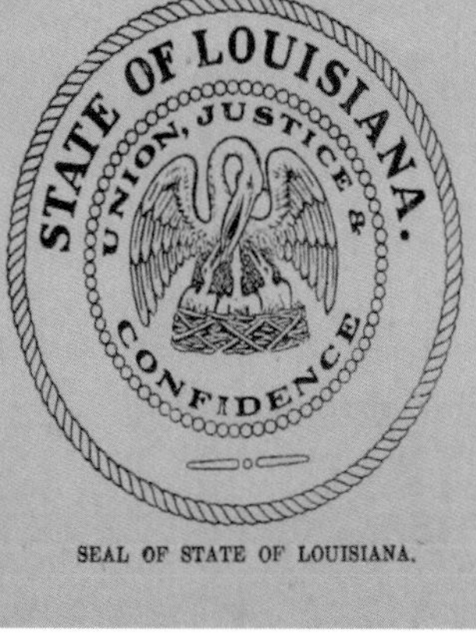

SEAL OF STATE OF LOUISIANA.

GOVERNORS OF LOUISIANA.

GOVERNORS OF LOUISIANA UNDER FRENCH RULE.

Pierre le Moyne, Sieur d'Iberville	1699-1700
Jean Baptiste le Moyne, Sieur de Bienville	1701-1713
Antoine de la Mothe Cadillac	1713-1716
De l'Epinay (Christian name unrecorded)	1717-1718
Jean Baptiste le Moyne, Sieur de Bienville	1718-1724
Pierre Dugué de Boisbriant (ad interim)	1724
Perrier (Christian name unrecorded)	1725-1732
Jean Baptiste le Moyne, Sieur de Bienville	1733-1743
Pierre François, Marquis de Vaudreuil-Cavagnal	1743-1752
Louis Billouart, Baron de Kerlerec	1753-1763
D'Abadie (Christian name unrecorded)	1763-1765
Aubry	1765-1766

GOVERNORS OF LOUISIANA UNDER SPANISH RULE.

Antonio de Ulloa	1766-1768
Alexander, Count O'Reilly	1768-1769
Louis de Unzaga y Amerzaga	1769-1776
Bernardo de Galvez y Gallardo	1777-1785
Estevan Rodriquez Miro	1785-1791
Francisco Louis Hortes, Baron de Carondelet	1792-1797
Gayosa de Lemos	1797-1799
Francisco de Douligny	1799
Sebastian, Marquis de Casa Calvo y O'Farril	1799-1801
Juan Manuel de Salcedo	1801-1803

GOVERNORS OF THE TERRITORY OF ORLEANS.

William Charles Cole Claiborne	1804-1812

GOVERNORS OF THE STATE OF LOUISIANA.

William Charles Cole Claiborne	1812-1816
Jacques P. Villeré	1816-1820
Thomas Bolling Robertson (resigned)	1820-1824
H. S. Thibodeaux, President of the Senate (Acting Governor)	1824
Henry Johnson	1824-1828
Pierre Derbigny (died in office)	1828-1829
A. Beauvais, President of the Senate (Acting Governor)	1829-1830
Jacques Dupré	1830
Andre Bienvenu Roman	1831-1835
Edward Douglas White	1835-1839
Andre Bienvenu Roman	1839-1843
Alexander Mouton	1843-1846
Isaac Johnson	1846-1850
Joseph W. Walker	1850-1853
Paul Octave Hebert	1853-1856
Robert Charles Wickliffe	1856-1860
Thomas Overton Moore	1860-1864
General George F. Shepley (Military Governor)	1862-1864
Henry Watkins Allen (under Confederate government)	1864-1865
Michael Hahn (under Federal government)	1864-1865
James Madison Wells, President of the Senate (Acting Governor)	1864-1866
James Madison Wells	1866-1867
Benjamin F. Flanders (under military authority)	1867-1868
Joshua Baker (under military authority)	1868
Henry Clay Warmoth	1868-1873
John McEnery (counted out by the Returning Board)	1873
Peter B. S. Pinchback, Lieutenant Governor (Acting Governor)	1873
William Pitt Kellogg, Governor de facto	1873-1877
Francis T. Nicholls	1877-1880
Louis Alfred Wiltz (died in office)	1880-1881
S. Douglas McEnery, Lieutenant Governor (succeeded Wiltz as Governor)	1881-1884
S. Douglas McEnery	1884-1888
Francis T. Nicholls	1888-1892
Murphy J. Foster	1892-1900
William Wright Heard	1900-1904
Newton Crain Blanchard	1904-1908
Jared Y. Sanders	1908-1912
Luther E. Hall	1912-1916
Ruffin G. Pleasant	1916-

INDEX.